# DALE WINTON
## MY STORY

# DALE WINTON
## MY STORY

CENTURY

First published by Century in 2002

Copyright © Dale Winton 2002

The right of Dale Winton to be identified as the author of this work has been asserted by him
in accordance with the Copyright, Designs and Patents Act, 1988

First published in the United Kingdom in 2002 by
Century, 20 Vauxhall Bridge Road, London SW1V 2SA

Random House Australia (Pty) Limited
20 Alfred Street, Milsons Point, Sydney,
New South Wales 2061, Australia

Random House New Zealand Limited
18 Poland Road, Glenfield
Auckland 10, New Zealand

Random House South Africa (Pty) Limited
Endulini, 5A Jubilee Road,
Parktown 2193, South Africa

Random House UK Limited Reg. No. 954009

www.randomhouse.co.uk

A CIP catalogue record for this book
is available from the British Library

Papers used by Random House UK Limited are natural, recyclable
products made from wood grown in sustainable forests.
The manufacturing processes conform to the environmental
regulations of the country of origin.

ISBN 0 7126 2368 X

Typeset in Garamond by MATS, Southend-on-Sea, Essex
Printed and bound in Great Britain by
Clays Ltd, St. Ives plc, Bungay, Suffolk

# CONTENTS

This book is dedicated to my mum

# ACKNOWLEDGEMENTS

I would like to thank my agent and friend, Jan Kennedy, and her husband, Tony Ball, for their love and support. Lisa Ratcliff, for her hard work and dedication, and all the other girls at Billy Marsh Associates – Suzanne, Ann, Vicki and Wenda. My editor, Anna Cherrett, and all at Random House. Barbara Nash, for all her patience and kindness while working with me on this book. Michelle and Sue for getting me organised and, most important of all, Mark Linsey, for his lifelong friendship.

Double lovely! xxxx

it was Bournemouth. I wasn't strapped into a car seat or harness because these didn't exist in 1956 when I was about fourteen months old. But I remember sitting on the back seat of the car, and for the very first time in my life, actually saying something. We had driven into a tunnel, and as we came out on the other side I recall my mother turning round, looking at me, then saying to my dad, 'Gary, he *spoke*!' Apparently I had said, 'It's very dark in there.' Those weren't the first words I had ever uttered, but they formed the first sentence I had ever put together. I couldn't understand why there was such excitement in the car, but I now realize that the first time your offspring manages a complete sentence it's a major milestone. And my mum, like most mothers everywhere, was absolutely thrilled.

From a very young age, Mum was an incredibly independent character who, having been born in a house on a Sheffield council estate, had her eyes set on bettering herself. Like so many other ambitious, pretty young girls, with hope in her heart and stars in her eyes she felt ready to leave home by the age of sixteen and went to live in a bedsit. It was owned by a landlady with the unlikely name of Robbie, which I guess might have caused a few raised eyebrows whenever Mum said who she was living with! Mum then decided to go to London and got a job as a receptionist in a detective agency, which I can only assume was the 1950s equivalent of going to Tec. Mum met my dad soon after, in 1953. I was never told exactly how they met, but I imagine it was in a reputable nightclub because she was very attractive and vivacious, and just loved to go out. She was sweet seventeen and very beautiful, and he was a slim, good-looking man in his forties. It was a truly phenomenal age gap. Mum's parents' marriage broke up after her dad returned home from the Second World War, and I often wonder if her choice of partner was influenced by the fact that she grew up without a father figure in her life. But although that may have had something to do with Mum marrying a much older man, I also believe she was very much in love with him. My father must have thought she was a very impressionable young girl, though, because he chatted her up with a story that he had ten furniture shops and a dozen vans when, in truth, he only had one little blue van and one shop, the Angel Bedding Company, in Islington.

'He always used to ride around in the *same* blue van,' Mum told me, 'and was always telling me it was a *different* van. But I wasn't daft! I could see the registration number was the same, and I knew he didn't have ten furniture shops or twelve vans.'

Fortunately for Dad, he had already won her heart before she realized this and he did very well with the Angel Bedding Company. Having got the necessary permission from my maternal grandmother to marry my mother when she was just seventeen and a half, they tied the knot.

However, the lead-up to their wedding was apparently not a bed of roses. My mother never really explained to me why she didn't get on with his family, but I suspect one of the reasons was that my father was Jewish and she was not. Although Mum converted from C of E to Dad's religion, there was obviously still tremendous family resistance. This may have had something to do with the fact that Dad came from a family of six sisters and one brother, and that he was the first of the children to marry. I will never know the real reason for their antagonism, but I do know that there was so much bad feeling between Mum and Dad's family that she insisted he change his name by deed poll from Winner to Winton, her version of his family name.

I know Mum and Dad were happy to begin with but, doubtless, the family split and all the related unpleasantness took its toll on the marriage – those kinds of feuds between kinfolk usually do. My mother was certainly *very* happy and thrilled when she had me when she was just nineteen, although it was quite out of the ordinary in those days to be such a young wife and mother. According to Mum, I was born three weeks late, by which time she thought I was never going to arrive. While Mum was heavily pregnant, she would take a taxi to the Angel Bedding Company and sit there with my father, waiting for something to happen. At last it did. I was born on 22 May 1955, right at the beginning of Gemini, and I actually believe I waited until then because I'm one of the truest and most mercurial Geminis imaginable – something that will become abundantly clear throughout this book. My mother gave me the name Dale because she was watching a highly popular cowboy serial called *Wells Fargo* on TV while she was in the clinic. Dale Robertson was the star of this and, because he was very handsome, Mum took a shine to him and to his name. It was just like her to pick a name that was different but, in 1955, she couldn't possibly have known what a great gift she was giving me for my later professional life. Many people have thought that Dale is a made-up show business name, but it has served me *so* well because it is different and stands out on its own. If I'd done a job outside show business the name would not have been so relevant, but it has certainly been a great asset to me in my chosen career.

Mum was a natural blonde, with lovely green-blue eyes, however, I she told me repeatedly during my childhood that she had always wanted a brown-haired, brown-eyed boy, and that she got *exactly* what she desired. Even if this wasn't true – and I'm sure it was – it's the sort of thing that a mother *should* say. For some reason, heaven knows why, I also remember her telling me that I was born one week after Moira Lister's child in the very same bed in the Welbeck Clinic, London.

'There were two wonderful things about having you when I was nineteen,' Mum also informed me. 'Your birth was easy because my young body made it so painless; and, because I was so young, I had a great relationship with you.' A bond between mother and son is unique, and what is brilliant is that Mum understood that bond even before it had a chance to grow. Also, because she was so young we were, from the beginning, more like best friends and playmates or brother and sister than mother and son. Later on I remember being very aware that other mums were quite matronly, but my mum was lively, playful and vivacious.

At the time, I'm sure we were reasonably well off because another of my early memories is being wheeled around Regent's Park in a pram by the nanny, Nanny Burke, who was dressed in the traditional starched uniform. Very posh! I can still see her in my mind's eye. She was stocky, but not fat, and had short, dark-brown hair. The pram was one of those wonderful high-wheeled blue perambulators with a hood that came up. For the full upper-crust effect, all I would have needed to perfect it was an infantile version of the royal wave! At the time we were living in a flat at Ivor Court, Baker Street, but when I was about three, my parents bought a house, No. 76 St Margaret's Road, Edgware, a three-bedroomed, semi-detached, Fifties-style house. We shared the drive with Mrs Marks, an old lady who was always complaining. Once, when the drive was being tarmacked, I had great fun jumping all over the sticky mess before it had dried and all hell broke loose next door. I remember Mrs Marks emerging from the house wielding a broom and quite clearly at the end of her tether. Even as a child I obviously felt the need to express myself – and make my indelible mark!

I wish I could say I loved my dad as much as I loved my mother, but my relationship with him was very different. This had nothing to do with his age because I wasn't really aware of the huge age difference between him and Mum until I was much older. As a child I just thought that dads were older than mothers. I knew that I had to pay him respect, but I never felt close to him. He was a bullish man who had a fiery temper, and I feared him in many ways. He never harmed me physically and I never saw him being violent towards my mother, but I was still frightened of him. However, I know that if he was ever verbally or physically abusive towards Mum she would never have let me know. Any row would have been kept behind closed doors because her instinct was always to protect me and not to alienate me from him. Subconsciously, I must have been aware of some tensions, though, because as a child of four or five I remember having recurring nightmares about Dad. In these it seemed he was always chasing me – on foot or in a car – and I was very frightened and running as fast as I could, but unable to get away from him. I don't remember more than that because I always woke up, as one often does, before the nightmare became even more unbearable.

*

Another of my abiding memories is being in the kitchen of our Edgware house when I was between five and six at the most. It is strange, isn't it, that even in situations where something has traumatized you, the details can remain so clear. I have a vivid recollection of that kitchen, its wall coverings, red work surfaces and the black-and-white speckled linoleum floor, which everybody seemed to have in those days. I can also remember the painted cupboards and drawers. When I look back on that kitchen now, I realize it was the kind of kitchen you saw in early 1960s kitchen-sink dramas. Kitchens were relatively stark places then, as opposed to now when they are considered places of beauty and major selling points in a house. Our kitchen was small and square, and tagged on to the back of our house. It was very functional and had an eye-level grill. To this day, I don't believe you can get a good slice of cheese on toast without one of those. Oh, how I miss them! If only they were as aesthetically attractive as they are useful. On this particular occasion, I was having breakfast with the au pair. I was always passionate about toy cars and had a number of them spread out on the table while I was making the usual 'vroom-vroom' noises as I drove them around. All of a sudden Dad came in and said, 'Now, stop that and do your four-times table for me.'

'Once times four is four,' I began, 'two times four is eight, three times four is . . .' I couldn't finish it. 'Three times four is . . . I don't know it,' I whispered, paralysed with fear.

Enraged, my father stepped forward and swept all my toy cars off the table. I was devastated. I lived for those cars. I wanted to drop to the floor, collect them all up and examine them for damage, but I was too scared. The au pair was frozen to her seat and Mum was out of reach upstairs.

'Three times four is . . . *what*? You *must* learn!' Dad kept shouting at me.

Breakfast ended in floods of tears.

Later, when we were out in the car, he started again. 'Right, three times four is . . . *what*?' Then, when I couldn't answer, he 'babied' me, making it simpler: 'Right. Two times three is what? Four times *three* is . . . *what?*' And whenever I stumbled or my mind went blank, he became even more incensed and started shouting again, 'You *must* learn!'

All this makes it sound as if I hated my father on sight, but I didn't. I just saw him as a strict father, and it's very hard to love somebody when you see them primarily as a person you are afraid of offending or upsetting, and especially when the prime motivation for your behaviour is to avoid saying or doing the wrong thing. When that is the only way you know how to be with a person, all other feelings get pushed aside. I don't really know whether his behaviour would be considered tantamount to mental abuse, but I certainly experienced it as bullying and verbal abuse, and the thought of anybody treating a child like that is abhorrent to me now. I absolutely adore my godchildren and, if anybody upset them in such a manner, I simply would not tolerate it.

Regardless of these tensions, we did lots of things together as a family and we often went out in the car. When I was about four, we would go to the seaside, just for lunch or for the weekend and I really looked forward to those day trips. On one occasion, I remember Dad wandering up and down the seashore collecting shells, which he then gave to me. 'If you put this one to your ear,' he said, stooping down beside me, 'you'll hear the sea.' As I stood there listening it was lovely, like being given a very special present. But, sadly, the next day when I wanted to repeat the experience I couldn't find the shells. I was very upset, not because I thought Dad would be angry with me, but because he had given them to me and I had lost them.

Being a car fanatic I also have fond memories of his bright yellow Zephyr convertible with the personal registration number GW20. He always had nice cars until he branched out from his bedding shop and began his own furniture business. This was meant to be a very exciting new project for him and a friend with whom he had gone into partnership. They had just developed a method of manufacturing padded headboards, which were becoming quite the rage in the Sixties. Headboards were considered a thing of beauty and padded headboards in particular were the 'in' thing. I remember Dad being very excited about plastic mouldings, studs, and all the other things that went into the making of the headboards and, not surprisingly, there were many tears and upsets when the business collapsed in 1964. He and his friend had probably gone into the venture too early, before they had perfected their methods. Now, whenever I think of Dad and his plastic padded headboards, I think of that lovely scene in the film *The Graduate*, when Dustin Hoffman first meets Anne Bancroft at a party. He is totally bewitched by her and her husband says to him, 'The future is in *plastics*, my boy. Get into *plastics*.' That film was made about four or five years after my dad's business had collapsed. The future *was* in plastic, of course, but not for my father!

By the time things got very bad with his business, Mum and he weren't getting on at all well. They had much less money than they used to have, and Mum was now helping to support him. I remember Dad had to sell his Zephyr convertible and buy a Mini Countryman which, along with shooting brakes or station wagons, were very popular then. His was turquoise blue, with the characteristic highly glossed wooden frame around the windows. I can still recall its number plate: HMF 130B.

It wasn't all bad between Dad and me. I never actually fell out with him. It's simply that, as I sit here now, aged forty-seven, there's no special corner of my mind that he occupies. I just feel he was rather Victorian in his attitudes and overbearing where I was concerned. But he could also make people laugh. My grandma always thought he was great fun. Perhaps they should have married each other! Like it or not, children are all conditioned for better or worse by their families, but, as it is, I don't seem to know as much about my father, his parents and his siblings as most of my friends seem to know about theirs. I never had the chance to meet my paternal grandfather because, sadly, he died during the Second World War, and I only had a very short time to get to know my paternal grandmother because she died when I was only six years old. What I do know is that my grandparents were of Russian-Jewish extraction and that, after they married and came to England, they had six daughters, Hazel, Betty,

Lily, Myra, Rita and Jill, and two sons, Terry and Gary. My father, Gary, was born on 5 April 1914.

I was never told why my grandparents left Russia. I only ever knew that they lived in Hampstead Garden Suburb and through hard work had opened two toy shops. Sadly, after Grandad's death, my grandmother was left to bring up the eight children on her own. The house, 1 Linden Lea, Hampstead Garden Suburb, was situated on a corner. It was a beautiful big house, with a garage on the left. It had a very large garden and a kitchen that you approached from the side through a utility room. The kitchen was a huge room with an oak table in the middle that was big enough to seat the whole family. On one side a window overlooked the garden and next to that was a huge dresser stacked with brightly coloured plates. We always sat in the kitchen when I was a child and also, in later years, when I popped over on my bike to see my aunts. The front parlour, which was only used for entertaining special guests(!), was a sea of Dralon with heavy drapes that were kept closed. I was always saying, 'Why is it *so* dark in there?' and once I asked, 'Why are the curtains kept closed?' Someone replied, 'Well . . . because if the curtains are kept open and it's a sunny day, the sun bleaches the fabric of the settee and carpet.' So it was an act of preservation – all to do with the sound domestic economy of not wanting to replace anything sooner than was necessary. I also remember thinking, 'They're quite posh, my family, because they have funny doily things on the backs of their armchairs and settees.'

During the Second World War, because my grandmother was now a widow with six daughters, she was told she could keep her two sons at home to help support the family. Amazingly, she said, 'No, they have got to go to war' and they did. She was obviously very concerned about Hitler's rise to power and was also totally patriotic about Britain, her adopted country. Mum always said that Grandma was a brave and formidable woman who ruled her household with a rod of iron. She needed to be, because it's quite a feat having to bring up eight kids single-handed and coping with her predicament of being left a widow in such difficult circumstances.

She clearly was a woman of courage, whom I regarded with awe. She had the power of parental authority honed to a fine art – and had looks that could kill at twenty paces. My most vivid memory of her is of a very large, typically Russian-looking matriarch presiding over the kitchen at mealtimes, with all her daughters gathered around her. Several of these, Myra, Hazel, Jill and Rita, got married, despite the fact that, for some extraordinary reason, their mother was always threatening to cut them out of her will if they did! Lily, a particular favourite of mine, remained unmarried and stayed at home. She was a robust matronly woman with a ruddy complexion, but a lovely face and a very friendly personality – everything an auntie should be. Every time I saw Auntie Lily she was warm and welcoming; she always wore an apron because she loved cooking and was indeed cook for the family. She made divine apple strudels, her mince pies were to die for and her roast chicken was finger-licking good, probably before KFC was a twinkle in Colonel Sanders's eye! I'm sad that she never married because I think she would have made a brilliant wife and mother.

The daughter the family used to whisper about most was Betty, my number-one favourite aunt, who also never married and just stayed at home. She was a hearty, witty person with a great sense of humour and a wicked laugh to match. She had shortish hair and wore glasses. She and Lily were very close and they often went on holidays together. But Betty also used to go on cruises with lady friends. Nothing was ever said outright and, anyway, I would have been too young to understand, but it was strongly hinted that Betty was *not* the marrying kind. I never quite got to the bottom of all that, but I think I now know what might have gone on!

Terry, my father's brother, also never married and remained living at home tied to his mother's proverbial apron strings. He looked very much like my father, but, poor fellow, he had extremely bandy legs and looked as if he'd been planted in a pot. I think his hips used to give him problems. He was a nice man, but more subdued than my father. By and large, although I had problems with Dad because he was such a strict disciplinarian, he was actually always quite jolly when he was with his brother and sisters. Mindful of all the circumstances, I think the Winners were quite a happy family. They were certainly great characters, every one.

I was much closer to my mother's family, whose surname was Patrick. My maternal grandma was always called by her second name, Joan, which my mother thought was a terrible shame because she loved Grandma's first name, Elizabeth. Grandma came from a very large family and was brought up in Caterham, Surrey, but during the war she moved to Sheffield, got a job there in the Stanley tool factory and stayed in that area until she died. She was always a very glamorous woman and although she was brought up in Surrey, she had obviously adapted to the northern way of life and was a very straight-talking person who didn't suffer fools gladly. She also had a great sense of humour and got on particularly well with my father. She had three children: first, my mum, Sheree, who was born on 4 November 1935, next, Mum's younger brother, Norman, then her other little brother, Joe.

My mother's father was listed as 'missing, presumed dead' during the Second World War and, soon after, my grandmother, who by then was seeing another man, became pregnant, the outcome being my Uncle Norman. It must have been a terrible shock to her when my grandfather suddenly returned from the war! All I know about the days that followed this event was that Grandma's lover made a quick retreat from the house, and Grandma and Grandpa were reconciled. The marriage, though, did not last. Soon after Grandma had had her final baby, my Uncle Joe, Grandpa left her to bring up the three children single-handed. Her mother, my great-grandmother, was a distant relative of the family who owned Lyons Corner House. When they left Grandma £1500 – which was a lot of money in those days – she could have left the Stanley tool factory but, as she was almost at retirement age and wanted the traditional gold watch, she put the money away and stayed on. She then moved upmarket and bought a big house in Millhouses, near Barnsley, South Yorkshire, and converted this into bedsits for students, which she and my Uncle Norman ran together. They only let rooms to girls, though, because they thought boys would be much more trouble and bring girls home to do unspeakable things! I remember Grandma staggering around this huge house, looking like a female version of Quasimodo, Victor Hugo's hunchback of Notre Dame, with a huge bunch of keys attached to her belt. She was very happy organizing all the students, giving them breakfast, making them up sandwiches and generally mothering them. To all intents and purposes, though, until the latter part of her life my grandmother had no money other than what she earned and she brought up her three kids in a council flat. As my mum had left home before her mother's £1500 windfall bettered the family's circumstances, it clearly makes me the son of a working-class mother who pulled herself up from humble beginnings and made good.

Even though Mum eventually lived in London and Grandma still lived up North, they remained very close during my early childhood. Mum used to give Grandma clothes and take her out frequently. Over the years, Grandma would come down to London to stay with us three or four times a year and we went to see her whenever we could. I loved her. I remember her looking twenty years younger than her age, and she always had her lippy on and nearly always a smile on her face. Like Mum, she was a natural blonde and, in her day, would have been quite a beauty. I remember saying to her once, 'Would you ever remarry, Grandma?'

'What would I want to do that for?' she replied. 'I've had my share of washing men's smelly socks and dirty underpants. What good is a man to me? No, I don't want a man.'

Norman – Mum's brother – was a tall, slim, studious man, with a good head on his shoulders. Mum was always very proud of him because he was the first member of her family to get a white-collar job. He was very charming and used to play chess twice a week of an evening. My other uncle, Joe, was also very lovable. He became the lead singer in Sheffield's top band called, heaven knows why, Tom Brown's Schooldays. He was very tall and handsome, and had always wanted to be a pop singer. Although the band never made it to *Top of the Pops*, they were very popular locally and Joe was a very good singer.

The only problem with Mum's side of the family was one of geography. We all lived too far apart to see each other as often as we would have liked. This, coupled with the pressures and demands of everybody's busy lives, did not make more regular visits possible. It was very sad but, I suppose, as with many other families, an inevitable fact of modern life.

The problem that arose in Mum and Dad's marriage was that my father had done all the partying he wanted to do before they were married. Apparently, just before I was born, he bought a television; and, although we were sufficiently well off for him to employ a nanny who could obviously babysit me, he no longer wanted to go out. Mum, who was still only nineteen, was bored and restless. She was full of life, wanted to get out and about, and continue to have the kind of good time they had had when they first met. The story goes that one day she said to him, 'You're *obsessed* with that goggle-box and, however dreary the programme, I can't drag you away from it.'

'If you're *so* clever,' he retorted, 'why don't you go and work on it yourself?'

This proved to be a seminal moment. Mum was up for a challenge. The next day she went out, got herself signed up with a theatrical agent and amazingly, two weeks later, she was on Michael Miles's TV show, *Take Your Pick*, as Box 13, dressed in a mink bikini! It was the beginning of her glamorous career in show business as a very successful Fifties and Sixties actress and pin-up girl who literally had the world at her feet and the press on her doorstep. My father was stunned when she got her first job, but he was very proud of her and from then on enjoyed the kudos of having a famous wife.

I'm not at all surprised that Mum took up his dare and got herself into show business. For the 1950s, when women were still tied to the kitchen sink (and we only have to look at 1960s footage to see how long this continued), she was a truly remarkable and unconventional woman. I guess these days we would call her a 'ladette', but that's not quite the right expression because she was always very much a lady. She knew her duties as a mother, but she was also one of the new breed of post-war women who were aware that they should have their own life. Mum's philosophy on femininity can be summed up by one of her favourite sayings, 'You can buy with a smile so much more than you can with a rolling pin or an argument – and it's *so* easy to smile.' I couldn't agree more – I'm always smiling.

Mum also knew that she was an exceptionally attractive woman, but she was never calculating or manipulative. Neither did she undermine men or forge bonds with feminist movements. She simply believed that women had their role, men had theirs, and men should treat the fairer sex with respect. 'A lady,' she always told me from my nursery days upwards, 'should have doors opened by gentlemen.' I obviously learned this lesson well. Even today when I'm out with female colleagues and friends, I have to walk around them so that I'm closest to the roadside. Some ask, 'Why?' but that was what was instilled in me. When I was working in Austria later in life, this created quite a dilemma when I was informed, 'It's *not* ladies first here, Dale. The man always goes in front.' The theory there is that a man should enter an establishment first to see if it's safe for the woman to go in. But old habits die hard – I still do what I was first taught.

Mum was always very conscious of the benefits of a good education and continually drilled into me the importance of being a good student. I guess this was because she had never had the benefit of a university or college education herself. I recognized the need for good reports, but was always one of the 'could try harder' variety. I much preferred being at home with Mum because she made this such fun.

On one particular occasion, I remember not wanting to go to school. I don't know why. I wasn't trying to shirk. It was just such a nice day. 'I don't feel very well today,' I said to Mum.

'What's wrong with you?'

'I just don't feel too good.'

'Really? You look fine to me. Are you just trying to take a day off school?'

I nodded, knowing she'd seen right through me.

Nine times out of ten she would have sent me to school, but on this particular occasion she said, 'OK, I understand. It is a long term and you'd like to have a day off. But you can't just have a day off whenever you please. If you want to have a day off today, I'll say that you have the flu and you can take a couple of days off. But this is the only time you can do this, this term.'

In today's climate she'd probably run the risk of being highly censured for such motherly foolishness, but she had understood my need for some special moments with her. 'She's the best mum in the world,' I thought. 'She's fantastic.' I don't remember exactly what we did together that day, but I know it would have been great fun.

My mother was very aware of teachers' reports and would study them extremely carefully, but she'd never just take someone else's word without asking me herself. If I was in trouble at school, she would get to the bottom of what happened before judgement was passed. If I was in the wrong she made sure I knew it – and then there would be hell to pay.

Around this time, I remember being with her in Woolworths in Edgware High Street. There was a Pick'n'Mix in there and, as we walked around the store, I dipped my hand into the sweetie selection, pulled out a toffee and popped it into my mouth without Mum seeing. When we came out, my mother looked at me, then said, 'What have you got in your mouth, Dale?'

'Nothing,' I replied, pushing the toffee well back.

Bending down, she hooked the toffee out, gave me a clip round the ear and said, 'We are now going back into the shop and you're going to tell the lady behind the counter what you've done.'

I was absolutely terrified and tried to stay rooted to the pavement but, with no more ado, she marched me back into Woolworths. 'This is my son, Dale,' she said. 'He's taken a sweet from your Pick'n'Mix and he's walked out of the shop without paying for it. How much is the sweet?'

It was *so* embarrassing, *so* mortifying. The shop assistant doubtless said, 'Don't worry,' but I was taught a very good lesson. This is one of many examples of how right and wrong was brought home to me from a very early age and, to be truthful, I believe these lessons have served me very well throughout my life.

Because I was an only child, Mum always made sure I had lots of friends to play with. My best friend when I was at Edgware primary school was Jeffrey Collier who lived in the same road, and my other friends were Jeffrey's sister Susan, Anthony Bull and his sister, Hillary, and Betsy Lyons who lived just round the corner. Mum also encouraged me to go to the Cubs, but it never appealed to me.

After Nanny Burke left, we always had au pairs. There was Erica, a blonde, earthy Swedish girl, who seemed to me like a giant from one of my early picture books. She, I remember, used to cook this thing with eggs, and both Mum and I used to say, 'Would you make that egg-thingy, please.' She also cooked wonderful soufflé dishes, which I can still taste to this day. Erica was followed by Bodil who came from Copenhagen, and who was so glamorous she looked like a movie star. With Erica I had my first real experience of right and wrong, and with Bodil I witnessed the art of attempted seduction. But more of that later.

We all know that kids can't resist touching things that don't belong to them and when I was fiveish I was obviously going through a very naughty phase. During this time I used to walk home from Edgware Primary with Betsy Lyons and Jeffrey Collier. Betsy was older than me and had obviously been put in charge. As I suffered from asthma and eczema, I was prescribed 'puffers' to help me breathe and Betnovate cream to keep my skin condition under control. In addition to being on my body and limbs, the outbreak erupted above my eyelids and, young though I was, I was very self-conscious about it. My skin also became very sensitive if too much of the cream was applied. I knew that I looked an absolute sight.

As Betsy, Jeffrey and I walked up past the railway station, as an act of sheer bravado I bought an ice cream, which for me had been strictly forbidden. For my own good I'd been told not to eat ice cream and ice lollies because it was thought they would give me a chill on my delicate chest. Needless to say, they were *the* two things I *always* wanted. Just past the shop was an alleyway which took us back down to our houses, and I can't begin to tell you about the awful the feeling in my stomach when I saw Mum's car waiting at the bottom of it. I knew that she had clocked me eating the ice cream as she drove past the top entrance. It was purely bad timing on my part and I felt very guilty for two reasons. One was because of the asthma, the second was the question of where I had got the money from to buy it. I knew both these questions would need to be answered when I reached the waiting red Consul Classic Capri. Realizing I was in serious trouble, I dumped what was left of the ice cream, but doubtless had the streaky white evidence still smeared all over my face.

'I saw you eating an ice cream,' Mum said, obviously not at all pleased. 'You know it's bad for your asthma and will make you cough.'

'I wasn't eating an ice cream,' I lied.

'I hope that's the *only* lie of the day,' she retorted. 'But, more importantly, *where* did you get the money to buy the ice cream?'

I was shamefaced – caught out. This was the moment when I knew I had to be honest. I'd actually nicked one shilling and sixpence from Erica's bedside table. When I confessed this to Mum, I was made to feel absolutely terrible; and, although it was Friday, when I was usually allowed to stay up late, I was sent off to bed early. Quite right. Children shouldn't steal things and, at five years of age, I did know that. Next day when we were out in the car, I heard Mum and Dad having a conversation I was meant to overhear: 'We've got a thief in the house, so we'll have to lock things up in the cupboard from now on.'

I was very upset, but it taught me a short, sharp lesson. We were living in a Jewish community, doing the Friday night Sabbath thing, and I was made to feel so guilty that, to this day, I've never forgotten how that felt. There's nothing quite like Jewish guilt – like *the* chicken soup, it works like no other. As a five-year-old I was taught an invaluable lesson: 'Don't touch that which doesn't belong to you.' It's a good lesson for life.

In truth, though, I always felt Mum would forgive me anything. She believed in being strict, but her love for me was real and unconditional. I was made aware of the boundaries and, to this day, I believe that's very important for children. They are free spirits, and must be encouraged to follow their own creative thought patterns, but as well as being loved they must also be monitored and guided.

So now for Bodil and the attempted seduction – not by me I might add! In 1962, when I was seven, we were on a family holiday in Bournemouth. As I look back on this, it seems like a scene that's unique to British black-and-white movies of the very early Sixties without any of the Hollywood gloss. British films then were raw and so was the language. The scene of Bodil's seduction was a very British seaside fairground. It was slightly grubby and everybody was standing around looking at the lights, the big dippers, the dodgem cars, the helter-skelters and the carousels, all with the current hits blaring out loudly. But, above all, I remember the smell of hot dogs and onions, and candyfloss, and the possibility, if I was lucky, of winning a goldfish in a clear plastic bag. This particular day, when Bodil was in charge of me while Mum and Dad were in the hotel, was my very first experience of a fairground and, for me, it was like being in a magical toy factory. And there I was with Bodil, whom I absolutely adored. She was very blonde, very glamorous and very Danish. Quite a speciality, I suppose, because she looked so Scandinavian and, when she spoke, she had a Nordic accent which, while she was struggling with her English, made her all the more mysterious.

I loved the dodgems from the moment I first rode in one and, while I was steering around in one of these with Bodil, bumping and ramming as many of the others as I could, a fairground Johnny, who was hanging around at the side, latched on to her and was obviously totally bewitched by the strange-sounding, gorgeous Scandinavian. He probably realized that the little fat, brown-haired boy was her charge, rather than her son; and, having initiated a conversation, he was charming. Bodil probably had no idea about how seductive and alluring she was as she tried to understand his accent, and the fairground Johnny – a real Jack the Lad – persisted in his efforts to pull her. Thanks to this, while Bodil was letting him chat her up, I was kept constantly amused with endless free rides on the dodgems, which pleased me no end. I can see now that he was obviously a pre-runner of the early-Sixties groovy guys, not by any means as 'cool', but with a good, if somewhat direct, line of patter. I can imagine him saying to her, 'You're a nice bit of stuff. Where are you from?' He must have had some good follow-up chat-up lines, too, because I was soon hauled off the dodgems with the bribe of an ice cream – and off we went. I'm sure she quite liked him, because we spent much longer than we should at the fairground, and he continued to escort us everywhere. Within a couple of hours they were holding hands and I remember wondering if they going to get married like Mum and Dad. It all seemed very innocent and sweet, although no doubt he had a different agenda in mind! When I say it was the first time I witnessed seduction, I don't mean I understood what was happening but, even without knowing what was what, I know I was witnessing sexual chemistry at its most potent. He really thought he was in with a chance and, given the opportunity without me there, goodness knows what might have happened. We certainly got back to the hotel very late.

The next day at breakfast, when Bodil was also sitting at the table, Mum said, 'So, did you enjoy the fairground, Dale?'

Like most children, I chatted away enthusiastically about the dodgems, the lights, the hot dogs, the candyfloss, and said it was all *fantastic*. Then, without thinking, I mentioned the man who had attached himself to us. Mum was quite curious and asked who he was. Without giving Bodil a chance to reply, I said that he had bought me ice cream and paid for me to go on the dodgems, and that he and Bodil had been holding hands. Now Mum was a very modern woman, who would never have had a problem with a man chatting up a woman in that sort of situation, but what did give her cause for concern was that her son was in the charge of someone who had spent time apparently engrossed in a complete stranger when she was supposed to be making sure that her son was all right. She was horrified and immediately wanted to know, in detail, everything that had happened, what was said and was I ever left on my own? I realized I was being put through the third degree and that poor Bodil was going to get it with both barrels for having neglected her duty. Her job was to take me to the fair, not get pulled by local rough trade.

Mum, who was always very clever at getting the right answers out of me, had the habit of saying, 'Dale, I know when you are lying because you get a red spot on each cheek.' So I knew if I told her a white lie or didn't tell her the whole story, she'd say, 'Dale, you have *two* little red spots on your cheeks, so I know you are *not* telling me the truth. Kindly do so.' At this point in the Bodil fiasco I thought, 'Oh, God, I've obviously got two spots on my cheeks.' I used to curse my cheeks because they always got me into such trouble. Like the innocent I was, I overreacted, relaunched into the dodgems, the guy who came along and escorted us, then I added, 'They had a kiss!' Why did I say that? They *hadn't*! Mum was absolutely furious and went loopy. I'd made matters worse and really dropped Bodil right in it. I remember feeling very upset and saying, 'But he was a *nice* man. He was such a *nice* man,' which then earned me the lecture about not talking to strangers.

Mum took an overview of the incident and decided that Bodil wasn't the right person to look after her little boy. This would have been a problem for Mum. Her primal drive was to be a good mother, a role she took more seriously than any other. As a result, although I didn't make the connection at the time, she went into protective overdrive and, once we got back to London, it wasn't long before Bodil's bags were packed and she was replaced by another au pair. At that time Mum was only in her mid-twenties but, because she had left home when she was so young and married so young, she had grown up incredibly quickly. She was never eighteen years old. Mum was one of those women who was always thirty.

If any of our other au pairs had the good fortune to have some fun on the side as well, I will never know. I was much too young, still in short trousers. But this was the permissive Sixties and, to the shock-horror of the older generations, life would never be quite the same again. The key word now was 'youth', teenagers were calling the cultural and the social shots, and the newspapers were full of the Profumo sex scandal. (John Profumo, the Secretary of State for War, had just resigned after he admitted lying to the Commons when he said there was 'no impropriety whatever' in his relationship with the 'model' Christine Keeler.) I remember Christine Keeler and Mandy Rice-Davies being talked about at home. I didn't know who these people were – how do parents explain such goings on to an eight-year-old? – but I remember it causing a great deal of interest in our household. Mum obviously thought Christine Keeler was an absolute stunner because I recall her saying, 'Christine Keeler is *so* beautiful.' Now, with hindsight, I realize how important the Profumo scandal was and why it was such a major story then. I also recall Beatlemania sweeping Britain with a string of number ones, such as 'She Loves You' and 'I Wanna Hold Your Hand'. Merely wanting to hold hands, though, seemed a thing of the past to the oldies in what was now a sexually permissive era.


In terms of my education around this time, between the ages of five and seven I was taken out of Edgware primary and sent to Rosh Pinner, a Jewish school, also in Edgware. I was only there for a short while – nobody ever told me why – then I went to Lee House School in Hampstead. Finally, at the tender age of eight, I was packed off to be a boarder at Orley Farm School, South Hill Avenue, Harrow-on-the-Hill. This was a prep school for Harrow, but Mum hadn't put my name down for that so I was never destined to go there.

Our annual family holidays were always spent in the South of France, which was fabulous. To this day, I laugh aloud when I remember that because I'd seen commercials on TV for Butlin's and Fred Pontin's holiday camps, with their little chalets, water slides and Big Dippers on the sky line, and felt deprived because they looked such fun. I then kept saying, 'Why can't we go to Butlin's?'

'You'll go to the South of France like you always do and you'll enjoy it,' Mum invariably replied. And enjoy it I did. The South of France was as exotic and as beautiful then as it is now. The Martinez in Cannes was our preferred hotel. To this day you are either a Martinez person or a Carlton person, and I now feel more comfortable in the Carlton. From childhood, I remember the wonderful approach up to the Martinez and all the exotic-looking French cars parked in its driveway. What was so unique about that area – and what separated Cannes from England and any other part of the world I visited – was La Croisette, the fabulous half-mile stretch of dual-carriage coastal road, lined with palm trees. That just sums up for me the lush luxury of those family holidays. In England you simply do not get palm trees on a dual carriageway with the ocean just in front of you and, as far as I was concerned, the South of France, with its wonderful dry heat, was a million miles away from my everyday life. If ever a film mirrored the reality of a place, it is the Grace Kelly and Cary Grant film, *To Catch a Thief*, which was set in the South of France. That place was – and is – just wonderful, and our holidays, sandwiched between azure-blue skies and white sandy beaches, were full of fun and absolutely great. Mum and Dad seemed happy enough to me then, but things are not always how they seem. I now know from what was said later that by the time I was seven they were unhappy together, and that the marriage had only lasted that long because of me. Mum always had a very strong sense of 'family' and would have done everything she could to keep the marital home together for my sake. I was oblivious, unaware of any huge tensions, just getting on, as kids do, with my life at school, playing with my mates, riding my bike and collecting my cars.

As I mentioned earlier Mum was a beautiful, curvaceous, voluptuous woman with an hourglass figure; a natural blonde bombshell who was always tagged by her public relations people as the 'English Jayne Mansfield'. Physically, though, she was even more attractive than Jayne Mansfield. I was always dead proud of her. I was never embarrassed by her fame, and loved it when she put her make-up on and got dressed up to go out. I used to think, 'Oh, *yes!*' I loved all the wolf whistles and attention she attracted, and I used to think,

'*That's my mum.*' She was a woman who would stop the traffic when she crossed the road. Most men are obsessed by women's busts and my mum's gave her a headstart in life! She was so well-endowed that this caused a strain on her back and she had to have a bust reduction when she was twenty-four.

One day, when I was about eight and out for a drive with Mum, a van driver pulled up alongside us and said to me, 'You've got a *lovely* mum, son. Just look at your mum. Isn't she *gorgeous.*' That happened often; and from childhood onwards I noticed that when she walked into a room, people would look up. She knew exactly how to make an entrance and work a space; and I grew up knowing what it was like to attract attention and be centre-stage. I guess that's why I'm in the business I'm in. I've inherited Mum's eagerness to be noticed and to please; and I know the show-off in me comes from her. In some ways I was, I suppose, tied to her apron strings, but I was also an independent little character. She always complained that I wasn't the kind of child who wanted to be cuddled or who crawled into bed with her to give her a cuddle, and that's probably as true of me as of many boys. Yet now I'm very much the reverse, and one of the most demonstrative, touchy-feely people imaginable. I just greet people with open arms. Perhaps I developed her warmth later. It is also interesting that anybody who knew her and who now knows me says, 'My God, Dale, you've turned into your mother's son. You're *so* like Sheree!' I sense that, too.

Mum was very busy with her showbiz career and was particularly popular with all the comics. She worked a lot with Roy Hudd, Bruce Forsyth and Bob Monkhouse, and was in the film *Dentist in the Chair* with Bob. She also had a small part in *Road to Hong Kong* with Bob Hope and Bing Crosby. I remember her saying how much she liked Bob, but that she wasn't at all sure about Bing. She loved Burt Lancaster, whom she met round about 1959, when they were working on *The Devil's Disciple*, and I know they got on very well together. When he came to London about ten years later, I remember her saying to me, 'Dale, I know where he's staying. Do you think I should contact him?' 'Go on,' I said, 'get in touch'. But she was going through a low self-esteem period then and she never did. Some years later I was given a coffee table compendium on all the great Hollywood movies. There, inside, was a picture of Mum sitting in a carriage and wearing her period costume for *The Devil's Disciple*. I also have a lovely picture, taken during a TV special, of Mum standing between Donald Sutherland and Terry-Thomas. Years later, I remember looking at that photograph and saying to her, 'Mum, that must have been a *great* show.'

'Terry was a very generous man,' she replied. 'And he was very smitten with me.'

She then told me that Terry was always pursuing her and saying, 'Come on, Sheree, why won't you be with me?' But Mum always liked people for *what* they were, not *who* they were. She was never into the biz of 'you're a star so I must be with you'. She really liked him, though, and found him very attractive and dashing. He once informed her over dinner that he was a 'big star in America' and that he had a lot to offer. He was, she told me, very disciplined when he was filming, but he also played hard and liked to drink. She couldn't, she said, handle someone who had two such different sides to their character. Later, she had a walk-on part in the James Bond movie, *Thunderball*, with Sean Connery, whom she liked enormously. I remember her coming to my school when she was working on this film. She was still wearing the make-up and the clothes, and all the boys went, 'Wow. Your mother's a Bond girl.' She collected autographs for me of all the people she worked with and I kept the book for ages. Then, idiot that I am, I lost it.

One of Mum's great virtues was that she enjoyed the company of women as well as men; and both girls and guys adored her. She was very good at girlie lunches and would gossip for hours on the phone with her girlfriends. But she also had platonic relationships with men which, I suppose, would have been considered quite unusual in those days. Where sexual chemistry was concerned, Mum's values were always very firmly rooted. She would make it quite clear from the outset that she was happy to meet up for a coffee, but that there would be no monkey business. From a man's point of view this probably made her doubly alluring because they were always trying to get to first base and found it very difficult not to pursue her in a physical way, but that was the way she was.

Her willingness to be a platonic friend went very wrong with one guy. She had obviously been introduced to someone at a social function who had taken a great shine to her. Mum thought he was an OK guy at first, but she changed her mind when she was repeatedly placed in the position of having to reject his advances. Most men would have given up at this point, but it made him all the more keen. This occurred towards the very end of Mum's relationship with Dad when Mum and I were living in Wendover Court, just at the top of the Finchley Road, north London. She was absolutely devastated when she discovered that the roof of her Sunbeam Alpine car had been ripped open and her portfolio of photographs had been stolen. There was also another occasion when she found that her car had been immobilized by coins being put into the petrol tank. The man was obviously obsessed with her and acting out of spite because he couldn't get his way. He clearly didn't take into account the degree of mental torture he was causing her. He started to follow her and she had to call the police several times to have him removed from outside the house. So keen was he to secure my mother in a relationship that he actually contacted my father without asking her permission. When she caught him on the phone offering Dad money to get a divorce, she was absolutely furious with him and with my father for even talking to the man. The chap had already completely alienated her and, even if she had been divorced then, he was the last person she would have ended up with.

There is nothing worse than someone following you and turning up at the oddest times and she made it clear to him, over and over again, that he had to stop. It got so bad that eventually the police said, 'Sheree, you keep on calling us and we keep offering to arrest him, but you won't press charges.' Mum was probably mindful of the fact that he was a married man with children and also a very successful businessman who was, I believe, about to be knighted in the next year's Honours List. She didn't want to cause him any embarrassment, but she *did* want him to stop pestering her. Finally the police said, 'You've now gone as far as allowing us to get a restraining order against him, but he's broken this repeatedly. We won't come again unless you press charges.' By now the man had driven Mum to floods of tears. She felt terrorized, a prisoner in her own home. In the end, having resisted pressing charges so many times, she agreed to do this and the police came and took him away. Much later I heard that when he was released on bail, he committed suicide. He obviously had very serious emotional problems, knew he would have to go to court and couldn't face the consequences. His death was a great shock to Mum, but she was placed in an intolerable situation where she had to take action in order to be able to get on with her life.

The man Mum *did* become passionately involved with, during the days when she and Dad were drifting apart, remained *the* love of her life. This relationship came about through a red-headed glamour girl actress whom she met at auditions and with whom she became great friends. The two of them, having bonded, formed a foursome with their husbands and the group started to go out to dinners and on holiday together.

My mother's lover, Peter Eden, always said that he fell in love with her the moment they were introduced in a restaurant, and Mum also fell for him, *big time.* I remember him as a very tall, slim, dapper man with a very good complexion. He was the kind of guy who walked with the air of someone who knew where they were going and what they wanted from life. Having started the affair with my mother and fallen in love, he rented a flat in Maida Vale and arranged that they should both tell their respective partners at the same time on the same day in 1964, then leave home and live together. By this time I was aged nine and a boarder at Orley Farm School, Harrow-on-the-Hill. Apparently my mother did tell my father and left. However, the relationship did not work out and, although Mum was devastated and still in love with him, they ended the affair. Despite this, she decided to carry on with divorcing my father. What I know now – because of events that occur much later in my life story – is that, right up to the day she died, Mum *never* got over Peter Eden

I don't actually remember when or how the subject of my parents getting a divorce was broached to me, but I do remember that Mum wasn't happy with Dad at this point and I think I knew that their parting was on the cards. It must have been handled brilliantly well because I don't remember it being a catastrophic experience. It's very hard for a child to know or understand the reasons why a marriage falls apart and fails. I don't recall it coming as a great surprise to me – I probably took it in my stride because it was sold to me on the premise that they would both be happier and that it would be a good move for all of us. All I really remember is being quite philosophical about it and thinking, 'Well, there's a couple of boys at school in the same situation as me. This is what happens.'

A little later in Mum's topsy-turvy emotional life, we secured the services of an au pair girl from a family who were very upset about her leaving them. The man of the house, Aubrey, turned up at our home to try to get the girl back. But, having taken one look at Mum, he was instantly smitten and fell hook, line and sinker for her. Mum, of course, was having none of this, and was only interested in placating him because he was so aggrieved that we'd taken his au pair. He obviously pursued Mum, though, because they ended up having an affair. Dad must have found out because I remember an incident when Mum was first seeing Aubrey.

I was in the car with Dad, driving up the Holloway Road, when we saw them together. I assume Aubrey had just collected Mum from a job. 'Look, there's your mum with that fellow Aubrey,' Dad said angrily. 'I don't know what she sees in him; he's certainly no oil painting. Have you seen his face?'

I was too young to understand what was going on, but I was old enough to appreciate that Dad was very tense and that I'd better watch my 'p's and 'q's.

Aubrey was a tall, good-humoured, good-hearted man who had a certain swagger about him. Although he was about the same age as my father, he definitely had more energy. His lifestyle was similar to Dad's but his business, which was the rag trade, was based in the Commercial Road, east London. He was absolutely besotted by Mum and he was very good with me. I really liked him and I would have been happy if they had stayed together for ever. Even though he proved to have an eye for the ladies, I think he really cared for her. On one occasion I remember hearing Mum giving him the third degree when she was accusing him of having a fling with a girl who worked in his office. Given half the chance, Aubrey might possibly have had affairs – but they would have been meaningless. Like many men, he knew where his home life was, but he was always a bit of a lad and clearly did what some men do in that situation when opportunity presents itself. But Mum did love him and I remember her being really happy with him.

After Aubrey came to live with us, Mum and I still went on holidays to the South of France together. She loved driving and was always the first to get the newest zippy sports car. In this, as in so many respects, she was ahead of her time. She knew all about pension funds, as well as fashion and performance cars. She read a great number of books and always wore gloves when reading newspapers so that she wouldn't get fingerprints from the printer's ink everywhere. She was, in fact, very bright, and there lies the rub because so many people mistook her beauty for stupidity – the 'dumb blonde' syndrome.

Her divorce from Dad came through in 1965 while we were still living in Wendover Court.

My boarding school days at Orley Farm School, Harrow-on-the-Hill, came into being just as Beatlemania was in full swing. I remember going to Kinch & Lack, the school outfitters in Victoria, for the uniform and having my name-tapes sewn into everything. I also remember my mother discovering nylon shirts, which I hated. The uniform was grey and short trousers were compulsory until your final year. Wearing this was to become a real problem for me when clothes became a really big issue and flowered shirts were the 'in', trendy thing. We all wanted to wear these and the minute we came home for exeat we couldn't wait to put them on.

Schools like Orley Farm have a smell of sandalwood and decay, which only seems to hang around downstairs, not upstairs. Like a Gothic mansion, it appeared gargantuan to me as an eight-year-old, but when I looked at it a couple of years ago it didn't seem half as big. In one of the corridors, which ran the full length of the building, were three rows of wooden lockers where you kept all your belongings – books, toys, whatever. Mine was number fifty-seven on the bottom row. Opposite this was a classroom and the headmaster's office, which I only visited for canings. The dormitories were upstairs and, as you progressed through the school, you were moved from dormitory to dormitory until you finally got a little cubicle space of your own. I remember Alastair Sim playing a schoolmaster in the film *The Belles of St Trinian's*, and that's how Orley Farm seemed to me.

Some kids love being at boarding school and embrace it wholeheartedly, some don't. I *hated* being a boarder, but I knew Mum had sent me there to give me the benefit of a really good education. Fortunately, we were allowed to go home four Sundays a term and our parents were encouraged to visit the school and watch the cricket or football, and come to sports days. Eight, though, was too young for me. I was really miserable at first, always misbehaving and getting the cane. I remember showing Mum the weals on my backside and thighs. 'My God,' she said, 'what did you do to get those?' I was a chatterbox even then, and my four or six of the best were usually for talking after lights out. I was caned regularly for this and lived in fear of the next punishment. Any boy who said 'bloody' also got six whacks. When I think about it now, I can see it was barbaric – the canings were really painful. I remember being at home one Sunday and going swimming with Mum. She was horrified when she saw the marks. But corporal punishment was standard practice, then, and not something for which parents removed a child from school.

I loved my grub, was prone to comfort eating, and was always a chubby child. The terrible thing then was that people didn't know as much as we do now about fibre, protein and carbohydrate. It was a case of 'chocolate is bad and cheese is good – have a piece of cheese'. But the fat content of cheese is twice as much as chocolate. Mum tried to help by dragging me off regularly to health farms with her, and when I was about twelve she took me to a dietician because I had become quite obese. Fortunately, although I was a chub and therefore not brilliant at sports, such as cricket, rugby, football or swimming, I was still popular because I was a 'character', a jovial, chubby child with the inborn ability to make my friends laugh. I was also very much an individual, an observer with a thoughtful side to my nature. I've always been best at one to ones, which is why boarding school, where you are encouraged to be a team player, wasn't particularly good for me. I *do* think it's wonderful to be part of a team, but there was always something within me that wanted to be the leader rather than a team member. You could call it spoiled only-child syndrome.

My mates also knew Mum was a pin-up girl and were forever asking me for one of her professional 10 x 8 glossy photos. As a jobbing actress, Mum understood that the photos were a tool of her trade, but she was always very embarrassed when I asked her for copies for the lads. As far as she was concerned, that was what she did when she went to work, not when she picked me up from school or came to visit me there. She certainly – and quite right, too – didn't want photos of her going around the school. In those days there weren't so many pin-up girls around and the ones who were didn't have to do so much to be well-known. TV was also comparatively new and everybody used to watch it. When Mum appeared on a Frankie Howerd or Benny Hill show, it generated masses of publicity. I really enjoyed having a famous mum who was always in the newspapers. It was *different*!

During the Beatles era, when I was about eight years old, Mum got a role in their film, *A Hard Day's Night.* 'You can come and meet the Beatles,' she said to me. She wanted me to do this because she recognized that they were a phenomenon. The other kids at my school would have been absolutely beside themselves at the thought of meeting them. Not me! I only wished it were Dusty Springfield whom Mum was taking me to see. I had first seen Dusty perform on telly in 1963 and, ever since then, I had been ecstatic about her and gone completely mad whenever I heard her sing. Whenever she had a new album out, *that* was what I wanted for my birthday or Christmas present. I was obsessed with her and didn't really get into any other pop singers until I was fourteen. Anyway, off we went to Teddington Studios where John, Paul, George and Ringo were filming some of their scenes. Mum, who had finished doing a couple of hers by then, had got on particularly well with John because he was a cheeky chappie who made her laugh. She told me he was her favourite Beatle, but she liked Paul, too.

There was *so* much going on in the studio – cameramen, sound-men, sparks, gofers – that I was agog. There were also screaming fans outside, deafening everybody in the vicinity. As Mum and I walked down a long corridor inside the studio, an actor, who was also in the movie and had a scene with Mum, was standing there. It was Wilfred Brambell who played Steptoe, the father, in *Steptoe and Son*. But as I'd never seen the television show I couldn't understand *why* I was being introduced to someone's father. That didn't make any sense to me whatsoever. Now, of course, I realize!

Paul McCartney and John Lennon were sitting in the de rigueur filmset canvas chairs and said, 'Hi, Sheree' as Mum took me over, so I could ask very politely for their autographs. Naïve as I was about them and their music, I just took all this in my stride. Some years later my Uncle Joe, who was still singing in a band, met Paul in London one night and was very surprised that Paul remembered his sister, Sheree Winton. And it was with some irony that I read many years later that Paul himself was fascinated by reality television shows and that, just after I had done *Touch the Truck*, he had actually commented that he really liked my programmes. I thought this was a great compliment. If Mum had been alive then, she would have been *so* thrilled and proud.

While I was at boarding school it wasn't possible for me to visit filmsets very often with Mum, but I did once go to Pinewood to watch her posing for a photo shoot, and I have a clear memory of going to the BBC and watching her record *Misleading Cases* with Alastair Sim and Diana Dors. Although I didn't know it at the time, all these events were sowing seeds for my own later career.

One of the things about a boarding school education is that it teaches you how to communicate by letter. Unfortunately, this is not a discipline that has remained with me. These days I always pick up the phone rather than write a letter, so if any of you ever receive a letter from me, please treat it as a great compliment! At school we were instructed to write letters home once a week. Having done this, we would give the letters to Mr Priestly, the deputy head, for him to put on the stamps. As borders away from home, every boy in the school used to relish the postal deliveries. The headmaster would stand at the dining-room table in the huge wooden-panelled dining room and, at the end of breakfast, he would say, 'Right, letters.' Every boy present would be sitting there hoping that he was the lucky one. A letter from home meant that someone was thinking of you and that there was news from the outside world. Mum was a brilliant letter writer who wrote on pale-blue paper with a pale-blue envelope. When I saw those Basildon Bond envelopes with her wonderfully legible left-slanted handwriting I was thrilled. Mum would tell me where she had been and what she had been doing, and her letters were a major part of my school life. I would tuck the latest one in my pocket and read it again and again until the next one arrived.

Although I was definitely someone who would have been much happier being a day boy and living at home, I wasn't permanently homesick at school. I was one of many boys and I just accepted that was what boys did. Mum was very good. She came as often as she could and so did Dad. Even after they separated and then divorced, there was always an air of stability. If there was any acrimony between them, it certainly wasn't made evident to me during my exeats or on my days off when either Mum or Dad would pick me up. Whatever else I thought about my father, he was dutiful in that respect. He'd take me out for Sunday lunches and even allow me to bring along a friend whose parents lived abroad. The parents of John Nadler, one of my best mates at school, lived in the South of France so, quite often, he'd come out to lunch with us and also come home with me for an exeat, which was really good fun.

The exeats, of course, were the highlights of the school term. At the start of these, all the boys would head for the windows to be on the lookout for the cars arriving and parking outside. Mum loved bright-red cars and nearly always had one of these. My happiest memories of school were seeing her arrive. We used to get four weekends a year, plus four Sundays off a term, and she would always make sure that something special was planned for 'Dale's Sunday' or 'Dale's weekend'. It would either be a lovely lunch out or go-carting or a visit to an airport or aerodrome for me to watch planes taking off and landing. It was always a tremendous treat and I *lived* for those days.

After Mum's divorce came through, Aubrey left his wife and sons and came to live with her. Mum was happy with him. I have some good memories of going out with him to restaurants and to work with him in the East End during the holidays when Mum was busy with her career. In particular, I will never forget the flowerpower era of 1967 when I was twelve. This had blossomed at hippy festivals, such as the one at Woburn, and it had its own fashions, language and free-love lifestyle. Love was now seen as *the* cure for the world's ills and the hippy revolution was fuelled along by the psychedelic hallucinogen, LSD, and pumped up to an even greater high by rock music performed by rock icons such as the Rolling Stones. Irreverent pirate radio stations were now up and running with the BBC trying hard to close them down; and Radios One, Two, Three and Four were replacing the Home and Third Programmes. The generation gap had never been wider. I, just bordering on my teens, was determined to be one of the flower children and was really into dressing cool whenever I was at home.

I did like some of the music but, most of the time, while the kids at my school were raving about what the press called the 'new aristocracy of pop stars' – the Rolling Stones, the Monkees, the Beatles and the Beach Boys – the only person I was still really into big time was Dusty. Some flower child I was! But I had my revolutionary moments. During this era, people used to wear bead necklaces and cow bells, and I remember going to Carnaby Street with Gary Simpson, a fellow pupil at Orley Farm, whom everybody wanted to be mates with because he was *so* groovy and good-looking. I came home with my very own cow bell, which obligingly jangled every time I moved. Aubrey was deaf in one ear and this drove him crazy, which made me, horrible piece of rebellion that I was, jangle it all the more to annoy him.

'Dale, *please* take that bell off,' Mum pleaded. 'Aubrey's going insane. You know he can't hear much at the best of times.'

'No,' I said. And I kept that cow bell among my possessions for years.

Even after Mum was divorced from Dad there was one more family holiday for the three of us. He came and stayed with us in a villa that Mum had rented in the South of France. I don't remember the sleeping arrangements, but I'm pretty sure he and Mum had separate bedrooms. I remember thinking, 'Are they going to get back together?' and, although I really liked Aubrey, I wanted them to do this. This may sound strange, given that I always feared Dad when he was in a mood, but he wasn't like that twenty-four hours a day, seven days a week. He was only like that some of the time. I was also older and understood the nature of the man a bit better. And, in a carefree holiday environment, he was different. Although he and Mum were now divorced, I guessed that he was still hoping for a reconciliation. So, seduced by the Côte d'Azur, I thought, 'Maybe this *could* work.'

By then Dad's health had not been good for some years. When he met Mum he was slim, but he had let himself go almost immediately and had got fatter and fatter. He ate all the kosher food and eventually weighed nineteen stone, which was dangerous for a man of about five foot five inches. I stand at nearly six foot two inches, so I clearly get my height from my mum, who was quite a tall lady. I know Dad's health problems began very early on in the marriage because Mum told me that when I was about a year old he was turned down for private health insurance. 'Mr Winton,' he was informed, 'we are *not* able to insure you. The condition of your heart, liver and kidneys is *very* poor; and if you do not lose at least five stone, you will be dead within a year.' He did lose weight, but he had obviously damaged his health beyond repair.

After they had separated and were living apart, I remember Dad being very ill while we were out for a drive in London. He was driving at about five miles an hour and I was thinking, '*Dad*! Go a bit faster.' He was clearly very unwell, though, and shouldn't have been behind the wheel of a car at all. After that I remember him going in and out of hospital. By then he had had a disaster with his furniture business and was now living in a flat on his own. He was never short of the company of women, though. Having lost some weight, he was once again a personable-looking macho geezer who would appeal to some women.

On the Côte d'Azur occasion, Mum flew back to England after a couple of weeks and Dad, who had joint access to me, took over for the final week. This proved to be disastrous because he suddenly began to feel very liverish and ill, and was hospitalized. I ended up staying with a family in Lyons for three days and nights. I felt very out of my depth, and couldn't wait to get home.

Sadly, Mum's relationship with Aubrey didn't last. By then I knew he was a *really* nice fellow and I liked having him around, but Mum was obviously having second thoughts and feeling that he wasn't coming up to scratch as her partner. According to my maternal grandma, who told me this much later after Mum had died, Mum had a secret liaison with a high-profile married man. I've no idea who this person was because Grandma didn't mention his name. But apparently this chap said, 'Sheree, we are going to be together. Let's buy a house in your name.' Having always been very canny with the money she'd earned, Mum had enough saved up to put a deposit on a beautiful double-fronted carriageway house in Hatch End, north London, the first she'd owned herself. But then he was killed in a car crash before they could set up home together. She was very unlucky in love.

I didn't know anything about this relationship at the time, but I do remember Mum buying the Hatch End house and being very upset soon after. She was no longer working, but had a mortgage and a son at boarding school, and there was no man in her life. Not surprisingly, she was not in the best emotional shape. The really tragic thing was that when she gave up showbiz in 1968, just as I was thirteen and about to leave Orley Farm and go on to Aldenham, my next school, she was only thirty-two, still young, and looked amazing. But she always claimed that her work was only a means to an end and that she had never really enjoyed it that much. I'm not sure I believe that. I think she was suffering from low self-esteem at this time, coupled with a fear of growing old, and that she felt her time had come and gone. In truth, she liked having her picture in the papers, liked being in films and on television, and liked being seen with famous faces. She was never a major star, but she was a much appreciated and admired working actress.

The three-bedroomed Hatch End house, which became my home for many years, was in Thornton Grove. When we moved into it I asked Mum what she was going to call it because our house in St Margaret's Road had been called 'Wintonville'.

'Nothing,' she said firmly, 'those days have gone. It's just going to be called Number 10.'

I was very happy there. Hatch End was a very quiet, safe area and during my school holidays I was allowed to disappear for hours on my bike, visiting my friends. The house was beautiful. Built post-war, it was light and airy, situated between two other big houses, and had an in-and-out drive, which I thought was sensational. To the left of the drive was a covered alleyway with a door that led into a garage, and beyond that there was a greenhouse. The garden, which had a rockery at the end of it, was lovely. Down the end of the street there were some semi-detached and detached houses. A lot of the boys I was at school with lived in that area. There was Andrew Searle who lived in a big white mansion, called Virginia Lodge, which had tennis courts; there was John Marenbon who lived across the road in another big house; and there was Malcolm Ashken, who lived just round the corner. Malcolm's father was an eminent doctor and his mother was a very hearty lady whom I liked very much. Their home, which was twice the size of ours, was called Oriel House because it had a big oriel window. Malcolm and I always played Monopoly together, but one day I kicked him out of our house because I thought he had cheated and he was claiming I had cheated. Mum appeared just as I was saying, 'I'm not playing with you any more, Malcolm.'

'What's the matter?' she asked.

'That's the last you've seen of him,' I replied. 'He's cheating at Monopoly.'

'For goodness sake,' she said. 'Make it up, you've been friends for too long.'

'*No*,' I said – and I never did.

One summer's afternoon soon after we'd moved into the new home, Grandma came down to see us. I was reading a book in the garden and I can still see Mum opening the kitchen window and waving the transistor radio at me. Mum, of course, knew I *adored* Dusty Springfield and was saying, 'Dale, they're playing one of Dusty's songs.'

I went rushing round to listen. Dusty was singing 'I close my eyes and count to ten'.

'It's a *great* song . . . a *great* song,' I kept saying as she finished.

'*What's* he saying?' Grandma asked my mother.

'Oh, it's Dale's favourite singer – Dusty Springfield,' my mother called back.

'Oh, I *can't* stick her,' Grandma said.

Having caught the expression on Grandma's face, I burst into tears. Looking back now, I can see it was absurd for me to be *so* upset just because my grandmother didn't like Dusty. But, at the time, I couldn't bear her being so nasty about my favourite singer.

By the time we were living in Hatch End, Aubrey had been gone for some months. However, there was clearly a reconciliation because he did move back in with Mum for a while. Like most people in the rag trade, he was always up or down ten grand and, at the time, his business wasn't doing so well. I think Mum could have been *really* happy with him, but by then she was intent on securing our future and she didn't think Aubrey was fulfilling his early promise as a businessman. I suppose there's nothing more seductive to a woman than a successful, powerful man. I remember Mum coming home one night after she'd been out to dinner with a friend and saying to me, 'I've just seen Aristotle Onassis at the next table. I can understand *why* women find him so attractive. He's short and not good-looking but, my God, he's *so* powerful. You can just sense his presence in a room.' This memory has reminded me that she loved glossy magazines. I suppose the 1960s equivalent of *OK!* was *Modern Screen* which, sadly, we don't get any more. Like *OK!*, this was packed with pictures of the great and the good, and I remember Mum looking at one of Princess Caroline, the daughter of Prince Rainier of Monaco and his wife, the film star Grace Kelly, and saying, 'Dale, one day I'd love you to marry – and Princess Caroline would be just right for you.' Mum always wanted me to marry well!

The last thing Mr Ellis, our headmaster, did for us at Orley Farm was to give us a talk on the Facts of Life. You would think that a room full of 'permissive-age' twelve- coming up to thirteen-year-olds would be sitting there sniggering with contempt, but we took it all very seriously. We listened intently and absorbed everything we already knew – bar one thing. Apparently, we were at the age when we might start masturbating. God forbid! The head spent a good fifteen minutes on the perils of this and how it would ruin our love life and render us impotent. So, picture the scene, a roomful of adolescent boys being told that another pleasure was about to be denied them.

When I was coming up to my bar mitzvah at thirteen, I remember Mum taking me to visit Dad in Westminster Hospital where he'd been for quite a while. He was *very* ill and most of his sisters were there, hovering at the end of the bed. I take my hat off to Mum for taking me there. It must have been terribly difficult for her. She had never got on particularly well with the sisters and felt it had always been a 'them-and-us' situation between Dad's family and her. She rose above it all beautifully and still never aired any of the issues in front of me. She didn't want me to witness or be any part of the conflict.

That day at the hospital I was aware of a bit of frostiness in the room.

'What's wrong with you?' his sisters kept asking.

Dad, being the kind of man he was, was revelling in all this attention and, full of self-importance, he replied, 'They've found something else now.'

'*What* is it?' they all wailed.

'Obesity,' he replied.

I was nearly thirteen, but even I knew what *that* word meant. I thought, 'This man's mad! Does he think they've found a new disease?'

The day after this carry-on around the bed, Mum said, 'Dale, we've got to go and see your dad in the hospital again.'

When I next saw Dad, I was shocked and, without thinking, I blurted out, 'Dad, *what's* that on your face?'

'He hasn't shaved, darling,' Mum said quickly.

But I knew it wasn't stubble. His skin was peeling off his face. Realizing that all was not as it should be, I fell very quiet.

'Can I talk to you?' I remember a nurse saying to my mother. And Mum went off into a side office with her.

In the car going home, Mum said, 'We have to go back to see your father later tonight or perhaps tomorrow. He's not at all well, Dale. You must prepare yourself, darling, because he's not responding to treatment and we can only make him as comfortable as possible. He's clearly not going to survive.'

I cannot lie and say I was devastated. I wasn't. I was 'cool', just took it in my stride and thought, 'OK, so Dad's *really* ill and he isn't going to be with us.'

But, then, in so many ways he hadn't been with us for a very long time. After he left home, we had slowly drifted away from each other – grown apart – and the emotional bond that had once been there had been severed. Since then I have often found that this is what happens in life. For a time you can be very close to someone, speak to them every day but then, through circumstances or the break-up of a relationship, you drift apart. I then find it heartbreaking that when you do meet up again the emotional bond is broken. I am someone who always tries to perpetuate the bond and keep it going, but sometimes I have had to give it up as a bad job simply because the other person doesn't have the passion within them to sustain it.

The next day in the hospital, my mother was very caring and said to Dad, 'Gary, you *are* going to get better, and you will be fine.' Knowing that he probably wouldn't live for longer than another forty-eight hours, she then added, 'You can come and recuperate at the house. *We'll* look after you, nurse you back to health and make it right for you.'

By this time they had been divorced for three years and Mum was living with Aubrey again. But her words perked Dad up and seemed to work a miracle. When we went back the next day he was off the drip, taking solids and talking about the future.

After that visit, I remember sitting dismally at our kitchen table with Mum and Aubrey. 'My God, *what* are we going to do?' Mum exclaimed. 'I've given him a reason to live and he's getting better by the minute. I've made a *promise* to this man and he could be here living with us within a week.'

She was obviously in a state of panic and honestly didn't know what to do. More to comfort herself than me, she added, 'Whatever else he's done, Dale. He *is* your father.' I thought about that, but it was too late for me to feel any real emotional grief about what was happening to him.

The other irony was that, because I was a non-orthodox Jew who had never attended synagogue on a regular basis, I was learning my bar mitzvah phonetically, and the thought that I was doing this for Dad and that he would be at the bar mitzvah was also working miracles. 'Your father's *determined* to be there,' Mum said. 'So you *really* have to do this, Dale. And, anyway, it'll be good for you.'

Mum always had a great sense of what was right and wrong.

Having converted to Judaism herself, she had made sure I attended Hebrew classes at school every Sunday and had always brought me up to embrace the wonderfully strong values of Jewish family life. It still makes me laugh that when, many years later, the *Jewish Chronicle* published a showbiz piece about me, it printed a picture *not* of me, but of my mother. This was captioned, *Sheree Winton. This is the mother of Dale, now on* Supermarket Sweep. *We always knew he was a Yiddisher boy.* It was so like the *Jewish Chronicle* to put a mother's picture in instead of the person they were writing about!

Those two weeks when Dad started to get better were like a black farce. Mum and I would sit there and he'd ask her questions like, 'How big is your garden, Sheree?' Then he'd say, 'This is a new start for us, Sheree.'

'Absolutely,' Mum would reply.

She simply couldn't break the illusion. Her promise was clearly giving him the will to live. Two weeks later, though, the illness kicked back in again and he relapsed. The idea, then, was that I should do my bar mitzvah in the synagogue with one other boy whom I didn't know from a bar of soap, then go with my tallis, cappel and the book, and read it to Dad in the hospital.

On the day of my bar mitzvah, half the congregation present on one side of the synagogue included my family and my father's sisters, and the other half was the boy's family. Having read my bar mitzvah phonetically and got away with it, what I couldn't understand as I stood there, very pleased with myself, looking out at the congregation, was that his half were looking joyous and my half were looking very upset – and crying. The good news, it seemed to me, was that I had managed to do the bar mitzvah; the bad news was that it didn't look as if it had gone down too well. I was bewildered. It wasn't until I left the synagogue that I understood what had happened. Taking me to one side, Mum kissed me and congratulated me, and made it very clear that she was very proud of me but then, putting her arm round my shoulders, said, 'Dale, I have something sad to tell you. Your father died earlier this morning.'

I stood for a moment trying to absorb this news and collect my thoughts, but I didn't feel a great sense of loss or grief. Then Mum explained that she needed to go and see to the rabbi. Clearly there were arrangements to make about Dad's funeral and, as the whole family were present, having comforted me and made sure I was all right, she had to do this. I remember Aubrey saying, 'Sheree, let me take Dale and sit in the car with him.' He was a wise old soul who knew that a son's bar mitzvah was a very big thing for a mother, and that Mum was now very upset and torn between remaining with me and dealing with the situation.

When we were sitting in the car, I asked Aubrey for a cigarette and, not surprised because he had once caught me smoking, he said 'OK', and allowed me to sit there quietly smoking it.

He and, above all, Mum, were absolutely brilliant with me that day. It was obviously totally inappropriate for us to celebrate, which is what normally happens after a bar mitzvah so, once Mum had returned from seeing the rabbi and the rest of Dad's family, we went home and spent the afternoon very quietly.

People say you should never knock your father because if it were not for him you wouldn't be here. Nevertheless, I think that Dad did fail in some of his parental priorities and obligations. A father, no matter what, should be your best friend as well as your guide through life. I was his responsibility. But on one of his days out with me when I was about ten he said, 'Your mother will always look after you, Dale, and make sure you're all right, so I'm going to spend *all* my money. I'm leaving you *nothing*.' That was a spiteful thing to say to a child and, what's more, he was almost true to his word. He left £284. When he died, I was thirteen years old and I didn't need his money, but it was somehow indicative of his way of thinking. And God forbid that something might have happened to Mum while I was still at school. With the benefit of hindsight, I can see that his spiteful words that day were spoken out of jealousy and bitterness, call it what you will, and that he intended me to carry the message back to Mum. I know this because, after he and Mum were divorced, he once said to me, 'I can't remarry, Dale. Who'd be better than your mum?' He had realized by then that he'd lost the best woman he could have had, and that's why he had become so bitter. He should have looked after her, but I guess he just didn't know how.

The day of his funeral, which was the first one I ever went to, remains a bit of a blur. I seem to remember it was a Sunday in September. It was a very hot day following a record-breaking heatwave, and Mum and I drove to the cemetery in Hoop Lane, Hampstead Garden Suburb, in her fabulous red Sunbeam Alpine sports car. The cemetery was a sea of gravestones that seemed to go on for ever. No graveyard can look anything other than what it is, and I found that one, full of grey marble and stone and overgrown in places, very depressing. Why would anyone want to be under one of those stones? Dad's sisters were present, of course, but I particularly remember my Aunt Jill – who I felt sometimes acted very grand because she had married very well and had two beautiful daughters, Madelaine and Gabrielle – and Aunt Myra, who was blue-rinsed, overly made-up, over-tanned. We're talking big, heavy gold earrings here! I have to admit that at times I found her a little intimidating, and I can't look at the Dustin Hoffman film, *Tootsie,* without thinking of her. Rita, the youngest, had inherited most of my grandmother's worldly goods, which was always a bone of contention for the rest of the family. There were also assorted friends, so the funeral was very well attended.

At the graveside when you shovel bits of earth into the grave, I remember my mother handing me a spade and saying, 'This is what you have to do, Dale.' Taking it all in my stride, I remember thinking, 'This is *really* weird.' And later, when I saw the film, *Far from the Madding Crowd,* where, at the graveside, the wife throws the spade in after the dirt, I thought, 'My God, I'd have loved to have done that at Dad's funeral and watched their faces!' Does that say something about me – or just about my relationship with Dad and his family?

After the burial, as I stood there in the cemetery with Mum, I remember the rabbi wishing us 'good health and good luck', and all the relatives and friends coming one by one to shake my hand and wish me the same thing. Then Myra touched my face with her hand and said, 'You will *always* have a home with us, Dale. We will *always* look after you.'

Mum was furious – and with good reason. The implication to us was that she was incapable of doing the same. 'Take your hands off my son *this minute*,' she said.

As everybody recoiled in horror, I looked at Mum. I knew that one more out-of-line word from the group would be dealt with in one fell swoop. And Mum would have been right.

As I stood, head bowed, not quite knowing how to deal with the situation, another relative said something I didn't quite catch that incensed Mum still more. '*Enough!*' Mum said. 'We came here out of respect. *Behave.*'

One by one they dispersed and we all congregated in the prayer room.

I admired Mum for telling them straight! I could pinpoint several family reunions over the years – bar mitzvahs, weddings, dinners – where they had demonstrated to each other and to me that they were more Woody Allen than any of his sketches. They were *unbelievable*. One hadn't spoken to another for years after they'd fallen out over a bit of fish! Was it a case of Jewish Alzheimers where you forget everything but a grudge?

It's de rigueur in the Jewish faith that after a funeral you sit shiva. For this, the curtains are drawn in the house and people sit very quietly. I suppose it's the Jewish way of having a 'wake' and a day of remembrance.

As we walked out of the prayer room, I could see Mum's car and I remember thinking, 'I've had *enough*. I just want to go.'

'Are you coming back to the house to sit shiva?' Jill asked.

Dad's family home was only up the road from the cemetery on Hoop Lane, and a couple of his sisters were still living there. As a result, it was decided that everyone would go there to sit shiva.

'Dale, it's up to you,' Mum said. 'Do you want to go and sit shiva? You've done your duty, but you can pay your respects if you like.

How do you feel? You're a man now, you can decide. I'll go along with whatever you want to do.'

'I don't know,' I said, uncertain for a moment. 'I don't really want to go there though,' I added.

'If you're sure, we *don't* have to,' Mum said. 'We'll just get in the car and leave.'

I nodded and, as we turned to walk towards the car, we quickened our pace.

'We *can't* believe you're not coming back,' they all started to call after us, waving their arms around like windmills. Then, as we quickened our pace still more, they began to follow us, quickening their pace too, until they were almost chasing us to the car.

When we reached it, Mum said to me, 'Just get in the car, Dale,' and we sped off.

I *know* we did the right thing. Had we stayed, the disharmony would only have been perpetuated threefold. We'd had a lucky escape.

Once home, we sat down at the kitchen table, played Monopoly and then had a pizza. Aubrey was there. Everything was fine. There was even a Dusty Springfield record on the radio, 'Son of a preacher man'. 'That's a *really* good record, Dale, a *really* strong song,' Aubrey said.

Suddenly, I was *so* glad he was there.

By that Christmas Dusty's song was in the top ten. But, sadly, Aubrey was no longer a part of our family.

# 2

## 'Learn to say goodbye . . .'

IN SEPTEMBER 1968, aged thirteen, I left my junior school, Orley Farm, and went to board at Aldenham public school in Letchmore Heath, near Boreham Wood, Hertfordshire. I already knew that area because, having been fascinated by planes as well as cars since the age of six, Mum had often driven me there so that I could watch small light aircraft taking off and landing at Elstree aerodrome. Whenever somebody asks me what my favourite journey is I reply, 'It's *any* day when there's a trip to an airport – not just to get on a plane but to *see* planes.' Even now I'm so fascinated by them that whenever there's a plane overhead, a Concorde, a 747, or even a more ordinary one, I *yearn* to be on it. This element of wanting to be somewhere other than where I am is something I often experience. Does this mean that I'm not as happy as I think I am? I don't honestly know. I just know that from early childhood onwards, it's how I have always felt.

To get to Aldenham, we had to drive past the aerodrome, which I thought was absolutely wonderful because I could see the planes taking off and coming in low. That area, which was very close to Elstree studios, was also used as a location for many of my then-favourite TV series, *Randall and Hopkirk (Deceased)*, *Department S* and *The Saint*.

My new school, Aldenham, seemed to be in the middle of nowhere and surrounded by fields. It was a good mile and a half from the aerodrome, but nonetheless it was still good for plane spotting. As you approached the school, which began its life way back in 1597, it looked like a magnificent series of houses, set in a huge courtyard. On sentry duty at the main gate was a guy we called Chief. He, I soon discovered, was also in charge of the Army Cadets side of things, and when I saw him wearing his medals and other trappings he looked like something out of *Carry On Cruising*! Adapted over the years, the architecture of the main school was nineteenth-century Georgian, but the bursar's office was quite Gothic-looking. It had really beautiful grounds and, like most public schools, it was very sports orientated, with well-kept playing fields for hockey, football and rugby, as well as courts where we played fives. There were also science labs and music rooms. I thought it was *very* big, somewhat daunting, but magnificent, and I felt very grown-up to be there. I started off in Kennedy's House, which was adjacent to the beautiful chapel and the only twentieth-century schoolhouse.

The teacher who taught us French was called Mr Tyson. No he wasn't a prize fighter, but he *was* French. To me he seemed about four foot six inches tall. He had a shock of white hair and looked almost like a bleached Oliver Hardy without the moustache. I've always been outspoken and, when he walked into our classroom for the first time saying, '*Bonjour*, boys, welcome to Aldenham,' I said aloud, 'How *sweet*! They've sent a Frenchman to teach us French!' There must have been something about the way I said this because he looked at me absolutely aghast. I doubtless was quite camp, even at school, but I never got bullied or beaten up for this because I always had the gift of the gab and found it easy to communicate with others. I have always thought that children who have a communication problem are often the most likely to be bullied.

There was, of course, a fagging system at Aldenham and I remember getting merit marks for this quite quickly. Since then, whenever I've seen films or programmes that portray fagging as an abusive relationship between older and younger boys it annoys me, as it wasn't a bit like that at my school. The way it worked at Aldenham was that you had a card, which you had to fill in each time you did a chore or duty for the allocated older boy. This could be anything from going to the tuck shop for a can of Coca-Cola to cleaning his shoes or tidying up his study. You would then get a merit entered on your card. It was a nuisance, of course, but I used just to get on with it, making sure I got my card filled up as quickly as possible so I could then concentrate on more enjoyable things such as playing records and reading.

From thirteen onwards, people would say to me, 'What do you want to be, Dale, when you leave school?' I was always nonplussed and thought, '*Why* do I have to decide that now?' I remember clutching for ideas in my mind and thinking, 'What am I supposed to say here? I haven't a clue what I want to be.' I knew I didn't want to be an actor because Mum had repeatedly said, 'Don't go into the acting profession, Dale. People who do this face possible rejection every day of their lives. Precious few succeed, precious few survive and make a success of it. Do something sensible like becoming a doctor, accountant, lawyer or estate agent.' Even dentistry reared its head, because Mum had heard that this was the career of the future. 'That's a really good job to have, Dale' she said, 'people are now taking much more care of their teeth.' The thought of spending my life prodding around in people's mouths was abhorrent to me. 'But that's all right, I thought, I'm thirteen and I don't have to make that choice yet.' Then Mum tried out journalism on me because she had wanted to be a journalist. 'Be a journalist, Dale. I think you'd be good at that.' She was certainly getting warmer! Since those days I have done journalism of a sort – radio journalism – so I did eventually fulfil one of her ambitions for me.

I wasn't surprised by Mum's job suggestions. I knew she wanted me to do well and was just trying to be helpful. Another reason she would have wanted me to avoid show business was because so few people manage to succeed in a field which is permanently over-crowded with heroes, hopefuls and people who are resting more often than they're working. Despite the difficulties, in my heart of hearts I always knew that I wanted to do something in the entertainment business. It was a spark within me that has inspired me all my life. I guess what I'd really have liked to be then was a pop star, as that would have been sensational. But I was overweight, didn't look the part, and I certainly didn't make the right sounds either in or out of the bath! Fascinated as I was by Dusty Springfield, though, I remained obsessed with music from a very young age. Music was my love and, by my middle teens, I knew I wanted to do something in that business. Until then, I brushed off the questions and went on thinking, 'Why do I have to decide what I am going to do now? It will come to me when it comes to me.'

By the spring of 1969 I was well and truly ensconced in my new life at Aldenham, but was in for a shock in my home life. One man who had always shown a great interest in Mum was Norman Isow. Norman was a very wealthy restaurateur and owned Isow's in Brewer Street, Soho which, like the Ivy today, was *the* showbiz restaurant in the Sixties. A very big, sumptuous restaurant then, it is now called Madame JoJo's. In those days as you walked up the marble steps into Isow's, you first entered a bar area before going through to the restaurant where you sat in very comfortable, padded, burgundy-coloured leather chairs. On their high backs, inscribed in gold lettering, were the names of regular customers. Your head would therefore rest on names like Cyd Charisse, Fred Astaire, Rod Steiger, Cary Grant, Judy Garland or Bette Davis. It really was a very smart restaurant and I have often wondered what happened to those chairs.

This Mecca of the mighty was always bursting at the seams with stars of stage, screen, radio and TV. Mum had been going there for many years. On those occasions she had often met Norman, who was a very hands-on restaurateur and was always there overseeing things. I'd also met Norman many times when Mum took me out to dinner with her. He was an attractive man, aged about forty-two, and had real presence. Of medium build, he had very short hair and wore what I thought were very distinguished glasses. He looked a bit like the actor, Ian Hendry, but in many ways he also looked like an accountant. He was obviously very happy in his own company – and very into soul music, which was unusual for a man of his age. I knew Mum was now seeing him because she had mentioned this several times in her letters. But I was completely taken aback when she rang me out of the blue at school to tell me that she was going to marry him. She went on to say that the wedding would be happening very soon and that on the day I would be collected from school to be a witness at the ceremony in Harrow Register Office.

I was old enough by then to understand that Mum had been having a terrible time for months. Dad had died, Aubrey had come and gone, and she had given up her showbiz career. But only now, with hindsight, can I see that it is at times like these that you are most likely to decide things in too much haste. When you're feeling depressed you can make choices that may seem to be the right solution in the short term, but prove to be hopelessly wrong in the long term. At that time, I can now see, Mum was obviously suffering from a serious bout of low self-esteem and desperately looking for some stability in her life. She wanted to be a wife again, Norman was there, and she was naturally looking forward to some emotional and financial support. As a result, she decided to marry a man who was a couple of years older than she was and who had been a bachelor all his life. Looking back, I honestly do not believe that this was a love match for Mum but, as I was just a schoolboy, I didn't think about the implications of this at that time.

On the day of the marriage Mum seemed happy enough to me. She looked magnificent in one of the black-and-white polka-dot dresses and hats that were so very fashionable in the 1970s. I thought she looked very elegant and truly stunning. Strangely, I can't remember who the other witnesses were or who else was present that day. All I recall is being there, going out to dinner in the evening, then returning to school. The post-wedding plan, I was told, was that Mum would keep our house in Hatch End and Norman would retain his luxurious flat in Knightsbridge. This would be the most convenient arrangement because he liked to go to Covent Garden fruit and vegetable market very early in the mornings to order the produce for the restaurant. He and Mum would then divide their time between Knightsbridge and Hatch End, but they would live most of the time in Hatch End, which was where we would all be when I came home for school hols and exeats. All that seemed fine to me.

When Norman whisked Mum away for an exotic six-week honeymoon in the Caribbean, Mum left all my pocket money at the school in advance. I must have been feeling somewhat emotionally unsettled, though, because I spent it all on comfort eating and put on at least a stone and a half. When Mum came back from her honeymoon, looking fabulously tanned and much better for the break, she was absolutely horrified by my appearance and, during my next exeat, dragged me off to a health farm to lose weight. This was absolute torture because, in those days, you were started on lemon water for three days, building up to plain yoghurt on the fourth day. Mum was very good, she followed the same diet as me and, although it wasn't called this at the time, she had a thorough detox. I knew why I was there and I just went along with the various regimes and treatments because I accepted that the juices and massages were doing me good. Above all, I enjoyed being with Mum.

'It's such a shame,' she used to say to me, 'but all of us in our family are prone to gaining weight if we're not careful. So, unfortunately, Dale, like me, you will always have to watch your weight and be mindful of it for the rest of your life.'

I've been a yo-yo dieter ever since then.

During that term's summer hols, Norman joined Mum and me at a hotel in Studland Bay, Dorset. Having been a bachelor all his life, I'm quite sure that being landed with a thirteen-year-old son came as quite a shock for him, and he didn't find his adjustment to this any easier than I found adjusting to him as my new stepdad. We didn't know each other *that* well and it was, to say the least, a difficult learning curve for both of us. Not surprisingly, a couple of days into the holiday, he and I had a row at the breakfast table, then he suddenly lost his temper and told me to 'scram'. I was furious. No one had ever spoken to me like that. I had always been an emotional child, who cried easily, and I was now an emotional teenager. I burst into tears, shouting, 'Don't you dare talk to me like that.' Mum, who was by now equally upset, backed me up and said to Norman, 'No, *don't* talk to my son like that.' With no more ado, Norman got up from the table, strode out of the dining room and went home to his Knightsbridge flat. Mum and I were left feeling shaken, but I was too full of righteous anger to feel guilty. It was particularly distressing because Mum was exceptionally good at making us both feel special. But Norman was not an easy man. He was one of life's loners, a belligerent man at times, which doubtless explains why he had never married before.

It soon blew over, but there was another memorable drama not long afterwards in our Hatch End house. I loved my bedroom there. It was wonderful. It had a fashionable Sixties-style G-plan unit, which went around the bed, so that for storage the bed could be pushed underneath it to create more space. The unit had padded doors that slid back and I used to keep all my classic toy cars and records in it. I had posters all over the walls, which, with the exception of Dusty Springfield, were changed from time to time to keep up with my current favourite pop stars. By 1969 I was crazy about pop music, especially Marmalade, Love Affair and Amen Corner, three groups which came on to the scene soon after the Beatles stopped touring. I was a huge fan of Andy Fairweather Low and, from the moment I'd heard 'If Paradise is Half as Nice', Amen Corner's number one in March 1969, I thought they were the best band in the land. I also put up posters of Clodagh Rogers and Steve Ellis of Love Affair. To this day, I think Steve Ellis, who recorded 'Everlasting Love', has the best ever male pop star voice. Even now I don't quite know what it is about Dusty that gets me going, but she does it for me every time. My friends often teased me about liking her so much when I was thirteen or fourteen, but they teased me all the more for liking Andy Fairweather Low, Marmalade and Love Affair. Progressive rock had just come in and they were into Deep Purple, Black Sabbath and Pink Floyd. To this day, in addition to listening to Dusty, I *still* play Andy Fairweather Low, Marmalade and Love

Affair all the time, but in recent years I've also developed a passion for dance music and good pop such as Blue and Ibiza House.

On the day of this particular drama with Norman, though, I was playing Dusty records in my bedroom while Norman, having come home from the restaurant in the early hours, was trying to sleep. I don't suppose there's a household in the country that hasn't had a mother or father of teenage kids saying, '*Turn that music down!*' and, on this occasion, it happened to me. Norman stormed into my bedroom, clad in only a T-shirt and therefore naked from the hips down. I was mortified that I'd woken him up but, at the same time, I was struggling to stifle my giggles. There's something very amusing about a man who's trying to make a point while he's standing there with all his bits hanging out. But I also remember thinking, 'He's absolutely right. The music *is* too loud.'

There were times when he was driving me to school or we were just out and about in the car together when we would talk about this and that, but our relationship always remained rather strained and ambivalent. I suppose I did resent him. Norman, like most men who live on their own for a very long time, was set in his ways and uneasy about sharing his space at home. I think he probably tried very hard with me, but he never quite succeeded. He smoked a pipe and I remember thinking, 'That's what old men do,' but I realized he *wasn't* an old man – he was only in his early forties. At least I liked the smell of his tobacco wafting around the house.

Aldenham School wasn't nearly as regimented as Orley Farm. We were older boys and allowed much more freedom to roam and go cycling in our free periods, and we were even allowed our own transistor radios. A little freedom, though, only makes you want more. I was now of the age where, having been allowed out on my own at home, I resented being confined to school premises day and night. So after a couple of terms of being a boarder, I started to kick up a huge fuss to become a day boy. I suspect that this also had much to do with Mum's remarriage. That change, coming relatively soon after the previous year's dramas of Dad dying, Aubrey leaving and my move to a new school, had taken its toll. I was suffering badly from asthma and so emotionally stretched that, on one occasion, when I was sent to the school's sanatorium, I was kept in and put on Librium. It amazes me now that anyone would administer such a strong tranquillizer to a young child and I dare say that this wouldn't happen today. But I was kept on it for at least six months. I was constantly drowsy and felt like a zombie. The Librium also made me gain weight, which was a disaster because I was already quite fat and in pretty bad shape. Perhaps this was why it was decided that I would be better off living at home under Mum's wing. I don't know for sure, I just know that I got my way and became a day boy. I was much happier then. Mum or Norman used to drive me to school in the mornings, which was lovely for me, but must have been a great chore for them. Mum was not an early-morning person and Norman had to go to Covent Garden Market first. Coming home, I used to walk across Five-Minute Field (that's how long it took to cross it) and into the village to catch a bus from Leavesden, which took me to Watford where I would get a train home. That journey, from school to home, took an hour.

Once I had become a day boy I had to move from Kennedy's House, which was for boarders, to School House, which put me in the unique position of being the only boy in the history of Aldenham to change houses. My best friend at school was Martin Leach. We were very like-minded, loved the same music and got on brilliantly well. As a student he was as carefree as I was and, although he could have been a great sportsman, he had a couldn't-care-less attitude and wasn't fussed about any of those activities. We used to spend as much time as we could together and particularly enjoyed going off cycling. After I left school we remained friends for quite a while before we lost touch. Chris Miller was another of my friends from those days and, much later on, I was best man at his wedding. Chris and I used to sneak off to Elstree aerodrome and watch the planes taking off and landing. In fact, Chris, Martin and I were like the Three Musketeers. Those two lads – and another boy called Lawrence Moore – were my closest buddies at Aldenham.

Sadly, I never really improved as a student. I remained a student plagued by 'could do better', 'must try harder', 'needs to work'. Perhaps the tranquillizers had something to do with this. I particularly liked Divinity, though, because I enjoyed the Bible stories. But I was the worst ever student at History. Mr Wood, the History teacher, had the nickname 'Creepy' because we felt he had a Christopher Lee feel about him, was very light on his feet and seemed like something out of a Hammer horror film. In reality, he was just a quietly spoken man, but you know what schoolboys are! They tend to seize upon a characteristic and make a big deal of it. He wasn't helped by the fact that all the masters, including him, wore long black robes. I also found his voice irritating, perhaps because he spoke so quietly it was difficult to hear what he was saying. I don't think he liked me much either and he was always saying I would fail my History O-level. Maybe this taunt spurred me on. The night before the History exam I revised and, to my total amazement – and certainly to the amazement of many others – I actually passed.

When I got the result, I remember Mr Wood coming towards me as I was walking from the music room to the football pitch. 'Good afternoon, Mr Wood,' I said smugly.

'Good afternoon, Winton.'

'Are you going to congratulate me?'

'I suppose so,' he mumbled. 'I don't know how you did it, Winton, but well done.'

In the end, though, I only got three O-levels: one for History, the other two for English and Divinity. If I had added Woodwork to that list, maybe I could have made a career as an undertaker!

I suppose, as I look back now, the highlights of 1970, when I was fifteen, had nothing to do with school, but with two social events. During the school hols, just before Grandma moved to Millhouses, Mum took me up to see her in Sheffield. We drove up in a friend's Vauxhall Viscount, a fabulous dark-green car with a black vinyl roof, which had 'powerglide', whatever that meant. As Mum parked this outside Grandma's council flat, loads of kids crowded around it because they had never seen such a luxurious car on the estate before.

When Mum got out of it, looking very glamorous, this also caused quite a stir. I was then deposited with Grandma for a week. At this time Uncle Joe had got a lovely new girlfriend called Lorraine, one of the go-getting girls of Sheffield, whom he later married and had several children by. Lorraine was slim, trendy and very 'hip', and wore lots of eyeliner. She knew all the records that were in the charts and it was great to be able to chat about the latest hits, such as 'Tears of a Clown', by Smokey Robinson and The Miracles, which were at number one around that time.

One evening Lorraine took me to a pub in the middle of Sheffield, the first pub I'd ever been into. This was in the days of the miniskirt and I was just blown away by the pop culture. I thought it was fantastic. I adored Lorraine. It was like being taken under the wing of a gorgeous older sister and I just thought she was the best thing ever. On reflection, I was probably just a fat teenager whom she'd been landed with, but I had the time of my life. When we were in the pub, I remember thinking, 'God, *this* is nightlife. I wish we could come up here more often!' It really was a shame that we lived so far from them because both Mum and I loved her mother and her brothers. Distance never helps to retain a really close bond, but nevertheless the bond was always there.

The second social highlight that year was the Isle of Wight pop festival, which every teenager, including me, wanted to go to. Free and Jimi Hendrix were appearing there, along with Procul Harum, Chicago, The Doors, Ten Years After, Joni Mitchell, The Who, the Moody Blues, Miles Davis and Jethro Tull. It was a monumental festival and Jeremy Askwith, the younger brother of Robin Askwith, the actor, and a friend of mine at Orley Farm, mooted the idea of us going. Although I was more into pop and Jeremy was more into rock, we both shared a love of music and had become really good friends. Jeremy was a brilliant drummer and I remember going to his house in Ruislip Manor where he had a drum kit assembled in the sitting room. The chief question that day, though, was how could we get our parents to agree to us going to the Isle of Wight? This, after all, was the era when they would have seen TV footage of pop festivals like Monterey in California where people lived in huts, didn't wash, were very scruffy and were always wading around in mud and rain. And, since it was the tail-end of the hippy era, they probably took lots of substances, too. Pop festivals represented everything that was probably abhorrent to our parents – the antithesis of anything they had ever done or believed we should do.

In the end a deal was struck that we could go to the festival provided we didn't sleep rough and went back to our hotel every night. So, armed with a big floppy hat which I thought made me look very glamorous (but actually made me look like a complete twit) Jeremy and I went off to the Isle of Wight, stayed in a hotel and went to the concerts on both days. There we stood, at least two miles away from the stage, up to our ankles in mud, surrounded by thousands of people, with Jeremy loving every minute of Jimi Hendrix, while I was longing for the comforts of home. At least I could say I had been there, heard Free and seen Jimi Hendrix and everybody else who was performing, but if I had been really honest I'd have admitted I would rather have gone to see a pop concert in a civilized environment like Wembley!

The other things I particularly remember about the late 1960s and early 1970s were Amen Corner being at number one in the pop charts with 'Half as Nice'; Thunderclap Newman being number one with 'Something's in the Air', Dusty releasing her album, *Dusty in Memphis*, and Robert Wagner appearing in a great TV series, *It Takes a Thief*, which I used to rush home from school to watch. Another great thrill for me was seeing Concorde, which had made its twenty-minute maiden flight in 1969. It was absolutely amazing. I remember looking up at it, thinking, 'Will I *ever* get to fly in that?' When I did, many years later, it was a dream come true. I'd achieved an ambition I'd always had from the first moment I saw it flying over London. I also remember that because Mum and I had so much enjoyed seeing Dustin Hoffman in *The Graduate*, she took me as a treat to a cinema in Tottenham Court Road to see *Midnight Cowboy*, starring Dustin Hoffman and Jon Voight. On this occasion, though, I recall feeling very uncomfortable during the scene in which a man performs a sexual act on Jon Voight in a cinema on 42nd Street. Mum looked at me as if to say 'I *can't* believe I've brought you to see this. . .' and I thought, 'I *can't* believe I'm sitting here watching this with my mother!'

By now, Mum's relationship with Norman was in trouble. She was very unhappy and they were rowing all the time. These arguments probably began with silly little domestic things, but then got out of hand. Mum was usually a very calm, placid person, but when she couldn't take any more and lost her temper she completely lost it and things could get nasty. It was wise to stand well back then. She never had any fear and, in a way, I don't either. I will push the envelope every time. When Mum was pushed she would say, 'Fine! *OK*!' and then really dig her heels in. On at least ten occasions she kicked Norman out of the Hatch End house and sometimes when they continued the fight on the lawn, the police had to be called to separate them. Some relationships are very fiery and theirs certainly was. They clearly brought out the worst in each other.

With hindsight, it was the sort of family life drama that even soap writers would find challenging to write about. Norman had proved to be a very domineering man and the marriage wasn't at all what either of them had thought it would be. Norman, of course, had never been married before and didn't know how to act with a person who would not give in to him and be downtrodden. When Mum said no, she meant no, and when she kicked him out of the house she meant that, too. But Norman would never just go. A very volatile man, with a terrible temper, he would shout back and the fights would become frightening. In the end Mum would say, 'If you don't go, I will call the police.' He never believed her, but she did. I remember the police coming several times when she and he were continuing their push-shove wrestles outside on the lawn. Probably nowadays the police would simply call it another domestic, but in those days it was all taken much more seriously.

I can't really recall any of this having a deep emotional effect on me because I always knew that it wasn't me in the firing line – and there'd always been an air of volatility in our family, anyway. I was never really frightened that Norman would do Mum physical harm because men *didn't* hit women and it never even entered my mind that he might. Had he done so, that would have been a different matter and a real shock. But they never came to actual blows. They only shouted and wrestled as she tried to chuck him out of the house or stop him coming back in, and keys were often thrown about on the lawn. It wasn't pleasant to witness, but I just thought, 'Norman's in trouble again – and quite right, too!' I was never a big fan of his so, on the occasions he had to go, I was quite glad to be rid of him.

About eighteen months into the marriage, Mum threatened him with a divorce and things became exceedingly unpleasant when Norman's father, Jack Isow, who'd been in trouble during the war for black-marketeering, rang up and threatened her. 'If you don't call the dogs off my son,' he growled, 'I'll have both your legs broken.'

Needless to say, Mum was very distressed.

After Mum separated from Norman she decided to do her own DIY divorce. During these proceedings it all got even more nasty. Norman put a charge on our Hatch End house so Mum couldn't sell it. She told him to take the charge off because it was her home. He refused, so she put a charge on his flat in Knightsbridge and, even more important, on a Swiss Bank account and a safe deposit box that he had in Pall Mall. The latter proved to be crucial because the information that Mum had about his safe deposit box was invaluable when it came to their settlement. It just goes to show how far a person will go when they feel the roof over their head is threatened, and Mum was certainly single-minded when it came to her rights. She used to ask her mother for advice and I remember hearing about one memorable summit meeting in a restaurant when Grandma laid into Norman about him not coming up to scratch as a husband.

During the school hols, I also recall Mum poring over law books in the dining room, checking for legal precedents. She was more than prepared to take Norman to the wire, but on the day of a court hearing Norman's solicitor settled and she got the charge lifted off the house, which was all she had ever wanted. This was one of the rare occasions she made the daily newspapers with a story that had nothing to do with her showbiz life and, as it was settled out of court at the last minute, the judge chastised Mum for wasting the court's time!

After this incident I remember Mum going to see Mr Griffin, my headmaster, to ask if I could be put on a scholarship because her marriage had ended and she had met with unfortunate financial circumstances. I wasn't in the least embarrassed by this and the headmaster was happy to oblige. Most of Aldenham's teachers, in fact, were very good to me because they knew that there was something theatrical and different about me. I'm sure if anyone asked them now, 'Did you think Dale would become a radio disc jockey and TV presenter?' they'd reply, 'Oh, God, *yes*! We could see that coming a mile off. He was such an extrovert.' Looking back, I can see that I did waste some of the privileges of a public school education, but I also suspect I'd have been less popular if I had excelled. There was fat chance of that, though. I was lazy and would only ever apply myself if I was enjoying something. By the time I was fifteen, all I wanted was to be out in the world doing something – *anything* – in the music business and earning some of that decimal currency that had just come into being. I think I always realized that university was a great opportunity for those who wanted to go that route but, to this day, when I meet people in their forties who are eternal students, going from one course to another, still trying to find themselves, I cannot get my head round it.

When, aged sixteen, I was allowed to leave Aldenham in the summer of 1971, I was more than ready to join the big wide world. Norman, despite all his problems with Mum, put in a good word for me with the impresario, Bernard Delfont, who was a regular diner at his restaurant. It wasn't difficult for him to do this for me with a friend of his and that's how I started up in the music business.

'If Dale wants to be in the biz,' Bernard replied, 'I can help him, but he must start at the bottom and work his way up.'

I was absolutely over the moon when Norman told me Bernard Delfont had got me a job in the stockroom of HMV, Oxford Street, stacking and shrink-wrapping records in Polyfilm. 'This', I thought, 'is a good beginning.'

When I arrived at HMV on my first day, I discovered that the stockroom was a long, narrow room at the rear of the first floor of the store, with a goods lift at one end that went straight down to a street-level door where the delivery vans arrived. It was the job of myself and the other lads to take it in turns to collect the records. The shrink-wrapping machine was at the other end of the room and we used to sit on high chairs with stacks of LPs and 45 rpm records placed in front of us, checking the stock off against an advice note. (Nowadays, it's all computerised.) The stockroom was a music-free zone, but I loved looking at the new releases as they came in. For me it was a job from heaven. In all other respects, of course, it was just like any other stockroom. Off to one side of it was an office, staffed by people who dealt with all the returns. Unlike our stockroom manager, Bill Webb, they didn't wear overalls.


When Mum became truly downhearted about three or four years after she'd given up her career, she used to say to me, 'I was just getting *really* established, Dale. I should have stuck at it.' I remember her agent ringing up one day and saying, 'Come on, Sheree, we'll get you back to work,' but Mum wasn't really interested. She did audition for the role of Purdey in the TV series, *The New Avengers*, but Joanna Lumley got that part. One morning, she also got as far as going for a new photo shoot. Even though she was wearing very little make-up for this because she was going for a more natural look, she still looked amazing. 'Mum,' I remember commenting anxiously, 'natural is *not* what you're known for. Go for the glam like you did before.' But she didn't listen; she'd lost her self-belief and I think she was afraid of going back. Thereafter, she continued to say, 'No, Dale, it was too hard. I can't do it any more.' I actually believe that she was kidding herself. She'd always enjoyed her work, however hard it was at the time. It was her loss of confidence and low self-esteem that was now preventing her from returning.

As far as I knew in those days, the first time Mum ever got really desperate about her situation and attempted suicide was in July 1971, the year I was sixteen and started work. Later I found a letter that she'd written in 1963 when I was eight, which made it very clear that there had been at least one earlier attempt. One line said, *I'm so sorry I had to leave you, Dale, but I always knew that I was prone to this . . .* On the 1971 occasion Bill Webb, who ran the HMV stockroom, rushed up to me in a panic and said, 'Dale, I've just had a phone call. You have to go home *now*. Your mother's not very well.' I tore home and Norman, whom Mum must have telephoned, was waiting for me and drove me straight to Mount Vernon Hospital. I discovered that Mum had taken an overdose of sleeping pills. By the time we arrived she had already had her stomach pumped, but it was, we were told, 'touch and go'. I was absolutely distraught, and I sat there for what seemed like an eternity before I was told that she had survived.

Once she was sitting up in bed, recovering and taking food, she was full of remorse. I was desperately shaken up and upset, and she promised me over and over that she would never do it again.

'Not to have peace of mind, Dale,' she kept lamenting, 'is a *terrible thing*.'

At sixteen years old, I didn't quite understand what she meant by not having peace of mind, but I do now. On the surface there was a beautiful woman, reasonably financially secure, living in a beautiful house, popular with lots of friends. It seems like a good life, but something was obviously lacking and eluding her, and when depression gets a hold on you, everything becomes magnified and nothing gives you the peace of mind you crave. I can only guess, but I think Mum's depression had as much to do with a fear of the future as her difficulties in the past. She had never had peace of mind where the men in her life were concerned and had always been emotionally vulnerable. That was a terrible tragedy because she was loving, witty, bright and glamorous, all the things that could be wished for in a human being, and people couldn't help but adore her.

I was due to take my driving test on the Monday while Mum was still in hospital, and she absolutely insisted that I should do this. To please her, I did and, amazingly in the circumstances, I passed. This meant that I could drive her home when she was discharged from the hospital, which I think was what she really wanted.

That, then, was the first of her suicide attempts that I knew about, but over the next four years there were several others when she was having serious problems with insomnia. It was such a shame that she had such awful problems getting to sleep because this always left her feeling very depressed. Ironically, her bedroom was a beautiful, restful room. It had wall-to-wall white fitted wardrobes, a big dressing table and a really lovely soft mauve carpet. There was a huge double bed, with a lovely antique wooden headboard, and an armchair alongside it. It was really restful and always smelled of her perfume.

There were times during this period when she was *very* upset, emotional and tearful. Once, when she'd been having a really hard time because of her insomnia, and had stayed in her room for two or three days, she came downstairs crying because she thought there was something wrong with her eyesight. It turned out to be a reaction to the sleeping tablets and, once she went back to bed again and slept it off, she could see perfectly normally again. More often than not, she was just quiet and dazed. I used to try to talk to her about her state of mind and attempted suicides, and she was always so remorseful afterwards. I would cry, and she would cry and say again and again, 'I'm *so* sorry, Dale. I *don't* want to leave you. I will *never* do it again.' But I lived in fear. A 'Do Not Disturb' sign would go on to her bedroom door and, during the bad times, she would become a total recluse. However, on good days she would talk to her girlfriends on the phone. It was a very strange and painful existence. I remember her doctor, Dr Maclaren, whose surgery was just round the corner from our home, prescribing her tranquillizers and goodness knows what else. On one occasion he said to me, 'In ninety per cent of these cases, the people who do this don't really want to die. They do it as a cry for help. But the terrible thing is that your mother *means* to do it every time. You can keep on trying to save her, but I'm very sorry to tell you that there will be an occasion when this will be impossible. Her mind is *absolutely* set on it.'

During this period there was a man who was besotted with her and, although he was never her lover, he'd do anything for her. This included going to his own doctor and getting sleeping tablets prescribed for himself, which he then gave to her. This was appalling. On some occasions Mum took so many she was in a terrible state and Dr Maclaren would have to come round to see her. Usually he just calmed her down, put her back to bed and told me she would sleep it off.

On another occasion, when Mum was in a terrible state after one of her suicide attempts, I remember saying, 'You're a braver person than I am – or will ever be – if you can consider doing such a thing.'

'Brave! It's not brave,' she replied. 'It's the coward's way out, Dale. It's simply that when depression hits you as badly as it hits me, it's the easiest thing to do.'

From the time I was seventeen, then, the worrying 'Do Not Disturb' sign, which meant that I was not to knock on the door and possibly wake her, appeared ever more frequently. Her sleep disorder was getting more and more troublesome, which was awful for her because she loved to sleep – it was her way of escaping from life. The appearance of the sign went through phases; sometimes she'd be her old self and up ringing her friends, then she'd feel bad again and it would go back on the door. To this day, whenever I see a 'Do Not Disturb' sign on a hotel door it brings back painful memories of this dreadful period. On Sunday mornings, when I was at home, she often didn't appear until two in the afternoon. The answerphone was always on so she could monitor the calls. This had more to do with shutting out the world than trying to avoid anybody in particular and she always found it easier not to respond than to make up excuses for not going to someone's house for lunch or dinner. It also gave her the freedom to ring back when she felt better. She was really very insular at this time, and would only speak to two of her closest actress friends, Caron Gardener and Marianne Collins. She wasn't socializing anywhere and I never came into contact with her friends, except for a very brief moment when I answered the phone to them.

There were so many times when I prayed that she'd be her normal self and not in a downer. I so much wanted my mum to be there but, at the same time, my own life was beckoning. Mum had spent most of her adult life making a life for me, but she completely understood how I felt. I could also, despite her frame of mind, still tell her most things – well, *almost* most things, as I was a sexually active young man by then. Despite her low spirits, she was very good about letting me be more independent. But she could still be strict. To the day she died, if she heard me say the word 'bloody' in the house, I'd get a clip round the ear as she exclaimed, '*What* did you just say? Are you going to say that again?'

'No, Mum,' I'd reply. 'It just slipped out. *Really* sorry.'


For somebody who was obsessed with the music business, HMV had turned out to be the best job I could ever have imagined. Even after a year in the job, I honestly thought I'd died and gone to heaven. Bill Webb, our stockroom manager, was a kind, sweet man, just like the character that Peter Sellers played in the film, *I'm All Right, Jack*. There were six other lads and I was the lowest on the rung. They'd all got their jobs from the Labour Exchange; I'd got mine by recommendation from Bernard Delfont. They had cockney accents, I'd come straight from public school and had a very posh 'stewed prunes' accent. They soon knocked that out of me. Working there was a whole new discipline for me. I'd get my wages at the end of the week and, after deductions, such as paying Mum rent or loans back to teach me the value of money, I would spend most of it on records. We were lucky, we saw all the new releases as they came in and we got a staff discount of twenty-five per cent. I remember buying the theme music from the movie *Shaft* and I was nearly catatonic when Dusty Springfield's album *See All Her Faces* came out. I didn't even know that was going to be released until one of the lads, who knew I adored her, said, 'Dale, there's a new Dusty album.' HMV's original order was for seventy-five copies and I remember thinking, 'Oh, good, she's still popular!' This was the time of Neil Young's *Harvest* album and Cilla Black's hit single 'Something tells me . . .', and I remember having to stack all these records. It was a labour of love, a joy.

I was always the extrovert and with my showbiz ambition burning ever brighter within me I got my first DJ job at a place called the Old King Lud. The King Lud was at the bottom of Fleet Street, a grotty pub frequented mainly by printers. My talents at the turntable were complemented with the gyrating presence of stripper go-go dancers. In a generous endeavour to show support for me, Mum made a huge effort one night and arrived in a mink coat, looking absolutely amazing. However, after taking one look at the pub and its customers, she exclaimed, 'My God, is this what I sent him to public school for?' She then added, 'Do a radio course, Dale. I know you're going to be a success. Be a DJ, if you want to, but *not* here! Let's find out how to get you a job on radio.' She was still trying to guide me and despite her personal problems, she wasn't permanently living in her room during this period.

Mum was by then very short of money but, bless her, I can remember two occasions when I wanted to buy another car and she said she'd lend me the money if I paid the loan back out of my earnings each week. From a very early age Mum had instilled in me the principle of repaying any money I had received to pay for the things that I wanted. It was only the principle of the thing she cared about, because she often found ways of giving the money back to me. I had a little book in which I wrote down the sums I owed, then, when I received my wages, I used to give her the cash to cover my debts, rent and bills, and tick them off. I can't have been that spoiled, even though she was always trying to make life easy for me.

On one of the change-of-cars occasions, I wanted a Ford Cortina which, with all the knobs on, looked like a 1600E, *the* car to have. When I found out how costly this was, Mum said, 'Why do you want to buy an expensive saloon car when you can get a *proper* sports car for less money? At the end of the day, Dale, sports cars are timeless. It doesn't matter how old they are and they're much more fun.' That had never occurred to me and she was absolutely right. She then tracked down an old Volvo, just like the one that Simon Templar drove in the TV series *The Saint*. I was thrilled. It was a 1966 car, about six or seven years old then, with the number plate MLT 255D, and it still looked amazing. It cost just £600 pounds and, once again, Mum lent me the money, which I then ticked off in a book each week as I paid it back. I felt like the King of the Road and ready for life in the fast lane.

I thought Mum was brilliant to advise and help me out in this way, but I knew she wasn't happy within herself. Doing things for me gave her a purpose and a temporary respite from feeling so awful, but she couldn't keep covering up just how miserable she really was and, sadly, she soon went into decline again.

It's very easy for me to say that work is good for the soul and that had Mum listened to her agent and her friends and returned to work during this time, her career might have kept her going and eased her depression. But she was obviously feeling too low most of the time even to consider this, and just kept on thinking, 'What's the point?' Also, because I was now grown-up and earning my own living, there was no longer the same impetus for her to be the breadwinner and to provide for my every need. I was twenty-one. I'd given in my notice at HMV and was a full-time DJ doing lunchtime and evening discos. I often left home at eleven in the morning and didn't return until 3.30 a.m. the next day, and the 'Do Not Disturb' sign might still be on the door when I left home again. I was a grafter, I *loved* being a DJ and working late at clubs.

Inevitably, as happens in every mother's life when a child grows up and becomes independent, Mum's role in caring for me had somewhat diminished in her eyes and, although she never said as much, this must have been an additional emotional factor in her roller-coaster life. Like most people in this situation, she needed more than ever to have her own loving partner, someone special who would always be there for her. Sadly, it was not to be.

When I did come home from work during the day I was never sure whether her bedroom would have the dreaded 'Do Not Disturb' on the door. I never ever got used to seeing this and, each time it was hanging there, I panicked, thinking, 'Oh, God! What do I do? If I ignore it and knock on the door I might wake her up.' Part of me was always scared but, after a moment or so, I would comfort myself with the thought that she had promised me faithfully over and over that she would never again attempt to commit suicide, and she had also told me repeatedly that the sign would only be on the door because she was catching up on lost sleep. Three or four times a week this was true. At some point she would wake up, come downstairs and say, 'I'm *fine*, Dale. I just wanted to be left in peace.' I realize now, of course, that the 'Do Not Disturb' sign was there to make sure that she wouldn't be interrupted when she made that final decision to end her life.

Mum had always told me that throughout her youth she'd never had a problem with her monthly cycle but, during the last couple of years, she mentioned that this had changed and she was now having very heavy periods. Much more is known these days about the adverse psychological effects of pre-menstrual tension, and how this can cause women to run the whole gamut of emotions and cause some to become verbally or physically abusive, shoplift, or attempt suicide. Some have even been cleared of murder when the jury accepted medical evidence that PMT affected the balance of their minds and caused them to act out of character. With hindsight, I am now very sure that, during the period from 1971 to 1976, when Mum was making her suicide attempts, PMT was at the root of her problems. The Christmas after she died, I actually found a diary in which she'd written, *I am feeling so unmaternal. I love my son, but I feel so unmaternal at the moment. This is not me. What's going on?*

Despite all her promises, she did make several other attempts on her life and, about six months before she died, I arranged for Dr Maclaren to have her admitted to Bowden House Clinic, Harrow-on-the-Hill, which was for people with addiction problems. Mum's was a sleeping tablet addiction, of course. She was in the clinic for a week or so, being treated for depression and withdrawal from the tablets, and she came out in much better shape. By then I'd also laid down the law and said, 'That person who's been getting you sleeping tablets which the doctor hasn't prescribed must *never* come into this house again.' She agreed and, on this occasion, we collected all the sleeping tablets in the house and flushed them down the toilet. It was a very brave gesture for her to make and she said, 'It won't happen again, Dale.' And, my God, she tried. She started going out with her friends again, accepted invitations to the theatre, went out to restaurants and became altogether much more social. For the last four months of her life, people were saying, 'Oh, isn't it wonderful – Sheree's back!'

On Friday 28 May 1976, Mum made me breakfast and waved me off to work, something she had not done for several years. As I left, I remember thinking what a beautiful day it was. That evening I was working at my residency at Charlee Brown's Nightclub, Tottenham. We didn't have mobile phones in those days and, in the middle of my gig, at about eleven o'clock, the manager came up to me with an anxious look on her face and said, 'Dale, your mother's on the phone.'

I was very surprised that she had rung me during work, but I went immediately to speak to her. 'What is it, Mum?' I said.

'Where's my prescription?' she said angrily. 'I told you to go and get my prescription from the doctor's.'

To this day I don't remember ever seeing a prescription in the house, or her telling me to go and get one. 'What prescription?' I asked, surprised by the unnaturally aggressive tone of her voice.

'*Don't* talk to me like that,' she snapped. It was as if she were deliberately trying to pick a fight with me.

'Mum,' I said, 'I'm working. If there is a prescription, I'll go and get it tomorrow.'

'Don't come home tonight,' she suddenly shouted down the phone. 'I'm locking you out. Don't come home. I've just about had it with you.' And she hung up.

Having been subjected to what I thought was a totally unjustified onslaught, I had to go back to work and get on with the gig. But, coming out of the blue as it had, the phone call had been a shock and

I was taken aback and upset. For the last few months Mum had been off the sleeping tablets. In the real world she had seemed to be herself again. When I had left home that morning she had waved me off and seemed absolutely fine. At the time, in worrying over the abruptness of the call, I felt that perhaps she was having a fleeting bad moment. But when I think about it now I realize it was very unusual behaviour for her to ring me at work. She had never done that before. When I finished the gig, I thought to myself, 'Whatever she's said, I've got to go home. She's never told me not to before, and by the time I get there she'll be in bed and everything will be forgotten by the morning.'

I drove out of Charlee Brown's, which was in a one-way system, and as I drove down the road a cat ran out in front of me, squealing. I will never forget that sound. For some reason it signalled that something *was* wrong at home with Mum. And even though some people will think I'm mad, I remember thinking, '*My God, she's dead*!'. I immediately tried to put this awful thought out of my mind, though. 'This is crazy,' I chastised myself. 'You're only thinking that because Mum rang you at work and had a row. But she's been brilliant recently, nearly back to her old self.'

When I got to our front door, I was still a bit shaken, but my first thought was, '*Has* she locked me out?' She hadn't, my key turned in the lock and, as I entered the house, all seemed quiet and normal. Tiptoeing upstairs, I saw the 'Do Not Disturb' sign on the door, stood there a moment, then decided to go to bed. I didn't know what else to do. We'd had a row and she had told me not to come home; and she had a temper on her. I didn't want to risk waking her up by going in to see if she was OK. On the Saturday morning when I got up, I noticed that the 'Do Not Disturb' sign was still on the door. But it was earlyish and I thought, 'I won't push this.' I went out to meet a friend, as arranged. I then carried on with my usual Saturday routine, which was to pick up Friday's newly released records and sort out the ones I wanted for my DJ work.

I eventually returned home at about four in the afternoon. The 'Do Not Disturb' sign was still on the door and I stood there wondering whether I should wake her before I went out to work. By that time I had rationalized the fact that we had had a most unusual conversation the night before. She'd been so good since she came out of the clinic that I genuinely thought her suicidal days were behind us. I just thought that she would wake up in her own good time while I was pottering around in the house, listening to my records, having a bath and getting ready to go out to my gig.

I didn't know that Mum had arranged to go out to dinner that evening with Robert Williams, who had recently separated from his wife and lived just up the road, until he phoned at six o'clock and told me so. Robert was a very distinguished-looking man, who owned Williams furniture shops and his company's TV commercial had the strap line 'That's the wonder of Williams'. 'Dale,' he said, 'can you tell Sheree I'll be round in an hour or so?'

'The "Do Not Disturb" sign's still on her door,' I replied. 'I don't know if she's remembered she's going out with you, Robert.'

'Go and knock on the door,' he said, 'and just ask if she still wants to go out. And if so, what time?'

I put the phone down on the table and went upstairs. I knocked on the door and called out, 'Mum . . . *Mum!*' but there was no reply. I then banged louder, but there was still no answer. I tried to open the door, but it was locked from the inside. Running back downstairs, I said to Robert, 'There's no answer. I don't know what to do. The door's locked from inside.'

'I'll come round,' he said.

By now very frightened, I went back upstairs and continued to bang on the door and call out ever more loudly, '*Mum!*'

When Robert arrived we broke the door open.

To our unspeakable horror, we discovered the desperate, heart-rending tragedy that haunts me still. Mum had taken a fatal overdose and had died. I stood there crying hysterically, feeling instantly ill and sick at the same time. In the room were two suicide notes. One was addressed to me, the other to Peter Eden, who had always been the love of her life. Robert handed me the two notes and ushered me out of the room. I remember holding them and thinking, 'These are private. People mustn't see them.' I put the notes in my pocket and rang 999. I spoke to the police as instructed by the ambulance service, then telephoned the man my mother had always loved. Peter responded at once and came to the house, where he met Robert, which was all very strange. I was in a state of absolute shock, totally unable to take in the arrival of the police, or the subsequent removal of Mum's body from the house. Phone calls were made to various relatives and, during one of these, I was persuaded to go and stay with my cousin and his wife. It must have been very difficult for them because they had a young child, hardly knew me and I had never even been to their house. But they were wonderful.

The next day I read my mother's suicide note, which had been written on a scrappy piece of paper. In the letter Mum apologized for what she had done, and asked me to water the geraniums and look after the house. I was utterly heartbroken, and still quite incapable of taking anything in.

In the meantime, while I was staying miles away in Boreham Wood, the whole process of the police removing forensic material from the house for the coroner and the arranging of the cremation was going on. After a week, I decided to return home.

It was desolate going back into the house. It was a truly terrible moment and defeats any words that I can write.

I had given the other suicide note to my mother's ex-lover, without reading it. When Peter called at the house I asked him what was in the letter. 'Your mum asked me to look after you,' he said.

I believe she would have done that.

The post-mortem revealed that she had died hours before I came home in the early hours of the Saturday morning; and even if she had been found on the Friday night, no one could have saved her. I also realized that she had timed her death for that time for a reason. That Friday, when she waved me off to work, was exactly seven days after my twenty-first birthday. I think she had lovingly waited for me to come of age before killing herself. Although she had appeared to be making progress, she was still desperately unhappy and depressed, and this was the time she chose. Since then, it has always angered me when the police or coroners say, 'This person took their life while the balance of their mind was disturbed.' 'You may say that,' I think, 'but in Mum's case she knew exactly what she was doing.' She always used to say to me, 'If I go, Dale, it's because I *really* want to. *Please* don't ever let anyone try to bring me back.'

That last week of Mum's life was to be more crucial than any of us realised. For the first time in many years she was making calls and arranging to meet friends. It transpired that in the seven days prior to her death, she saw as many friends as she could, and those she couldn't see she spoke to on the telephone. It now seems that this was her way of saying goodbye. She had asked her best friend, Caron, to arrange a lunch for the two of them, plus a couple of other friends – but she had asked Caron to arrange it for the day *after* she killed herself. I know that Mum was relieved when Caron changed her original idea of venue from a restaurant to the house of one of the girls, probably because she knew she wouldn't be there, and was happier that they wouldn't be sitting in some restaurant waiting for her to turn up. Over the phone, the night she died, Mum asked Caron to take care of me. It was all planned incredibly carefully, and proves she had thought everything through.

One really miserable thing that I had to do after Mum died was to go to the police station and collect everything they'd taken from the house for forensic evidence. Nobody prepares you for such a moment and it was truly awful. One of the items I was given back was a very Sixties, pink-and-gold, frosted glass tumbler, the rim of which had been sealed with cling film by the police. It still contained the remains of the liquid that Mum had been drinking when she took the pills that killed her. I stood there looking at it in a state of acute shock and disbelief. I didn't know what to do with it, so I took it home with all the other items and, sobbing inconsolably, placed it gently on the kitchen table. It was heartbreaking.

I had some really desperate personal moments soon after Mum died and, on one occasion, I telephoned the Samaritans and went to see one of their volunteers. Whatever people say to comfort one, suicide is chiefly thought of as the ultimate rejection of loved ones, as well as of life, and those who are left need time to get beyond these thoughts. What is marvellous, though, and I want to emphasize *this*, is that although it is very easy to believe that suicide *is* the ultimate rejection of you as a person, I never felt that. Mum was always full of remorse after her many suicide attempts and I agreed with Dr Maclaren that this was not just a cry for help, but something she was determined to do. When, from the age of sixteen, you are put in this position and it goes on for five years, of course you say to yourself, 'How *could* you do this? How *could* you think of leaving me?' But what I was left with then – and now – is the thought that she was a brilliant mother, who brought me up very well with values and principles that have remained with me and saved me. But she was too depressed and emotionally vulnerable to save herself.

Immediately after the shock of bereavement, well-meaning people think that you need protecting and looking after, and everybody you meet seems to have advice for you. I would urge anybody confronted with a similar situation to mine to take their time before accepting anyone's advice. Where fundamental decisions are concerned, the early days of bereavement are not a good time to make hasty changes in your life. Taking a breather is essential. Mum had left a will, naming me as sole beneficiary and executor, so that I could do what I thought was right. There was no mortgage on the house and her savings meant that I could put by some of the money after meeting other expenses. People, however, kept saying 'Sell the house, Dale, and buy a flat', or 'Move into town, Dale', or 'Go on a holiday, Dale'. 'Do this, Dale . . .' 'Do that, Dale . . .' In fact, what I needed was a period when I could take stock and let things settle down. What I actually did was plough myself back into my work and just carry on.

Norman and my mum had become friends again after their divorce and, after she died, he came round a few times to see if I was OK. On one of those occasions he said, 'You know that time when your mother revealed that I had a safe deposit box in Pall Mall. Well, that opened a whole can of worms and caused me no end of problems with the Inland Revenue. It cost me a fortune because they went through everything.' By then he obviously wished he had not put a charge on the house and that he and Mum had settled things amicably. I lost touch with Norman soon after this.

In 1991, when Lionel Blair and I were guests on a TV show, Lionel, who knew Norman from Isow's restaurant, broke the news to me that Norman had died. 'I'm sorry,' he said, realizing that he had given me a shock. I knew that Norman had gone on holiday to the Caribbean, met someone there and married very quickly, but I didn't know that he had died.

It was a good year or so before I was able to face up to coping with Mum's belongings – her clothes and her personal effects. One thing that had bothered me throughout this entire period was that I couldn't find a gold chain that she used to wear nearly every day. Margaret Rutherford, the actress, had given this to her when they opened together in a play with Sid James at the Saville Theatre in London on 4 May 1965, and Mum loved it. There was a ruby on the chain and the date to mark the occasion. It really disturbed me that I couldn't find it. One day, I decided to go through all the pockets of Mum's clothes in her fitted wardrobe, but there was still no sign of the chain. I then sat on her bed, trying to think where she might have put it. She had two housecoats, one orange, one pink. As I sat there, a voice sounded in my head and, to this day, I'm sure this was Mum speaking to me. 'Left-hand pocket of orange housecoat. That's where the chain is.'

I got up from the bed, walked to the bedroom door and there, hanging behind it, was the housecoat with the chain in the pocket. My relief was phenomenal. It had had so much sentimental value attached to it for Mum. These days, I still pick it up, hold it and think ever fondly of her.

Like Mum, I have always been drawn to the unknown and fascinated by psychic readers, horoscopes and anything to do with self-knowledge. Although Mum loved all these, too, she always drilled into me from an early age that if anything ever happened to her, I should not go to a psychic reader with the specific purpose of getting in touch with her. 'If anybody ever says when I'm gone that we can be in touch,' she said, '*don't* do it, Dale. Apart from anything else, I don't want you to reach me. If I've gone, I want to be left in peace. *Do not disturb me.* You must respect that.' But in many ways she gave me mixed signals about this. Although she feared me being taken advantage of by a charlatan after she had gone, she consulted them herself.

I honoured her wish for three years until work placed me in a situation where I was to interview the world-renowned medium Doris Stokes as a guest on my radio show in Nottingham. Just before we were going on air to plug a book she had written, Doris said, 'Before we start, Dale, I've got a message for you from a spirit.' She then described my mother very accurately and told me that the spirit wanted me to know that she was OK. The spirit then talked about my friend, Mark, and what a good person he was, and how he was going to be important to me. (I am now godfather to his children.) The phrases that were used that day were those that my mother would have spoken. This wasn't a disturbing experience. It was just brilliant to know that Mum was happy and at peace, and I found it very comforting to have my feelings confirmed that she was still there somewhere. It made me feel very happy. It didn't change my attitude to religion, though. Although I had been brought up in the Jewish faith and had my bar mitzvah, I never got involved in practising one particular religion because I have always believed that there is good to be found in all of them. To this day, any kind of fanaticism where religion is concerned worries me. My philosophy is that if you lead a good life, don't hurt anyone and do your best by everybody, that's a good starting point. I do think religion is important as a guide, but I believe that you have to take from it what works for you. I also believe that an afterlife exists in some shape or form, and I still occasionally go to a clairvoyant because I find looking into the future through their eyes fascinating. From time to time, Mum has come through to me with some directions for my life. I've always believed that my success, coming as it did about ten years ago, so late, has saved me from certain disasters that are prevalent in showbiz. And I've felt that Mum is here with me as an ongoing, guiding force for my good.

In the days when she thought she might one day be a grandmother, she used to say, 'Never marry a really beautiful woman, Dale, because every man will try to take her from you.' She also used to say, 'By the way, when you *do* get married, remember it's just as easy to fall in love with a rich one as a poor one!' She had such a good sense of humour. I will always be sad that she was so desperately unhappy and so vulnerable where the men in her life were concerned. I'm especially sad now when so much is going on in my career and life. She would have been so thrilled. But I'm sure she sees everything.

For a long time when I was working, I wanted to please people, wanted them to love me. Often I knew from the way they looked at me that they were thinking I was too eager to please and that I wanted adulation. That may have been true to a certain extent but, to be fair, whatever my place is now and may be in the future, I feel I have earned it through commitment and sheer hard work. Even though this may sound immodest, I am very proud to have succeeded beyond my own expectations and wildest dreams. Part of me, of course, is still trying to please Mum. To this day, I think, '*God*! What would she have thought about this? What would she have said about that?' I remember Tony Gruner, who was one of the people who helped me get my first big break on *Supermarket Sweep*, coming into my dressing room, where I had a picture of Mum, and saying, 'Just before you go on, Dale, think of your mum. Do it for your mum.'

That was so wise of him and now I always think of her before I go on camera. She was in the business and I believe even now she understands exactly what's going on. The loving memory I have of her will always be an ongoing source of inspiration to me.

# 3

## 'I'll try anything . . .'

WHEN MUM DIED I was ill equipped to deal with day-to-day, nitty-gritty domestic matters. I was well prepared in the ways of etiquette and how to behave as a person, and I had an established sense of right and wrong, but I was completely unworldly in other ways. Mum had always taken care of so many things. I had a bank account but I remember sitting at the kitchen table, thinking, 'How do I pay my gas, electricity and phone bills? Do I use my chequebook?' At twenty-one, you'd think I'd have known how to do this, but I meet kids of less than ten years old these days who are more switched on than I was then. I marvel that they know all about credit cards, computers, hard drives and software when today, aged forty-seven, I am only just mastering the Internet and e-mails. It's strange, really, because I've been gadget-mad all my life. Looking back, I think I must have been particularly unswitched on. I was so soft about so many things. But I grew up quickly.

Fortunately, I had a good head on my shoulders. I'm amazed, knowing what an addictive personality I have, that I was never seduced by drugs or alcohol. I was very young to have inherited a house and Mum's money, and I could have gone to town on all sorts of things. I can only assume that the horrors of drugs and alcohol were instilled in me at such an early age that the fear of them was greater than the promise of any pleasure they might bring. Now, in later life, I also realize that this says a great deal about me as a person. The thought of taking anything that could cause me to lose control has always been abhorrent to me. There have been many times in my life when people have tried to force drink on me. 'Come on, Dale,' they say, '*loosen* up.' But actually that's the one thing I don't want to do – I think I'm loose enough as it is! My inborn zest for life is something I treasure. It's always been enough for me and that, plus my love of music and natural *joie de vivre*, were what kept me going after Mum died. I loved my life. My only ongoing pain was that Mum hadn't been happy and that I hadn't known what to do to make her happy.

It's hard to know if I would have found Mum's death easier to cope with, or been a different kind of person, if I had had a brother or sister. I never actually minded being an only child because I always thought Mum and I were complete. Knowing me as I am now, though, I think things would have been different if I hadn't been an only child. I probably had been a bit mollycoddled, but I guess that's what happens to a lot of kids whose parents come originally from a working-class background. When, like Mum, they make good, they naturally want their children to have an easier start in life than they had, and this can amount to a bit of over-indulgence, especially if, like me, the kids are told that their mum (or dad) is their best friend who will refuse them nothing. Mum always said, 'If you have any problems, Dale, come to me. Nothing will ever be too much trouble.' Kids need to know that they have someone in their life, such as a parent or other relative, whom they can go to for unconditional love and non-judgemental advice, and I always felt that Mum was my best friend as well as my mother.

I've always been a typical Gemini and, as anyone who's familiar with the zodiac knows, people born under this star sign are considered to be the chatterboxes, the charmers, the happy-go-luckys. Mercurial to a fault, so the sign says, they can apparently coax birds down from trees and they exude the kind of self-confidence that can remove more obstacles than a bulldozer. They look on life as their schoolyard, know exactly what they want and have the savvy to go about getting it. *But* – and it's a big but – beneath all that bravado is somebody who sometimes finds the world a rather complicated place and who's often a bit lost. Geminis, whose symbol is twins facing in different directions, epitomize a split personality. That just about sums up my character from adolescence to twenty-one – and it's still pretty accurate now.

At home, because of Mum's state of mind, I always suppressed the flamboyant and comedic side of my personality, which was why between sixteen and twenty-one I felt as if I were two different people. Outside the house, I was off the leash in the music biz at HMV, and when I became a DJ in pubs and nightclubs, I could be the showman and as extrovert as I wanted to be.

One day, not long after I started in the stockroom of HMV, one of the lads said, 'Dale, d'you wanna come round to the 'og in the Poun' for a drink at lunchtime?' The Hog in the Pound was a pub in South Molton Street in London's West End. I thought it was *great* to be asked. I was in with the lads, one of them, being included. Off I went, really pleased. The pub had a go-go dancer and a DJ who was playing records. When I looked at him, it was as if I had found the Holy Grail. 'That's what I want to do!' I thought. 'I want to be a DJ in a pub playing music.' Fired up, I marched straight up to the pub's manager. 'Where do you get your DJs from?' I asked.

An obliging man, confronted by an eager, pushy youth with a grapefruit juice in his hand, he replied, 'From an agency – DJ Enterprises – based out in Streatham – run by Edna and David James.' He then explained to me that Edna and David James visited pubs and venues all over London and talked managers into letting them install flashing lights and other gear, and persuaded them to employ DJs and go-go dancers.

Back at HMV, I rang the agency. 'My name's Dale Winton,' I said. 'I want to be one of your DJs.'

Edna, who had a wonderful Welsh lilt to her voice said, 'Have you ever done it?'

'Yes,' I lied. 'I'm good. I can do anything.'

I *was* sufficiently clued up to know that I could do what the chap in the pub had been doing. At the very least, I thought I could introduce records and talk on a microphone. Me, allowed to talk and play records – the idea was heaven! In those days, DJing in clubs and pubs was so different from how it is now. Today's DJs hardly ever utter a word. They do what is called 'mix and segue' (play records without a pause), but in those days, if you just stood there playing records you'd have been out of a job. You were expected to entertain as well. I was sixteen and, as far as I was concerned, it was a case of 'Let's do the show right here.'

'OK,' Edna said, 'we'll give you an audition.'

I put down the phone, stunned. It wasn't easy to concentrate on shrink-wrapping and stacking records in the stockroom that afternoon.

A couple of days later Edna James phoned me. I was, she instructed, to go to a pub miles out in the sticks of Surrey for what she said would be a 'try-out'. The pub was so far out, she added, that she would meet me – her 'new protégé' – at the train station. When she drove up in a Jensen Interceptor, quite a racy car to have at the time, I thought, 'Wow! I'm impressed with this.' In fact, I was so impressed that I don't recall anything about her. I was just *so* relieved that I had either looked much older than I was, or my tender age had not fazed her.

The organ-and-drums group that night was called Dragonmilk. They were obviously very popular with the locals and had pulled in a large beer-swilling crowd. The resident DJ, primed by Edna, let me do a few minutes and was then told, before she left, to report back to her on my performance. I wasn't very good, but I couldn't have been all bad because the next time I spoke to Edna she said, 'Right, go to the Redcliffe in Earls Court and do a proper audition.' I was in with a chance – and in London this time. I did my homework very carefully for the Redcliffe and sorted out all my latest records.

The Redcliffe was on the corner of Fulham Road and Redcliffe Gardens, and I remember it very well. An intimate venue it was not!

It was a huge pub, with a big open space of a room, where Geoff Bailey, king of the pub DJs at that time, was doing the auditions. As I was still working at HMV I had managed to get the latest records and I played two new releases, David Bowie's 'Star Man' and Elton John's 'Rocket Man'. '*Very good* choice of music, lad; *very nice*,' Geoff Bailey said. I was aglow! I was still too young to drink even if I wanted to, which I didn't, but there I was, standing on the stage, head and shoulders above the boozers now filling the huge space, spinning a line, playing my choice of records, and being a DJ.

Clearly unimpressed after my first performance, Edna James wasn't about to give me a gig. However, after that confidence-boosting experience I drove her mad. I rang her every week and, in the end, Edna caved in again and said, 'I want you to go and see Peter Tait, one of our top DJs, who's working in the White Hart, Willesden.'

This pub, which looked like a Bernie Inn from the outside, was another huge, vacuous place that reminded me of an aircraft hangar with optics and beer pumps, but the DJ made up for that. He was the best I'd ever seen or heard. Slim, with shoulder-length hair, Peter Tait *looked* the part, just like every DJ I'd seen on *Top of the Pops*. He also *sounded* like a DJ and was really into his music. I thought he was brilliant. Half an hour later, as I clutched my box of 45s, we were introduced. Peter clearly viewed my arrival on a quiet midweek night as an opportunity to have a well-earned break. 'Go on,' he said, 'let's see what you can do.'

With my usual bravado, I got up on the stage and, to my surprise and joy, Peter left me for nearly an hour playing my choice of records while he, who obviously had an eye for the ladies, stood at the bar chatting them up. It was great. At the end of the evening, he said, 'I think you were very good. I'll ring the agency and tell them that.' We'd hit it off straight away. We left the pub together, took a bus to the station and off he went to Croydon, Surrey, while I went in the opposite direction to Hatch End, Middlesex. A true friendship began that night, which has lasted to this day.

Once Peter's praise got back to Edna, she gave me my first proper booking at the Old King Lud pub at the bottom of Fleet Street. I was over the moon. With Mum's help, I had just bought my first Austin 1100 and now had my first real gig. I was set and more than capable of handling my two jobs: working at HMV during the day, and being a DJ at night.

'They've given me the Old King Lud,' I said to Peter.

'It's a rough old pub,' he warned. 'As it's in Fleet Street, it's always full of printers and there's always a fight there. The manager's a very tough, abrasive Irishman called Sean. Good luck! You're going to need it.'

The Old King Lud was on a corner site and had two entrances. As you walked in there was a ring of red velvet banquette seating, which had seen better days, running all around the central bar like a well-worn collar on an ageing poodle. The DJ's section was just a corner space by a door, which I soon discovered kept being opened and closed because it led upstairs to the ladies' loos and a room where the dancers changed. I saw immediately what Peter had meant. It was *very* rough. It's now a very fancy wine bar, but in those days it was far from fancy. There were two or three go-go dancers; and the DJs were expected to bring all their own gear – including lights – and wire it up and plug it all in.

Sean turned out to be a big, burly man with a ruddy complexion and a moustache. He looked exactly like the sort of man who would be at home running a rough pub and challenging all comers to a spot of arm wrestling. Giving me the once-over, he merely nodded and grunted. I was very overweight then, some eighteen stone, so I always used to wear what was comfortable. It may sound very strange for someone who is now known to be very clothes-conscious and always likes to look the part for television, but it never entered my mind then that I should try to dress differently. As far as I was concerned, the only thing that mattered was what you sounded like and the records you played. I always put on a clean shirt and trousers, and I sometimes wore a sweater, but how I looked was something I never worried about.

I smiled nervously back at Sean. I was an ex-public schoolboy, completely out of my depth in a spit-and-sawdust place. 'Right,' he then said, 'you've got two exotic dancers tonight.' Two sexy girls walked in obligingly, looked me up and down, and raised their eyes to heaven as if to say, 'Another DJ who doesn't know what he's doing – *and* a babyface one this time, who's still wet around the ears.' They then told me what records they wanted to dance to. These were always raunchy numbers such as Suzi Quatro's 'Can the Can', Sylvia's 'Pillow Talk' and Michael Jackson's 'Ain't no Sunshine' – that would get the printers in the mood to cast all their cares and inhibitions to the wind while they leered and jeered at the girls.

When I'd finished setting up the gear, I took a deep breath and started the gig. The girls, now scantily clad, responded to my DJing straight away. Obviously, second impressions were better than first. I might have been a babyface, but they thought I was good. I was so happy to be there, doing my first paid-for gig. At the end of the evening the girls, now relaxed, dressed and friendly, told me that no DJ had ever managed to survive five nights at the Lud, because it was so rough, and the manager was looking for a resident DJ. My ears pricked up and my heart skipped a beat, but Sean, the manager, hadn't said a word to me since the beginning of the evening. I packed up my gear, put it in my car, then stood for a moment on the pavement. I'd earned £4, the going rate, but I had to wait for that because it was paid to the agency first, so that Edna and David could take their commission.

Having paused, I geed myself up with the thought of how rude Sean had been to leave me totally unacknowledged and unwatered all evening, and went back into the pub. 'Sean,' I said, going up to him behind the bar. 'I'm the DJ. You may have noticed me. I've worked for you all night, packed up my gear and loaded it into my car. I didn't have a break all evening and *you*, the landlord, haven't even so much as offered to buy me a drink.'

The bar area fell silent. It was like, 'How would anybody dare speak to this man in this way?' But I wasn't being nasty, I was just making my point. It's always been my philosophy that you should have no fear and, even if you do, you should never show it.

Sean gave me the kind of stare which reminded me of Long John Silver without his parrot. Everyone present obviously thought he was going to give me the Irishman's equivalent of a Glasgow kiss. '*Ya what?*' he said.

'You heard me,' I replied. 'I've worked for five hours without a stop. I've taken the gear up and down the stairs of this pub. I've now packed up, having kept your pub full tonight, and you haven't even bought me a drink. I don't think that's very good.'

Silence reigned. Everybody was wondering how this young upstart dared to speak to Sean like that when they were all terrified of him.

'Would you *like* a drink?' he said to me.

Everybody breathed a sigh of relief.

'Thank you very much, Sean,' I said, pacified. 'I'll have a grapefruit juice, if you don't mind.'

'*A bloody grapefruit juice?*' He obviously thought this was the funniest thing he had ever heard and burst out laughing, but he said to the barman, 'Give the boy a *grapefruit* juice.'

The next day Edna James rang HMV, asking me to ring her back during my break. 'I don't know what you've done to Sean,' she said. 'But he's insistent you start there next week – *five* nights a week – as his resident DJ. Good *boy* – you've got a residency.'

I had just turned seventeen. I still hadn't the foggiest idea what the legal situation was for someone below the age of consent for a pint or a short to be working in a pub. Doubtless I shouldn't have been there at all. *But* . . .

There then followed the occasion when Mum turned up one night after she'd been to the theatre. She looked amazing, fully made up and wearing a full-length ranch-mink coat. All the printers thought Christmas had come early. Their jaws dropped and their eyes popped out on stalks. They thought she looked familiar, but they were not sure who she was. They probably hoped that she might be one of the go-go dancers – with class. She stood looking around the pub and I could see she was absolutely horrified. There I was, working in a corner of the bar, with no stage and only a makeshift wooden board on the floor for the girls to dance on. That was the moment she whispered to me, 'I'm not happy. I don't like you working in a rough pub like this, Dale. It could be dangerous. If you're going to be a DJ, you're going have to do it properly.'

Actually, that was very forward-thinking of her, but I loved that job and I certainly wasn't prepared to give up the pub just like that. Mum, though, with her ever-helpful eye for my future well-being, discovered a company called Roger Squires, which had a studio in St John's Wood. There, for £25, you could have five one-hour sessions and learn how to operate radio equipment and project your voice. You then came out with a demo audition tape. You have to understand this was before Capital Radio, and every other commercial station that we now take for granted, was on the air. On offer then for pop fans were Radio One and Two, and Radio Luxembourg. But everybody knew that commercial radio was about to explode and that within the next two or three years, every town in the country would have its own commercial station. Budding DJs knew that if they wanted to get on in the radio business that was on the verge of blossoming, we needed to get on the first rung of the ladder straight away. The theory was that after completing five hours with Roger Squires we came out with a demo tape, which hopefully would be our intro into a successful job in broadcasting. Not surprisingly, there was hardly any room to move at Roger Squires's studios for would-be presenters turning out one audition tape after the other. In fact, most of the people broadcasting today would, at some time in their early career, have passed through Roger's hallowed studios in St John's Wood High Street. I duly did my demo tape and sent it off to the BBC's Radio One.

While I awaited the response, I continued to enjoy being a DJ earning regular money. I didn't care where the gigs were. There was a pecking order on the London circuit and if you were *really* good, you could work for Goodhews, which had popular pubs, such as Charlee Brown's in Tottenham, Boobs in Croydon, and Cheeky Petes and Brollies in Richmond. These were discos for proper DJs, DJs who had to look right and play the right records. Even more important, for the privilege of appearing there the fee went up, for example, from the £4 that I was being paid at the King Lud to a princely £12 for a full session in a proper nightclub. Oh, the giddy heights!

Mum proved to be right about the King Lud being 'dangerous'. One night, after I'd been doing gigs there for several months, I learned a very good lesson – never let a drunk fall asleep in a pub because when he wakes up he'll be nasty. On this particular evening, a drunk had fallen asleep on the banquette seating, which was very close to me. The pub had a circular bar in the middle and the barman, a tall, slim guy, had just called last orders. As the pub began to clear, I started to put the gear away. I'd just taken out a wire and was fiddling about underneath the equipment to disconnect it, when I noticed that everyone had now gone, but that no one had noticed a shabbily dressed drunk still asleep on the bench. At that moment he woke up, like the proverbial bear with a sore head, and the first person he saw was me, putting away all my gear. There was an empty beer bottle at his side. For no reason whatsoever he picked this up, smashed it on a table and, leaping towards me, he grabbed me by the throat and dragged me across the equipment. My hands were trapped underneath me and he was about to stick this vicious-looking beer bottle in my face when, fortunately for me, the barman moved like lightning, hauled the fellow off me and threw him out of the pub. *Phew*! 'Sorry, mate,' the barman said when he returned dishevelled, 'we should have seen him.'

It had frightened the life out of me.

Once I was safely back home, I thought, 'This isn't for me!' I'd got my wings – nearly been supplied with angel ones – and it was time to get a better gig. The next day I rang Edna James and was very straight with her. 'I've done my time,' I said. 'I'm ready to move on.' To my relief, she agreed with me. Effervesced, I decided now was the moment to go for it. I gave up my job in the stockroom of HMV and my new routine became lunchtime gigs in pubs on Mondays, Wednesdays and Fridays. These were the days when every pub, it seemed, had a lunchtime disco with a couple of go-go dancers. I was now doing gigs six nights a week in addition to these lunchtime slots and, on days I wasn't working, I could be found buying records and seeing friends and other DJs, discussing the new releases for hours over endless cups of coffee.

Among the places I went to during this time was the Lord Raglan, near St Paul's in the City of London, and the Target in Northolt, Middlesex. RKI also booked me for a pub in the Harrow Road. I was paid more when I worked for that company, but the Harrow Road pub proved to be as rough the Old King Lud. Here they had novelty acts as well as go-go girls. On one particular occasion one of these novelty acts came in, dressed to kill and all tasselled up. She gave me her cassette tape and said, 'That's for my act.'

'Right,' I said. 'I'll make sure you get a good round of applause when you come on.'

'No need to, love,' she said, 'it's all on the tape.'

I thought that was incredible. She'd edited her tape to include a round of applause!

'What's the act?' I asked.

'Very simple, love, twenty-five minutes. Just fire the tape and it will all take care of itself.'

'What do you do for twenty-five minutes?' I pressed.

'Well . . . I tread on broken glass, eat fire and play with a snake.'

'Oh!' I replied, 'this will be interesting!'

On she came. The pub was packed. I put the tape in the deck, pressed 'Play', and a cacophony of applause echoed around the bar. You'd have thought the Beatles had just walked on stage. She winked at me as if to say, 'Here we go . . .' and then she trod on the broken glass and did her fire-eating. Everyone in the pub had seen it all before and the men, behaving very badly, were all coming up to her, jeering and booing. I really felt for her. It wasn't fair. She was an act and didn't deserve all that. I looked at her as if to say, 'Sorry, love, but what can I do?' She winked, mouthing, *Watch this*,' and pulled a long sinewy snake out of a wicker basket and started to do a really sleazy dance with it. All the men quietened down a bit then, and when she started to weave in and out of them with the reptile I'd never seen boozers move so fast. She brought them into line in two seconds. It was brilliant. Fortunately, I'm not bothered by snakes, but there were many macho guys present who were. To see all these men recoil in horror and absolute fear at the sight of a snake made me feel like the butchest man in the room!

I had quite a long stint at the Harrow Road pub and while there I became good friends with the other DJs. We socialized with all the girls who performed there and often went out for a late-night curry together. I loved those days. It was on one of my gigs that a dancer I'd never seen before arrived. She was very tall, incredibly voluptuous, exquisitely made up and, dressed up to the nines, looked absolutely gorgeous. 'Can I go through your records, Dale, to pick some to dance to?' she purred in a suitably husky voice.

'Fine,' I said.

She sorted out some records and said, 'Right! I'll go on now.'

I was on the stage behind the DJ console and she began dancing in front of me, facing the audience. As she worked through her act, she created a storm among the guys who were going absolutely mental. Then, doing a sudden spin, she came up to me, sweating profusely and, while wriggling her bum for the audience, slipped her right hand into her left bra, pulled out a false boob, wiped her forehead with it and put it back in again. I was gobsmacked. She was a man! It was my first experience of a drag go-go dancer. She winked at me as if to say, 'Bet you didn't know that, darlin'.' She was right, and I learned more in three months working the pub circuit than I'd learned in fifteen years of education!

At the end of the evening as I was packing up the gear, I heard the most almighty bust-up coming from the ladies' toilet. The go-go dancer had gone in there to get changed and two drunken girls, who weren't at all happy with the act anyway, had realized he was a man and all hell broke loose. It took six guys to separate the three of them.

There were always fights in the pubs and I was working in the roughest ones imaginable. The licensing laws in those days meant that the lads had to get as much drink in as they possibly could before last orders at ten thirty. Because they also wanted to pull a bird, we had to play ten minutes of slow smoochie records at the end of every night. If they hadn't grabbed a girl there'd be trouble. I remember doing the Railway Tavern, Putney, on one such occasion when there was the most horrendous rumble outside and the police and a convoy of ambulances were involved. I didn't see much of the fight, but the next morning Mum banged on my bedroom door, saying, 'Dale, what on earth happened last night?'

'What do you mean?' I said, rubbing the sleep from my eyes.

'Were you in a car crash? Did you hit someone? What have you done?'

By this time I had a really nice car, a Volvo P.1800 S, the model driven by Simon Templar, the hero of the TV adventure series, *The Saint*, and I had parked it right outside the pub the previous evening. Someone had obviously been cut up by a bottle during the fight and he had rolled the entire length of its top on to its bonnet. The car was covered with blood from one end to the other. I hadn't noticed this when I had reloaded the car in the early hours of the morning. Mum thought I'd killed at least three people; and when I told her that there'd been a pub fight she said it was time I got better gigs. All this, though, was a very good education for me. Having come straight from the protection of a public school into a found-for-me-job at HMV, I was now out in the world on my own, using my wits and the gift of the gab to look after myself. I was toughening up.

On the pub circuit it didn't really matter what DJs wore or looked like. If you were working in a grotty pub, in the wrong end of town, on the wrong side of the tracks, that didn't matter either. Just as well. Bless me, in those days, I never looked the part. I had yet to define my image. I still weighed eighteen stone and trendy flared trousers, which were de rigueur then, just did not suit me. I couldn't even get away with a floppy baggy top because these were worn with thick wide belts that would have emphasized my non-existent waistline. Men also wore their hair long, not a good look for me. But, like everybody else, I grew mine anyway. With hindsight, I looked like someone who had auditioned for, but failed to get, a part in *Charlie's Angels*! I wore gingham shirts, with jeans as tight as I could bear without passing out and, yes, belts. Now, when I dare glance at photos taken at that time, I break out in a cold sweat with embarrassment. It *wasn't* a good era for me! Those days were part and parcel of the Seventies, and when you look at adverts for that time, everybody has thin shoulders, thin arms and waists. Compared with me, they all looked like stick insects. I'm fairly presentable now but, my God, I wasn't then. I had yet to learn the golden secret: wear black; get a suntan; get a haircut!

On the Goodhews circuit it was all *so* different – all about image and how to present yourself. Their DJs had to look the part, because they worked in proper nightclubs with disco equipment that they didn't have to assemble and put away personally, and the dancers had their own podiums and a disco light show. Their disco consoles looked like the cockpit of a 747 jet, all nailed in, wired up with a sound-to-light system that included strobes and coloured lights. There was a world of difference between working these nightclubs and working the pubs; and everybody, including me, wanted to get on to this circuit because it had prestige. The DJs were not considered to be only as good as their records, but on this circuit the patter also mattered. The rule of thumb was that, as well as playing records, DJs *had* to talk and be entertaining. It was a case of one segue mix every hour: three records in a row, then talk. It was bliss! And the managers of the DJ agencies would tour the clubs and better-class venues to check up on the acts and rate the DJs.

It was all very good groundwork for broadcasting and showbiz. The DJs learned microphone technique and how to work a crowd. If they had an empty dance floor they weren't whipping up the punters to the right kind of frenzy and that meant they weren't coming up to scratch. All the best radio DJs – people like Emperor Rosco and Tony Blackburn, who had their own individual style and were very good at the required patter – were emulated by the other DJs. I was 'Tony Blackburn' and, to this day, as far as DJs go, he is my mentor. I love him, he's great.

Astonishingly, given my then image problem, someone from Goodhews, who saw me at one of my gigs, must have thought I was all right because I was eventually offered bookings and despatched to do fill-in work for various other DJs. The disappointing thing was that these were not my own shows in my own residency club or pub, and the hours were either a one or a two o'clock finish. The main DJ would be on £12 to £14 a night and a support for the turn, like me, would only be on £7. All I had to do was two half-hour spots to give the other DJ two half-hour breaks.

At this time, Peter Tait was DJing in the Gunnersbury Fair, Ealing, and I supported him, then did the same for Freddie Jansen at Boobs in Croydon. After that I was asked to go to the Castle, Richmond, which had two huge rooms, one called Brollies, the other Cheeky Petes. Steve Allen was the resident DJ at the Castle. He was long-haired, blond, knew how to work the crowd, was quick-witted and sharp, and good with his patter. To this day he is one of the brightest and best UK radio broadcasters with his wicked sense of humour and a waspish wit. He learned all this, as I did, doing the pubs and clubs.

At the time of being sent to the Castle, I was working at the Railway Tavern, Putney and, never one to miss a trick, I told all my regulars – by this time I had developed quite a fan base – that I would be at Cheeky Petes on the Saturday night. When I arrived at the Castle in my beautiful newly acquired Volvo sports car, I noticed a guy with a shock of blond hair, unloading records from the back of a Mini. 'Are you Steve?' I said.

'Yes. Are you Dale?'

He looked at my car, then looked at his. I could see him thinking, 'Well, the car's very nice, but Dale . . . He's not very attractive. But he is *only* my relief DJ. I don't think he'll be very good, but . . .' As I approached this massive venue, I knew I had to pull out all the stops and make my mark.

Inside the pub, he told me which records to play and not to play while he was taking his breaks. 'Yes, Steve. No, Steve. Three bags full, Steve,' I thought. Still, it was his gig. There's always a pecking order and he was the headliner. Supports never argue or tell them how an act should be done. I knew my place.

'Fine,' I said. 'When do you want me to go on?'

'I'll start,' Steve replied, 'and you go on at nine to nine thirty and eleven thirty to midnight.'

Two half-hour periods! It was a great gig to be a part of and I was just so pleased to be there. I thought Steve was very glamorous and looked exactly as a DJ should. Then, when he started to talk, he was everything a DJ should sound like. The one thing in my favour was that while I didn't look the part then, I did sound it. God had given me a great voice for DJ work and I knew how to use it. Plus, I had my own collection of tried and tested records.

The reason I survived so well in the pubs and clubs in those days was because I used to buy all my records on import. I would travel to the Record Centre on Rayners Lane, Middlesex and Contempo on Hanway Street, London to get them as they arrived from America, and I had built a reputation for breaking in records. On Steve's night, I had a big club record, which had just come over from America, called 'Rock the Boat' by the Hughes Corporation and another called 'Short Stopping' by Veda Brown. I also had three or four records that were not yet available to the masses, which I'd proven with my audience at the Railway Tavern, Putney. Both became instant dance classics.

Come nine o'clock, Steve introduced me, saying, 'Here's someone new to you, who's going to be here while I take a half-hour break. It's Dale Winton.' He was in for a surprise. Up went this cheer from all my Railway Tavern fans, about forty or fifty of them, who had come all the way to the Castle, Richmond because *I* was there. Steve looked at me in disbelief. I was very nervous. This was an important gig for me and I wanted to be on this circuit. When I played Veda Brown's 'Short Stopping', which Steve had never heard of, the whole room erupted and started to dance. Then, as I went into my patter, I dropped my voice in the way that I'd been taught at Roger Squires's studio, so that it was very deep and butch.

I could see Steve looking at me with new respect. 'Where did that voice come from?' he enquired. 'And what was that record?'

'It's called voice projection, Steve,' I replied.

'I must try that,' he said, impressed.

'The record's Veda Brown's 'Short Stopping'. It's not out here for another six weeks.'

At the end of the night Steve and I went for a coffee and cemented our friendship there and then. We've been the closest of friends ever since. In fact, thirty years on, rarely does a Saturday night go by without Steve and I having supper together.

Soon after our first meeting I had my own nights and my own residency. Steve was always very popular in Richmond and, after the Goodhews clubs, I found north London was where I went down best. I was at Charlee Brown's, Tottenham, a very big venue, where I did Thursday, Friday and Saturday nights. Coming into Tottenham, you approached Charlee Brown's on a huge gyratory one-way system. As you turned right at the top of the brow of the hill, there it was on the right. The actual pub was called the Robert E. Lee, but the disco attached to it was Charlee Brown's. This was a huge galleried nightclub, with a massive dance floor and a wide staircase going up to a balcony where people used to hang out. To the right was a smaller bar area. The DJ's console was slightly raised and sited above the main dance floor. Alongside this was a go-go dancers' illuminated raised podium. Occasionally I would also go back to the Gunnersbury Fair, Ealing. By now I was a seasoned performer with many gigs under my belt and only nineteen years old.

I worked this circuit as a full-time DJ, doing lunchtime and evening gigs. Financially I was doing quite well, getting about £120 a week which, in the Seventies when the average working wage was £30–£40, was actually quite good. But nothing like the sums DJs earn these days! The trouble was that, in order to maintain that position, I had to spend a lot of my money on records. So out of the £120, thirty to forty per cent would go on buying the new releases to maintain my reputation, and a good bit more went on petrol and other expenses. But I was still able to say to Mum, 'I'm doing quite well, now.'

The difference between the pubs and Charlee Brown's, where both Steve and I now worked, was that we had doormen – Ray and Henry

– who wore black ties. They were huge bouncers and were the sort of guys you wouldn't want to mess with. It was the era of the cops-and-robbers TV series, *The Sweeney,* and Ray and Henry each had the de rigeur *Sweeney* Jaguar. This was the 1970s club culture that was building up to the disco boom and John Travolta in *Saturday Night Fever.* I guess that's why that film was made – the producers were aware of this movement.

I remember Mum coming to Charlee Brown's on her own one night to check out the gig. She was obviously going through one of her good spells and she told the bouncers that she'd come to see Dale. I was expecting her and I'd told the lady who checked in the coats. Mum walked in and Henry was in the background, ogling her as she came over to me and started to chat. As she was standing beside the DJ console, she looked amazing, as she always did. Henry, who was really a great big teddy bear of a man with a shock of blond hair, and popular with everyone who knew him, came over and tried to chat her up. 'What's a gorgeous blonde like you doing with an overweight disc jockey like that?' he said.

'He's my son,' my mother replied.

Henry was mortified and *so* apologetic.

Mum never looked her age. She would have been about thirty-eight at that time and I always looked older than my years because of the weight.

When I was working at Charlee Brown's I had a support DJ who was quite camp and clearly gay. One night one of the north-London boys went up to him and said something that caused the DJ to look visibly shaken.

'What's up?' I said to him.

'It doesn't matter. Don't ask,' he replied.

So I went up to the punter, a macho guy, who had a pint in one hand. 'What did you say to him that upset him?'

'I just asked 'im if 'e was a bleedin' iron.' ('Iron' is cockney rhyming slang for 'poof': iron=hoof=poof.)

'Do you have a problem with that?' I asked.

'Why?'

'Just answer the f\*\*\*ing question. Because if you've got a problem with that, you have a problem with me. Get it?'

I learned another lesson that night: never back down to a bully. Always stand your ground.

'Fair play to you, Dale,' he said. 'Fair play. I've not got a problem with you or anybody.'

'Glad to hear it,' I said.

Having worked the club circuit for up to six or seven nights a week, Steve, Peter and myself were all professional DJs – 'have records will travel'. Knowing that independent radio was coming, we were all busy making tapes. I was fiercely ambitious. I kept going back to Roger Squires's studio to make new demo tapes to send to Radio One, doubtless along with 10,000 other hopefuls.

Another way of gaining experience was hospital radio, which tended to be staffed by guys wearing anoraks. Despite my best endeavours and willingness to always play doctors and nurses, I didn't have any luck there. I then met Paul King, a DJ who was doing part-time work at UBN – United Biscuits Network. UBN was an industrial radio station in Isleworth, Middlesex, set up by United Biscuits to broadcast twenty-four hours a day to five of its factory locations around the UK. The reason the radio station worked so well was because the biscuit factories were so quiet – all ovens and no noisy machinery – so the workers could hear what was being broadcast. The company had launched the network to keep its 20,000 employees happy while they knocked out fig rolls, fairy cakes, chocolate fingers – you name it. Above the conveyor belts, where the biscuit-makers were mixing, adding flavourings, icing or whatever, there were loudspeakers and every two biscuit-makers had their own speaker. The cost of the radio network worked out at something like a penny a day per employee to run.

Having met Paul King, I started to send my demo tapes to UBN. I wanted a job there *so* badly. This was 1975 and radio stations, such as Capital, LBC, Radio City in Liverpool, BRMB in Birmingham,

Piccadilly and Manchester were about to open. These had to be staffed, and the UBN disc jockeys were all busily sending off tapes to them and getting jobs because they'd worked at UBN. 'This,' I thought, 'is a good moment for me to get in there.' I was always more ambitious than Steve and Peter, always the one who kept saying, 'Come on, let's do tapes.' I was obsessed. United Biscuits Network would be perfect experience for anyone who wanted a career in broadcasting.

Meanwhile, always one to keep my eyes peeled, I bought that week's copy of the *Record Mirror*, a publication that's sadly no longer with us. In those days, this was *the* bible for DJs. As well as listing the top fifty records, it was crammed full of news about new releases and pop scene gossip. A really great magazine, it also had several pages of classified ads in the back of it. One afternoon when I was looking through these, an ad caught my eye that said, 'Looking for DJs who would like to do radio' and included in it was an invitation for hopefuls to send demo tapes to an address near Carnaby Street. When I checked it out, word on the street was that Radio Luxembourg and Radio One were taking this unusual route in their search for new DJs, and that everybody – including me – should bang out new demo tapes.

After my next gig at the Old King Lud, never one to let the grass grow under my feet, I decided to drive to the back of Carnaby Street and personally drop my demo tape in *Record Mirror*'s PO box. When I got there, to my dismay I found it was a solid door with no letterbox. Downhearted, I climbed back into my car, put the tape on to the passenger seat and lit a cigarette. Parked close to Le Valbonne, one of *the* swish venues at that time, I was looking at the huge flames leaping out of the top of its two wrought-iron poles, when a magnificent Bentley pulled up and parked behind my car. Glancing in my rear-view mirror I saw that the driver was none other than David Hamilton, the huge Radio One star, who was doing the afternoon show and who also seemed to be on telly most of the time. 'Ah-ha,' I thought, very excited, 'now there's a man who could change my life. If he thinks I'm any good, he'll put in a word for me with the people who matter at Radio One.'

Thinking back, I can't help saying to myself, why on earth would David Hamilton go out of his way to help a complete stranger? But fired with the unquenchable enthusiasm of ambitious youth, that certainly wasn't how I thought then. I leapt out of the car and rushed over to the Bentley. Somewhat startled by my sudden appearance, David let the window down a fraction of an inch and said, 'Yes? Can I help?'

'You don't know me from a bar of soap,' I said. 'My name's Dale Winton and I have just tried to deliver a demo tape to *Record Mirror*'s offices, but there's no postbox. You're on radio and television and I'd just *love* you to listen to my tape and tell me what you think of it. All my details and address are inside this envelope.' And, before he had time to reply, I pushed the package through the tiny aperture in the window, ran back to my car and drove off.

As I was going up Regent Street, I came to my senses and thought, 'What a prat I am! What was I thinking of? He'll probably think I'm mad and it'll be a complete waste of my demo tape!'

This, of course, was also the Seventies when IRA bombs were going off, left right and centre in London, and my next thought was that he might think I was some kind of terrorist and would be wondering if there was something sinister in the package and debating whether or not to call the bomb squad. Spinning the car round, I drove back to Le Valbonne. But the doorman, having eyed me up and down with his eyes of steel and a heart of stone, wouldn't let me in. Perhaps it wasn't surprising. It was a very exclusive club and I was certainly not appropriately dressed.

'I know David Hamilton's in there,' I persisted, 'and I need to have a word with him. I gave him a demo tape about ten minutes ago and I must have it back.'

'Then you'll just have to wait until he comes out,' the doorman replied firmly.

Defeated, I went back to my car and sat there forlornly until four o'clock in the morning. When David Hamilton came out and saw me, he doubtless thought, 'Oh, no – not him again.' But I went up to him and said, 'You may remember me. I gave you a tape earlier on. I'm really sorry, but I had no business doing that. Can I have it back, please.'

'With the greatest of pleasure,' he replied, looking relieved.

Having reclaimed the tape, still feeling a bit of a prat, I drove off home.

The next day, about eleven in the morning, when I was sitting having coffee with Mum, I told her about my chance meeting with David Hamilton.

'But, Dale,' she said, 'you were right. David Hamilton might have been able to do something to help you.'

So, spurred on by Mum, I wrote to David, saying, 'I'm the nutcase who gave you my demo tape, then asked for it back, but I really would welcome your opinion . . .' Then, complete with the demo tape, I took it to Broadcasting House on Portland Place. Several days later I received a helpful letter from David, which I wish I had kept. He really was most encouraging – and, some years later, when we were both working on Lifestyle television, I couldn't resist reminding him of my demo tape incident.


One night Paul King, who was doing night shifts at UBN, took me inside the factory to show me what the DJs did. In addition to playing music twenty-four hours a day, they made health and safety commercials, such as 'Wash your hands before leaving the lavatory', 'Beware of fork-lift trucks'. They'd play requests for 'Jane in Tollcross, Scotland, on chocolate-wafer biscuits' or 'Sally on conveyor belt No. 5', or 'Maureen on Penguins in Harlesden, Middlesex', and if someone was getting engaged, married or having a baby there'd be requests for these occasions, too. UBN was run like a tight radio ship. It had three studios and also broadcast specialized programmes for minority audiences. It was 'rip-and-read' news, backed up by a Reuters news link. The marvellous thing was that this allowed the DJs, who worked six-hour shifts, to learn at first hand how to edit and present programmes, as well as to edit or rewrite Reuters news bulletins. It was brilliant; and the seductively distinctive smell of chocolate in the factory was simply divine.

'God,' I thought as Paul showed me round, 'this is *fabulous*! This is the next step for me. Without a job here, I can't progress.'

I made a tape, sent it in, got it back. I made another tape, sent it in, nothing happened. I was learning a lot, though, about how to set out my stall. But confidence and persistence are the keys to success in life. When it came to the next tape, I decided to drive up to UBN in my Volvo and hand-deliver the tape myself. I wanted to be absolutely sure that the right person got it. Having been in the building with Paul, I knew where everything was and that once I'd got through the electric security barrier, I could park the car and walk down to the UBN studio, which was just beyond Quality Control. Armed and loaded with my third tape I drove up to the security barrier like a latter-day John Wayne as if I owned the place.

'Yes?' the security guard queried.

'UBN,' I replied, trying to ignore the nervous twitch in my left buttock.

'Are you expected?'

'Absolutely.'

Up went the barrier and in I drove. Having parked the car, I walked straight to UBN's reception. Graham Dean, who later went on to Radio City, Liverpool and then hosted the breakfast show on Capital Radio, happened to be sitting at the reception desk.

'I have a tape for Adrian Love, the programme controller,' I said, seemingly full of confidence.

'Who are you?' Graham asked suspiciously.

UBN was used to representatives from record companies coming in and out, but they were not used to would-be disc jockeys getting through the net.

'I'm Dale Winton,' I said. 'I'm a DJ. I wanted to bring my demo tape in.'

'How did you get in?'

'The security guard let me drive through the barrier.'

'You shouldn't be in here,' he said. 'You can't just walk in like that.' He was firm, but smiling, really rather nice about it.

'Look,' I said, 'I'm going. But would you, please, make sure Adrian gets the tape?'

'Absolutely,' he said.

Something about the man made me believe him.

Mission accomplished, I left.

Two months later there was a phone call at about four o'clock one afternoon. I'd done a lunchtime disco, gone home and was just about to go off again to do a gig in the evening.

Mum answered the phone. 'Dale, it's for you.'

I picked up the phone and a voice at the other end said, 'Adrian Love here. When can you come in?'

I thought this was a hoax call, a wind-up from a friend, but I really wasn't sure and I decided to play safe. 'When would you like me?'

'How long will it take you to get to Syon Lane, Isleworth?'

'It's rush hour – about forty-five minutes.'

'Be here in half an hour.'

I put down the phone. I still couldn't believe it. 'Someone's having a laugh,' I thought, 'this can't be true.' So I immediately rang back. 'Can I speak to Adrian Love please. It's Dale Winton.'

'What? Yes?' Adrian said.

'I didn't quite believe it was you.'

'You should be on your way by now,' he said, amused. 'Just get here.'

'*I'm on my way! I'm on my way!*'

I can only equate that moment to the delirious excitement akin to winning the National Lottery. I broke my neck to get there in record time. On arrival, I was taken to Adrian Love's office. Adrian was a tall, gangly, bespectacled man and he was wearing this wonderful belt which had 'Love' printed on it. I remember thinking that was a very clever touch, that I would like a belt with my name on it, but that it must be a lot easier to find a belt with the name 'Love' on it than to find one with 'Winton'. He chatted away and asked me why I wanted to work for UBN.

'I love being a DJ,' I enthused, 'and I think this radio station is great.'

'We're going to give you an audition,' he replied. 'I want you to go into Studio Two and audition for me. I'll show you how the equipment works and then I'll listen in my office. Here are some records and some jingles, play these and make up a programme. Start in five minutes.'

'OK,' I said, with my heart hammering nineteen to the dozen.

I was absolutely terrified. I was being thrown in the deep end. I'd had no chance to prepare anything and I was desperate to do well and get the job. Here, at last, was my chance to have a career in broadcasting, and without this kind of experience I wasn't going to get anywhere. It was the equivalent of an actor doing 'rep' in the theatre, or a director making a good art film before doing a movie – you need experience. Since then, I've met a lot of people who say, '*I could do what you do.*' I used to be the same: I'd listen to the radio, watch things on television and think, 'I could do that.' But, actually, 'flying' time is everything. You need the experience, you need the knowledge – and you never stop learning.

About forty-five minutes into the audition, Adrian came in and sat down on the side of the desk. 'Did you enjoy that?' he asked.

'Oh, did I! It was fantastic,' I replied.

'Well . . . I listened to you, but I don't know what to say, really.'

As he paused, my heart was in my mouth.

'I *do* know what to say, really,' he added. 'Do you fancy having a job here? Would you like to work here?'

I couldn't believe my luck. I felt like punching the air. I was the first out of all the DJs I'd been working with in the clubs to break through. This had to be the best news ever. I could hardly wait to ring Steve and Peter and tell them.

'There is one problem,' Adrian said. 'Your name. Dale Winton sounds like a phoney, made-up, transatlantic, North American name.'

'But it's my *real* name,' I protested. 'It was what I was given when I was born. My initials are D. J. Winton, my middle name is Jonathan.'

'Well, it doesn't sound right.'

Quite honestly, they could have called me 'Joyce'! I wouldn't have minded. I'd have still taken the job. 'What do you take exception to?' I asked.

'Well . . . the Dale especially.'

In those days it was the fashion for DJs to have two Christian names which sounded good on the jingles that introduced their shows. So there were disc jockeys with names like Richard James, John Peters, Adrian Paul, Tony Alan.

Adrian Love passed me a list of suggestions to consider and some jingles to listen to.

'Well, at a push,' I said, 'if I put "Simon" together with "York", I could be Simon York. Then I could say something like "Hi, Sy". That would be quite catchy.'

So, under great sufferance and against all my natural instincts in wanting to keep my own name, I became Simon York and was given the 1 a.m to 6 a.m night show, the graveyard slot, which was where everyone started and worked their way up. The money wasn't brilliant – I was only paid £240 a month – but, quite frankly, I would have paid them for the job, it was that important to me. I decided to continue doing my usual gigs until midnight at the Gunnersbury Fair, Ealing, then drive straight to United Biscuits at Isleworth.


I spent a year in the graveyard slot. I worked hard, learned something new almost every day and I loved it. Then, when Adrian Love left UBN to start LBC, Alan King, our new programme director, moved me up the pecking order and let me go back to using my own name, Dale Winton. Eventually I worked my way up to the morning show, which included doing hourly monthly specialist programmes for Harlesdon, Isleworth, Liverpool, Manchester and Glasgow. For these programmes, I'd travel up by train or plane, stay overnight in a hotel, spend a day going round the factories, then return to London. I felt quite the high flyer! I loved it. I'd take my tape recorder with me, meet the biscuit-makers and play their requests. It was good experience and I learned my interview technique in those days.

The record companies – CBS, EMI, Decca, Polydor, Phonogram – all wanted their records played on the radio and, knowing that UBN had 20,000 listeners, they were happy to bring their stars in to be interviewed. More important, they knew that the contacts they made would serve them well as the DJs started to get radio jobs around the country. I remember one absolute disaster when Johnny Nash was promoting his record 'I can see clearly now'. CBS brought him in and I interviewed him – brilliantly! How it happened I shall never know, but for some reason I forgot to switch my tape recorder on. I was mortified. In desperation I asked CBS if he could come back, but I was told not until he came over to the UK on his next visit. I was horrified. But UBN forgave me.

I was then sent to interview Barry White who was staying at the Intercontinental Hotel, Hyde Park. The record companies always put up their stars in swish hotels and paid all the expenses for the DJs to come to London to do the interviews, conveyor-belt style. Because I was representing UBN, I was always last on the pecking order to go in. While I was in a room outside the suite waiting to interview Barry White, DJs from around the country were going in, one by one, to do their interviews. Maggie Norden, Denis Norden's daughter, was there for Capital Radio. When she came out saying, 'He's *great*,' it was my turn to go in.

'Where do I sit?' I asked Barry's record agent.

'Most people', he replied, 'have been sitting on the floor and lifting the microphone up to him.'

'This is not good for interaction,' I thought, 'it will also make me appear subservient, which won't lend itself to a good interview.' To get the best out of someone you have to meet them on an equal footing. 'I really *don't* want to sit on the floor,' I said.

I could see this guy from the record company thinking, 'Who is this man from United Biscuits Network?'

'I would really feel more comfortable in a chair,' I added. 'Would you mind if I pulled this chair up?'

Everybody in the room was obviously terrified of upsetting Barry White, so I turned to him and said, 'D'you mind, Mr White, if I bring the chair to you?'

'Quite right, too, man,' he said, roaring with laughter and gave me the best interview ever.

Then there was David Cassidy. Having left Bell Records and had a year out of the business, he had signed with RCA records, who then spent a fortune flying him to London and booking him in to a really nice hotel. A buffet lunch was put on so that he could sit there and give interviews. This was actually an unusual set-up. RCA had offices just around the corner from the hotel and normally stars did their interviews there, but for some reason David Cassidy was doing his in the hotel.

All the local radio DJs were quite full of themselves and enjoying the thought of meeting this big-name star. Peter Powell, who was then a huge Radio Luxembourg DJ, arrived and all the other DJs, aware that they had a national DJ in their midst, avoided him, leaving him to sit on his own across the room from me. I was in the same boat as Peter Powell, being ignored by all the others from Capital, BRMB, Radio City, all of whom were big fish in little ponds, but for a completely different reason. I was a nonentity, working for a biscuit factory and, as usual, the very last in the interview line. The guy from the record company came over to Peter Powell and said, 'Would you mind waiting? I know you want a bit longer with David than the others.'

'That's fine,' Peter Powell replied.

As the DJs came and went, only two or three of us were left, awaiting our turn. Then, surprise, surprise, Peter Powell suddenly stood up and came over to me. Sitting down beside me, he introduced himself, and said, 'What's your name?'

'*What* a lovely man,' I thought.

'I'm Dale Winton,' I said.

'Where do you work?'

'I work at UBN.'

The easy conversation just flowed from there. He was so genuinely interested in what I was doing, and so interesting to talk to. I was just bowled over. This star DJ had actually taken the time to come over and talk to little me. I learned another lesson then. Everyone is worthy of attention and approachable, and you should just go up and talk to people. This was one reason why I was not surprised that Peter

Powell went on to become a huge Radio One and TV personality, as well as being a tenacious and successful businessman. He clearly valued people, understood the art of communication and knew that it cost nothing to be friendly. In fact, looking back, I remember more about meeting Peter Powell that day than interviewing David Cassidy, who seemed to be really tiny, not particularly forthcoming and had a dodgy complexion.

I also interviewed the singer, Andy Williams, whom I was also destined to meet much later in my career when he was a guest on *The National Lottery*. You always remember if the people you interview are total nightmares or absolute pros and Andy Williams was a total pro. He didn't need to do UBN, but agreed all the same to an interview with me. All I could think at the time was, 'This man has the most perfect teeth.' His nails were also beautifully manicured and he was wearing clear nail varnish. I'd never seen a man groomed to such perfection. He looked so immaculate – and every bit the star. American stars know what style and quality in personal presentation is all about. They are communication-friendly, image-conscious and for them the performance is everything. That's actually something that's been going through an unfashionable phase recently in the UK, but it's something I've never compromised on. I think you *should* look and behave the part, and not let the public down.

During my time at UBN the Sex Pistols appeared on Bill Grundy's TV show. It was a momentous moment in television because it all went very pear-shaped and four-letter expletives were used. I rang their record company and said that I would like to interview them which, when I think about it now, was foolhardy, to say the least. Why on earth would I *want* to interview the Sex Pistols for a biscuit factory? I suppose it was because they were front-page news everywhere at the time and this had brought out the journalist in me. For a person who usually has no fear, though, I was rather anxious on this occasion. They were perceived as violent, anarchic, angry boys and I thought 'What will they do to me?' At the same time I felt I *had* to interview them. When I spoke to the record company I was told, 'Yes. You can come along and see them rehearse.'

'This', I thought, 'is incredible.'

When I went to do the interview, I took Steve Allen along with me. We headed towards Denmark Street – the Tin Pan Alley of the music business – where the Sex Pistols were rehearsing. On the way there, as we were trying to find the rehearsal rooms, something surreal happened. As we passed a public phone box, there, on the phone, was Billy Idol, who was a newcomer on the music scene then and attracting a lot of publicity.

'Steve, what shall I *do*,' I said. 'I've got the tape recorder. Do I stop and do Billy Idol and risk losing the interview with the Sex Pistols?'

We decided to give Billy a miss and go for the Sex Pistols.

The rehearsal rooms were in a hideous building, a real hovel that smelled disgusting. We climbed the dirty, rickety stairs and walked into a room that looked like a doss area with a single-bar electric fire standing on the floor. There was Sid Vicious looking unkempt and angry, Paul Cook looking bemused and another man who wasn't introduced to us. I started the interview, expecting a series of expletives, but none came. At one point I thought, 'Oh, God, this is probably *the* most boring interview I've ever done. These lads have absolutely nothing to say for themselves.'

After I had switched off the tape recorder, what made me laugh was that Sid Vicious had obviously realized that he hadn't been his usual controversial angry self, and that his image and the person the press were making him out to be hadn't quite come across in my interview with him. The occasion was before he got heavily into drugs and he was really quite a sweet guy then. Having looked at me, he clearly thought, 'Oh, dear, I'm going to ruin the illusion here. I'd better do something anarchic.' So, with no more ado, he spat at the one-bar electric fire, which made such a loud hissing noise that everybody in the room jumped and said, '*What's that?*' It was the only attempt he made at being vicious all afternoon. I was tempted to say, 'Would you mind doing that again, so that I can catch it on tape?' but I thought, 'No, this is horrible. The place smells and it's boring being here.' So Steve and I left.

It's extraordinary now for me to look back and think that I cut my teeth interviewing people like that. It was an experience that served me very well over the years. To this day, though, it has never ceased to amaze me that at times artistes are *not* what you think they are going to be. I've certainly had my share of stars who are, to coin a phrase, 'tired and emotional'!

Ever ambitious to go on to the next thing and feeling I had served my time at UBN, I started to fire off tapes again to Capital Radio. This was very much in keeping with my Gemini character. Gemini people are very mercurial and their enthusiasm always insists on pushing them to the front of the queue. Once there, however, they're ever restless, which is why so many of their plans stall before coming to fruition. In short, Geminis have more skins than a Spanish onion. I loved UBN, but Capital Radio was *the* jewel in the ILR (Independent London Radio) crown. It was a station that had already employed well-known people from the BBC and big stars from pirate radio. It had taken on Kenny Everett and Dave Cash. So Capital Radio was the star DJs' station, but it was impossible for a DJ like me, albeit with a background of good, sound experience, to get work there. That would have been a bit like getting the leading role in a major movie, having only done a bit of rep. It just doesn't happen. But Geminis are renowned as individuals who keep moving forward against all odds – I was twenty-one and more than prepared to do just that.

Not having had any luck with Capital, I sent off tapes to Beacon Radio, Wolverhampton. I then travelled up with Phil Sayer, another DJ at UBN, for an interview there. Phil got the job. I then sent a tape to Radio Trent, Nottingham. Mum had recently died, and I was feeling a little lost and even more desperate to get a job in network radio. By then, I had been promoted to Head of Music at UBN. It was a job that carried kudos because it meant not only was I dealing with record companies and labels on a day-to-day basis, but I was also selecting the music that the radio station played. Nevertheless, I still wanted to move on – and move up.

Newly bereaved, I must admit I had taken my eye off the ball a bit and, as luck would have it, there was a certain character at UBN, who shall remain nameless, who was doing his best to take advantage of this. Whenever I made the slightest false move or did anything out of line, he would make sure I was picked up for it. Punctuality, for example, was not always my strong point and if I was five minutes late back from a lunch break, or if he caught me larking about a bit, then he'd make sure things got very heavy. He had what I call a menial clerk's mentality. For him everything had to be done to the letter – which is not usually right for show business. Rightly or wrongly, though, he still managed to cause me a good deal of grief and, to my horror, nearly got me fired. By then it was 1977 and I was twenty-two. I had done three years at UBN, was still doing gigs in clubs from time to time, but I was becoming bored with it. One way and another, I felt it was definitely time I got a proper job in a proper radio station. However, twenty-two was still very young for this. Most of the other DJs who had succeeded were in their mid- to late-twenties. But, undeterred, I sent off tapes to Radio Trent and, to my joy, they *liked* them. I didn't know much about Nottingham, other than that it was on the way to Sheffield, where I used to visit my grandmother and the family, and was famous for its pretty girls, its Goose Fair – and Robin Hood!

When I went to Nottingham for the interview, I met a lovely guy called Dennis Maitland and his PA, Pauline Stone. Dennis was a very warm, friendly man who responded to my sort of personality. More important, with his experience of dealing with 'star' DJs at Radio Two, he knew his business. He understood show business and clearly loved it. Having listened to my tape again, Dennis interviewed me and said, 'Fine. Thank you for coming in.' I left disappointed, but full of hope. A couple of days later I received a letter which basically said, 'We liked you but don't call us, we'll call you.' As it happened, though, there never was a more sincere letter. Dennis, it emerged, had one job available and two presenters he liked – myself and Len Groat, who was working on Metro Radio, Newcastle, but wanted to move to a different part of the country. Len was more experienced than me so he got the job, but they told me I was earmarked for the next one. Again it was disappointing, but I was hopeful. Sure enough,

# 4

## 'Brand-new me . . .'

THE PROGRAMME CONTROLLER at Radio Trent was an influential guy called Neil Spence, formerly known as Dave Dennis, one of the best-ever DJs on pirate radio. By the time I came across him, he was in his forties and a very hard taskmaster who took no prisoners and could be terrifyingly blunt and honest if he didn't like your performance. A tall, slim man, always in a suit, he had a shock of dark hair that he was forever flicking off his face and forehead. Having sized me up, he gave me the Saturday lunchtime show. I could hardly believe my luck. I knew I was being tested, but I wasn't really nervous. I'd done my time as a club DJ and UBN presenter, so I felt I had a wealth of hard-earned practical experience that would now stand me in good stead.

These days when I watch the TV programme *Frasier*, I'm always reminded of my days at Radio Trent because that TV series depicts what a radio station should look like – double-glazed panels to the left and the right, wood panelling and carpet for sound insulation and the obligatory table, desk and console. Having waited so long for this chance to prove myself, I felt more than ready for my first show, but I was also acutely aware that broadcasting to 20,000 listeners at UBN was very different from broadcasting to people who were listening in their homes and cars or on personal stereos. This was *real* radio and I was so excited. I loved every moment of that first Saturday show and came off air feeling I had found my spiritual home. Radio Trent was, without doubt, the most exciting thing that had ever happened to me professionally.

The following weekend when I went back to do another show, Neil Spence, true to form, pulled my performance to pieces with all the skill of a friendly surgeon without the use of anaesthetic. But I couldn't have been that bad because he invited me to join the station, doing the afternoon show from one until five every day of the week. I was home and dry! There were, I soon discovered, several other DJs there who also wanted that particular spot, but I was always a 'Mr Showman' and I was the lucky one who got it. In my view, radio DJs fall into two categories. The first group are the radio hams, who love radio but who are *not* entertainers. These are the 'That was Diana Ross . . . this is Spandau Ballet. It's ten past two.' (I love them because they are so passionate about radio.) The members of the second group are the entertainers, the natural extroverts, who love chatting to people. I am very much of the latter and, as far as I was concerned, being on radio gave me the opportunity to be myself and talk to as many people as I possibly could at any one time. As luck would have it, my chat proved to be very popular with the housewives; Radio Trent's ratings went up and up, and within a year I was promoted to the mid-morning show, which was only one step away from the star DJ's spot, the breakfast show. (To be honest, I never really wanted that slot because it was too early in the morning for me. I'm not good in the mornings and, when I did eventually do it for a year, I hated every minute of it, as mid-morning was about as early as I could manage!)

The mid-morning show was an all-encompassing magazine format, an exciting mix of music, chat, news, phone-ins, and I just took off. It was one of those magical times when the audience was right, the timing was right, my performance was right, radio was blossoming and it just flew. Whenever I finished a show, I always came out on a high, looking forward to the next one. A lot of radio DJs pre-record some of their pieces, but that was never my style – I just loved being live on air.

During my Radio Trent days the IBA (Independent Broadcasting Association) was very strict about what it called 'meaningful speech', such as details of jumble sales, charity events and special localized events. This was tagged around public information cards that were left in the studio so that the presenters could do two or three of these an hour. In fact, the IBA in those days would only grant licences to the local radio stations that agreed to meet its requirements to educate and inform as well as entertain. So, following my programme, there would always be a speech programme between twelve and two that included a phone-in or debate, and then Peter Tait, who was now working at Radio Trent, would do his afternoon show, from two to five. This was great for me because, as he did most of his prep in the mornings, we could meet up for a sandwich lunch and a chat, then I'd go off to Marks and Spencer to get a bit of food for my bedsit fridge. I'd then watch a bit of TV and, having unwound, do my prep for the next morning. If I was also doing a local evening gig, I'd finish that at about three in the morning, then need to unwind again with a video and some toast. Believe me, you can *never* just come home and shut down. Whether it's radio, a gig or telly, you're on a high when you go in, but on an even bigger high when you come out.

Jingles set the tone of a radio show. My first was 'Get that good day feeling with the Dale Winton show.' Ever an optimist – a one-man commercial, really – I wanted the listeners to memorize my name. My jingle had a long and short version and I could do the time checks over it. To this day it's still played occasionally when I do guest spots on radio. The actual jingles are made by two companies, Jams and Pams, in Dallas, America, which is the home of the radio jingle. My friend, Len Groat, whom I first met at Radio Trent, is jingle crazy and has a collection of these, second to none, from all over the world. He used to spend hours listening to them and, whenever I went round for dinner with him and his then-wife Anne, I had to listen, too. He was always trying to talk Radio Trent into splashing out more money for new jingle packages. To be fair, though, the station was very good about upgrading these and that was one of the reasons why it was so successful. Jams and Pams used set backing tracks and a selection of singers, and you could tailor your own words to one of the many jingles that the company had available on its demonstration tapes. In addition to the jingles, I always began and ended my shows with the catchphrase, 'Have a good day, now . . .'

Shows like the mid-morning show, where I soon became known as the 'housewives' DJ', take on a life of their own. It wasn't just a case of filling every hour with music. It worked because the audience was comfortable with the format and knew when their favourite moments were coming up. The horoscopes from nine to ten, for instance, were always followed by a record and commercial breaks, with the news on the hour; then local information followed by the coffee break medley until 10.50, with the final ten minutes to eleven given over to promoting what was happening from then until noon: a phone-in or celebrity guest promoting a book, record, film or play, or something on TV.

From a DJ's point of view, the coffee break medley was wonderful, an opportunity to reflect your own taste and balance this with the kind of music that the listeners wanted to hear. These days this is not possible because every record is surveyed by market researchers who use a catalogue of Beatles' tracks, for example, and then choose a selection from the top ten all-time favourites that they're sure people *will* want to hear. That's sad, really, because people who'd like to hear the lesser-known tracks don't get the chance, and this kind of computer-ruled programming eventually shoots itself in the foot because the favourites get overexposed. For my show I had a play list of seventy records, divided into three sections, A, B and C. The A records would be from the top twenty, or those that were up and coming; the Bs would have been around for a while or were new releases that hadn't yet had much airtime; and the Cs were our 'records of the week' and personal-request choices. It may sound an old-fashioned approach now, but the ratings proved it worked.

The phone-ins were the most difficult part of the show to organize. I used to scan the papers for relevant topics that would appeal to our listeners and then encourage them to ring in with their opinions. In those days we had to play much safer than broadcasters do now, but we also wanted some controversial debates. Good standbys were always the royal family, or a big storyline in a soap, such as the previous night's *Coronation Street*, *Emmerdale* or *Crossroads*. It was a case of: 'Did you see that?' and 'What did you think?' And, occasionally, guest stars, like Larry Grayson who lived in Coventry, would do the phone-ins for us.

Celebrities on a show always bring in audiences and I thought my best programmes were when I had a top-notch person to interview. Stars were actually in plentiful supply then, especially if, like me, you actively sought them out. Daytime TV programmes, such as Richard and Judy's *This Morning,* didn't exist. There was just Michael Parkinson on evening telly and Jimmy Young on Radio Two. Radio One was all music, so there were no 'plug' opportunities there. This meant that record, theatre and film companies and publishers maximized local radio when their artistes were out on the road. EMI, for example, might want to plug a Cliff Richard album, and Cliff would then do Nottingham in the morning and Birmingham in the afternoon as part of his promotional tour. Nottingham had two big theatres – the Playhouse and the Theatre Royal – both of which featured major stars in good summer season and winter panto productions. The main difference that I have found between interviewing guests on radio, as opposed to television, is the freedom to prolong an interview. The first time Elton John came on to my programme I was told that I could only have him for ten minutes, but he loved being there and we chatted for an hour. Eventually I had about six interviews under my belt, which the listeners kept requesting to be played again and again. I still have those particular tapes, but goodness knows how they would sound twenty years later.

When I interviewed Kenneth Williams he proved to be the only guest ever who corpsed me on air. It was hysterical. I still laugh whenever I listen to that tape. Kenneth came on saying in his camp, nasal voice, 'It's *so* nice to be here, Dale. Mind you, listeners, I'm sitting in the basement of the studios and I had to go up five flights of stairs just to use the lavatory. You'd think they'd supply a commode for a star of my stature. After all, at the end of the day, I *am* a cult figure. People point at me in the street and go "*He's a cult*".' I absolutely doubled up with laughter, and couldn't believe he was being *so* risqué!

The beginning of my time at Radio Trent also coincided with the shock-horror arrival of the punk era, which many people think was over by 1979, but it actually reached Nottingham in 1978. Before I go into this, I'd like readers to bear in mind that I was a DJ on a friendly entertainment-based programme that was catering chiefly for housewives. Having had a few glimpses of outrageous punk bands, with heavy-duty unglamorous names, such as Generation X and The Skids, snarling their pop songs on *Top of the Pops*, I didn't feel my listeners would feel comfortable about me having anything to do with them on my show. I knew the punks were endearing themselves to the youth of the nation, but I also realized they were frightening the proverbial out of mums and dads and the grandparent generation. They were becoming increasingly difficult to ignore, though, because the record companies were going full throttle in promoting them, and they themselves were very eager to get airtime because they knew that would sell their records. At the height of this furore, I remember A&M Records saying to me, 'We've just signed this *great* new band. They're going to be *h-u-g-e*. And you can have all three of them because they're doing a promotional tour. They're called "The Police".' Completely oblivious of who they were, I thought, 'This is *not* for me. They're obviously hard-rock anarchist types who will not go down a bundle with the housewives.' and I didn't even bother to listen to the record I'd been sent. A short while later, when they'd taken the country by storm and every TV and radio show was trying to give them airtime, I realized to my chagrin that I'd turned down the chance to do an exclusive interview with all three of them when they were promoting their very first record.

The same thing nearly happened with another rock phenomenon.

One morning Melanie, our receptionist at Radio Trent, rang me, saying, 'There's a pop singer here who's asking to see you. I've told her you don't do ad hoc interviews, but she says she doesn't want to talk on radio, she's just got a record she wants to give to you personally. She is, I must say, a *very* bizarre-looking thing.'

'Is she a nutter?' I asked.

'No, she's not a nutter,' Melanie replied. 'She's just a pop singer who's doing a gig in town tonight.'

'OK,' I said, 'send her down.'

And in walked Toyah Wilcox!

I thought her way-out hairstyle was wonderful. I played her record off air, realized it really had something, played it on air, and interviewed her there and then. I don't know what the housewives were thinking, but I thought she was sensational.

During my time at Radio Trent, then, I was continuing to develop my skills and I loved it. It was great, I was doing the kind of shows I liked and, with only Radios One, Two, Three and Four as competition, our station was getting a forty-six per cent share of the ratings across the East Midlands, Derbyshire and Leicestershire. Nowadays networks would die for ratings like those, but today's radio bands are chock-full of commercial stations and they are lucky if they get ten per cent.

Looking back now, I can't even begin to count or remember all the celebrities I interviewed between 1977 and 1985 because there were *so* many flowing in and out of the studio on a weekly basis. Not surprisingly there have been many times since when I have bumped into people who say, 'Dale – I met you at Radio Trent.' I must seem rude, but really I'm just embarrassed because I don't remember them all and my stock cover-up is, 'Oh, God, *that* was another lifetime.' The ones I do remember are either those who made me laugh, those who filled me with horror, or those who really were mega.

One day, for example, Sophia Loren popped up in Nottingham to promote a fragrance or a book, I can't quite remember which. And whenever there was a star of Miss Loren's status he or she was always given a suite at the Albany Hotel, which was just across the road from our studios. 'Would you like to come and interview her at the hotel?' the PR asked me.

'*Of course!*' I said. 'She'd be perfect for my show.' I was so excited. I knew the local press and TV would be around her like a swarm of bees, and the thought of being close up to such an amazingly beautiful woman from an era when glamorous women were super-glamorous was a total thrill.

When I arrived at the hotel and met up with the public relations man, he said firmly, 'You have three minutes with her and, within that three minutes, you can ask three questions.'

'Fine,' I said, but, as I picked up my tape recorder to go in and see her I was thinking, 'This'll be a waste of time.'

'Where do you think you are going?' he muttered. 'I haven't given you the questions yet.'

'Oh – right! OK.'

I sat down again, still trying to decide whether it was worth doing the interview. But she *was* Sophia Loren and the questions were obviously the only ones she was prepared to answer, so I decided to accept the situation. When I went in I was overwhelmed by her perfect bone structure and the charm of her broken English. She was even more stunning in the flesh than on the big screen. I asked the three permitted questions and left. The interview was so short I don't think I ever put it out on air, but I certainly relished those three brief minutes seated alongside a true screen goddess.

My next brush with a female movie star proved to be an error of judgement on my part that meant I missed out on a unique opportunity to interview an actress who was going to become a *huge* screen star. This omission came about because at the time, I was actually in Park Lane to interview Dustin Hoffman who was promoting his latest film, *Kramer vs. Kramer*. The production company had hired a function room in the Intercontinental Hotel and spent a small fortune on a big press junket that became a total bun fight as interviewers jostled each other and held their microphones aloft. I eventually succeeded in forcing my way to the front to ask some questions, but I never really got a decent interview with Dustin Hoffman and spent most of the time wishing all the others would shut up. That, though, is how these occasions are and I did at least manage to get five minutes of airtime out of it. I thought Dustin was incredibly charismatic (and remarkably short!) and I was left in no doubt whatsoever that, apart from being a brilliant actor, he had lashings of that magical, indefinable X factor. But the most extraordinary thing about that day was my missed opportunity. While I was watching the bun fight still going on around him, a film company guy came up to me and said, 'The other star of the film is sitting over there having a cup of coffee. This is her first major movie, but she's going to be *very* big. You could have a fifteen-minute one to one with her.'

'Who is it?' I asked.

'Meryl Streep,' he replied.

I glanced over at the slim blonde starlet sitting there on her own, sipping her coffee, with no journalist present interested in talking to her. 'Maybe I'll talk to her later,' I said. But stupidly I had no intention of doing so. Hoffman was why I was there. Can you believe that? When *Kramer vs. Kramer* hit the screens, Meryl Streep was a wow, an overnight success, and the rest, as they say, is history.

My biggest personal pressure at Radio Trent, as I said earlier on, is that I've never been an early-morning person. The mid-morning show, from nine to twelve, which I actually did for nearly seven years, was just about fine. But for most of that time the management, aware that I was pulling in excellent ratings, was trying to persuade me to do the number one slot: the breakfast show. Eventually, when seriously heavy pressure was brought to bear on me, I did agree to do the slot, but I hated functioning that early (seven until ten) and I returned the moment I could to the mid-morning show. My other problem – and this is one that remains to this day – is that I'm tardy, always running five minutes behind. For a recorded radio or telly show, five minutes doesn't matter much, although it's obviously not good to keep anyone waiting. These days, if it's TV, I always say to producers, 'I need time to get my head around what I'm going to do, so the longer the gap you can give me from the dress rehearsal to the filming, the better the show will be.' This way, I also save them time in the edit, because I don't make mistakes that often. But what people, including radio and telly directors, producers and researchers, often fail to understand is that an entertainer – 'the talent', as it's called – has to work to his or her own rhythm. I'm at my best when my adrenalin is kicking in because I'm racing to get to a studio. On the mid-morning show, when I was on air at nine, I *should* have been there at eight thirty at the latest, but the best shows I ever did were when I shot in, adrenalin pumping, at eight forty. None of my colleagues ever quite understood that I preferred to read the papers at home or while I was having breakfast at the Maid Marion Café. Many's the time that the programme director said, 'Dale, you're sending the wrong signals to the management.'

'Why's that?' I'd reply. 'I've *never* missed the start of the show.'

'No – no! It's your car. It's parked outside the radio station on a yellow line. It's now Friday and you've been given a parking ticket every single day this week. It gives the impression that you just drive in and walk on air.'

'I virtually do,' I said, 'but has the show suffered? No. I've already done my prep at home, I've kick-started my adrenalin and, as far as I'm concerned, as long as I'm here, ready to do the job at nine, that's fine. But I promise to park more prettily in the future.'

That was how I liked to work – at my own tempo – but they were always trying to get me there an hour earlier. And even on the odd occasion when they succeeded, it never worked because I would be sitting there twiddling my thumbs as my adrenalin and enthusiasm died. Then I really would need a kick start.

On telly, when a show is being recorded, it's different. Everything runs late anyway. So even if I do arrive on time, nothing starts for at least forty-five minutes. That's the way TV is, except for a show like *Supermarket Sweep*, which is run like a military operation because, when you're recording five shows a day, any delay costs huge sums of money.

My other problem at Radio Trent was that, although I was very happy in the job, I was still missing London like crazy. For the first couple of years, the moment I finished broadcasting on Friday afternoon, I'd be off in the car on my way home to Hatch End, where I'd retained my mother's cleaner, Joan, who was wonderfully reliable and always on call. In many ways my life felt as if it were in suspended animation: Mondays to Fridays I'd do the job, then at weekends – Friday night to Monday morning – I'd just enjoy being back in the house, watching TV and relaxing. Once again, just as when Mum was alive, I was living two lives. But at least I'd become great friends with Len Groat, one of the other DJs at Radio Trent and, thanks to him and Peter Tait, I did have a weekday life up there.

On the domestic front in Nottingham, having moved from one bedsit to another, I decided to rent a very nice one-bedroom apartment in The Park, a smart, tree-lined area, very close to Radio Trent. I could walk to the studio from there, but I rarely did. That was naughty because I was overweight and needed the exercise. Nowadays, I work out regularly and conscientiously at a gym with a tough and rigid discipline, but in my Radio Trent days I used to think that people who went to health clubs were a very strange breed who were totally obsessed with keeping fit and jogging all the time. I had never wanted to be a fat child, or teenager, and I didn't want to be a fat chap in my twenties. But I was. One day, when I was thinking seriously about this, I remembered how Mum used to take me off to health farms and how proud I'd felt of myself when I lost weight. I also remembered her taking me to a dietician in Essex when I was about ten or eleven, certainly pre-puberty time, and him saying I was the fattest little boy he had ever examined. After this visit, Mum took me to Grayshott Hall health farm fairly regularly, where I usually managed to lose a stone in ten days, but I always put it back on again. I guess I was a yo-yo dieter throughout my entire teens. The one time the weight actually fell off me was during the traumatic period after Mum died, but then I put it on again because I was working for United Biscuits Network and eating too many of their delicious products. When I reached sixteen stone, I took myself off to

Grayshott Hall, thinking, 'This is what Mum would have told me to do,' but I didn't lose weight because my heart wasn't really in it and I cheated by going down to the village shop. Interestingly enough, though, when I got the bill I realized I should have taken it very seriously. I'd no idea that health farms cost so much and, now it was my money, it really hurt! However, I still love Grayshott Hall and go three or four times a year. Another reason why I gained weight after Mum died was because after I left London for Radio Trent, the bedsits were far from ideal for a healthy diet. Until I got settled in my own place, I was eating all the wrong convenience foods and having a full fried breakfast at the Maid Marion Café each morning. I would then go into the studio and sit there for three hours, eating biscuits and sandwiches and, not surprisingly, I ballooned to eighteen stone. The funny thing is, when you lose weight you still think you are fat, but when you are fat you look in the mirror and think, 'I'm not *that* fat.'

By twenty-two, I might have been the highest-rated DJ in the Midlands, but I was also one of the fattest. One of the most requested songs at that time was 'Lip up, Fatty' by Bad Manners. Never was a record more close to my heart than when I went to do a live radio broadcast from the Broadmarsh Centre. As I was compèring the show, some of my female listeners, followed by a couple of football fans, wearing red-and-white Nottingham Forest scarves, came in. A few minutes later, one of the football fans started to heckle me with shouts of 'Lip up, fatty'. All the women leapt to my defence and turned on him, but I was devastated because I knew he was right. Later, I decided that I had to do something and that weekend when I came down to London I made an appointment to see Dr James, a woman doctor, who had taken over the practice from Dr Maclaren. Having had a talk about my weight, she said, 'Please, get on the scales.'

'OK,' I answered, 'but please don't tell me how much I weigh. I know that already.'

Having looked at the dials, she simply said, 'Right – I'm going to put you on some appetite-suppressants for a month.'

The tablets she prescribed for me are not available any more, but I loved them. They obviously had some kind of stimulant in them that gave me a real buzz. I was feeling even more energetic than usual, and I was doing some really great shows. I called them my 'happy tablets'. 'This is great,' I thought, 'I like this approach to dieting' and, at the end of the month, I went back to Dr James for more. By now, I was convinced that the tablets had magic properties that would make me thin no matter what I ate.

'Step on the scales,' Dr James said, 'and let me see how you've done.' But when she looked her face registered horror. 'I'm absolutely appalled,' she exclaimed. 'You've put on four pounds. You're certainly not having any more tablets. I'll give you some diet sheets instead.'

I was really upset. I knew I had to do something about my weight, but by then I'd got fixated on the idea that amphetamines, which curb your appetite, were the answer to my prayers.

These days I cringe when I look back on my foolishness. It isn't for nothing that amphetamines are a strictly controlled drug, subject to abuse and generally bad for the mind as well as the body. However, when somebody told me about a London doctor who was willing to prescribe amphetamines for a fee, I rang him up, made an appointment and went to see him. He told me that I needed to lose weight fast and prescribed Duraphet. 'These particular pills', he warned me, 'are *very* strong amphetamines.' He then explained that the white ones were 7.5mg, the black-and-white ones were 12.5mg, and the solid black were 20mg. Being me, I went straight on to taking the black ones. They were phenomenally strong. On one occasion I didn't sleep for three days, and wasn't at all surprised when I subsequently heard that they were given to long-haul pilots to keep them awake. They were obviously 'speed' but, because they were prescribed by a doctor and I was losing weight and doing great shows, I didn't care. The thought of buying the same thing from a dealer at King's Cross would have filled me with horror, but because I was getting them from a pharmacist in London I never questioned what I was doing. This would have been about 1982, when I was twenty-seven, and I was on them until 1986. Having lost a phenomenal amount of weight, halfway through this period I was asked to present an innovative live radio campaign for Radio Trent called 'Diet with Dale'. For this, we picked five women from my listenership, who had weight problems, and employed a marvellous researcher called Sue Ward, a fabulously trim girl, with a great brain, who put together brilliant healthy-eating and exercise diet sheets and managed the whole thing. It proved to be a hugely successful campaign and, on the day of the final outside broadcast, people queued up, four abreast, around the block. So, long before the days when Richard and Judy and other TV presenters were doing diet programmes I was pioneering ours on radio.

By then, although I now looked great, I was still taking the amphetamines. One month's supply was now lasting three or four months, so I wasn't using them all the time, but I had got a bit dependent on the highs they gave me and every now and again when I had a gig at night as well as a show the next day, I popped one into my mouth. When I was down to my last six tablets I went up to London to see the doctor again but this time it was bad news.

'They've taken the tablets off the market,' he said, 'so you can't get them now.'

'Oh, God,' I thought. 'I've only got six left.' But, believe me, I made those six last so long they probably went past their sell-by date.

Fortunately, soon after this, I interviewed Barbara Cartland and, thanks to her, I became a vitamin junkie. (And the only stimulant I'm addicted to now is coffee.) I guess, looking back, I was lucky because, although the amphetamines gave me a 'high', I never got the 'low' when I came off them. I'm just one of those irritatingly happy people who always puts his best foot forward and smiles. Of course, like everybody else, I *do* have days when I feel a bit down, but I just have a good cry then, if I need to, and get it out of my system that way. The only time I ever get *really* low is when my faith in someone is shattered or if someone, in those famous words, draws their sword upon me without cause. I am *very* sensitive and I don't mind admitting that when this happens to me, I find it impossible to hold back the tears.

*

When I joined Radio Trent in 1977, my original contract stated that I was to do six shows a week. This meant that if the station gave me a daytime show (these were called strip shows, which meant that they were stripped across the week) I was also obliged, if asked, to do a weekend show. Two years down the line, when I still had the house in Hatch End, they wanted me to do a Saturday show. I was sorry to decline the request, but I knew that would ruin my weekends in London and I wasn't ready, then, to relinquish my southern base. The compromise they then came up with was for me to pre-record the Saturday shows. I agreed to do this, but it became the bane of my life. It's one thing to record a TV show, but quite another to record what is meant to be a *live* radio show. The essence of a live show is spontaneity and, with all due respect, you cannot make it sound live and spontaneous if it's pre-recorded on tape! The show became full of disjointed clips that didn't work. My heart wasn't in it and I used to dread recording the next one.

'What *do* you want to do, then?' I was asked. 'The problem is that you've leapfrogged everybody on the station to get the prime mid-morning show, and now you're saying that you don't want to do the obligatory weekend show that goes with it. If we agree it will be bad for morale and will make the others envious. Why should you be exempt from this?'

'Why don't you give me an evening show, instead?' I suggested.

'But what would you do on an evening show?'

'Soul – I'd like to do a soul show.'

I'd always loved soul music – R&B – and I was thrilled when they eventually agreed to this. From then on, in addition to the mid-morning show, I did a soul show from eight to ten on Monday nights and I loved it. I now had an excuse to carry on buying imported records from America and this time I went to a little shop called Arcade Records in the Nottingham Arcade. It also proved to be a clever additional source of income for me – DJ work in local clubs. By then I'd long left behind the days of doing six arduous hours in sweaty London pubs but, as a local radio presenter, I could do an hour's guest spot, which paid me considerably more. By doing the soul show I was attracting an audience who also visited clubs so it all made sense professionally and economically. To this day, people still come up to me and say, 'I *loved* that soul show you used to do.' All in all, I was becoming quite well known in Nottingham and its surrounding areas, and I was now a bit of a local celeb. This was obviously not quite the same as being a name on telly, but people who listen to you every day and come to local gigs do gradually get to know you and they make you feel very special and welcome when you're out and about in restaurants or attending local functions.

One way or another I was beginning to feel more at home in Nottingham, a city which became then – and is now – a very special place for me. At least three times a week I would go out with Peter Tait for great Italian food at the Trattoria Antonio on Trent Bridge (which I still go to when I'm working in Nottingham). And, having decided I needed more living space, I rented a house in Sherwood Rise, owned by Len Groat, who was by then Assistant Programme Controller, where I stayed until he sold it. I then moved into a modern two-bedroom flat on Mapperley Road, an area which everybody who visits the annual autumn Goose Fair knows well. I persuaded my lovely cleaner, Edna, from next door, to stay with me until she retired; then I had another cleaner, a wonderful Irish lady. By 1981 I was gradually becoming a bit less attached to London, settling into the Midlands, and enjoying life on and off air.

While I was busy behind the mike, doing my mid-morning shows, people used to come in with messages, and we also used to have regular visits of all kinds, from local organizations to visiting VIPs and potential advertisers. The studios at Radio Trent were in the basement, which was a bit of a labyrinth, and I made it quite clear from my earliest days there that I didn't want to be a goldfish in a bowl. When I'm focused on a show, I don't want to be gawped at by eight people who are touring the studios, even if they are VIPs. This became a regular bone of contention when visits were arranged because I always thought it was outrageous that strangers could just wander in and out of the studio when I was in full flight, and I even found it distracting when they just stood there looking at me through the glass in the next studio. I might be in the middle of a phone-in when I'd look up and there, for example, would be eight Japanese businessmen standing still or walking about. So I was grateful when Radio Trent agreed not to bring them into my studio.

One particular day, however, proved to be an exception to my own rule. Len Groat was always very good at public relations and, when people wrote in and wanted to visit the studios, he would let them. That morning, I saw Len on the other side of the glass and heard him explaining to a young man that I didn't like to be disturbed while I was doing a programme. It was a day when I must have been feeling extremely benevolent or in a wonderful mood, or I just felt like showing off. Being the nosy parker I am, I buzzed through to Len on what we call 'talk back' and said, 'Good morning, Len. Who's that with you?'

'It's a student from Leicester,' he replied. 'His name is Mark Linsey and he's doing media studies.'

'Come in and say hello,' I said.

'Are you sure?' Len queried, surprised, and I heard later that he said to Mark, 'Well! You're honoured. Dale *never* lets anyone into his studio.'

When Len brought Mark in, I liked him at once and, completely out of character, said, 'If you like, you can stay and listen to the rest of the show.' I've always read faces and this man had the kindest face I'd ever seen and a really sweet disposition. We chatted away and I discovered that day was his twenty-first birthday, which means at the time of writing I now have known him for twenty years. At the end of the show we exchanged telephone numbers and I said, 'If you ever want to come by again, *do*.'

'I'm about to write a dissertation on local radio,' Mark replied. 'May I call you and pick your brain?'

'Not a problem,' I said. It was weird, but I really wanted to help him with his studies. It's so rare to meet people one really responds to and I knew instinctively that this man was a kind soul who had no hidden agenda. When we went out to dinner we just hit it off, chatted and chatted and, within three weeks, we became firm friends.

One night, soon after this, Mark asked if he could come and see me doing the soul show.

'I'll tell you what,' I said, 'come over and see the show, and afterwards we can have a burger at the Hot Brick Café.'

When the show finished at ten I told Mark, who was driving a Volkswagen Golf, to follow me in my Vauxhall Carlton to the restaurant. At that time the Lace Market was a labyrinth of streets that were never very busy on Monday nights and, true to form, it was deserted. You had to drive very slowly down these roads and, as I drove out of the studio, down Castle Gate, past Marks and Spencer, up the road and was about to turn left into the Lace Market, two shadows suddenly leapt into the street. I screeched to a halt, but I bumped into one of them who then ran away. Mark was a little way behind me. Before he could catch me up, a policeman suddenly leapt on to the bonnet of my car, flashed his badge at me and then, jumping into the passenger seat, said, '*Follow that man. Put your foot down.*' Startled, I did what I was told and hightailed off on a full-speed chase. Glancing in my mirror, I could see Mark putting his foot down, too, and we all proceeded to race around the Lace Market and in and out of the back streets. (All Mark had seen, he told me later, was a shadowy figure leaping on to the bonnet of my car, then jumping in. He didn't know it was a policeman and thought I was being abducted!) When the officer eventually yelled, 'There he is – *over there.* Pull over and wait here,' I screeched to a dizzy halt. A few minutes later the policeman came back alone, saying, 'Thanks *very* much. You can go now. I'll get it sorted.' I was *so* stunned that I didn't even ask him what he thought the fellows had been up to.

Reunited with Mark, I told him what had happened.

'My God, Dale,' he said, 'it was like something out of *The Sweeney.*' I agreed – and, being a cops-and-robbers fan, I said, 'I've *always* wanted somebody to leap out at me and yell, "*Follow that car!*"'

My friendship with Mark just grew and grew. He was like the brother I'd never had and we became inseparable. He used to drive over from Leicester to Nottingham and, whenever I could, I would visit him. When he finished his media studies he came to work at Radio Trent, doing the Care Line, a non-profit-making, community-based service with regular broadcast bulletins. At this stage he thought he wanted a career in front of the camera but, as it turned out, he became a very successful television executive and managing director of his own production company. We have lived through countless highs and lows together and I trust him with my life. I also love his wife, Sarah, and I am now godfather to their three sons, twins Benjamin and Louis, who were born on 10 December 1998, and Joshua, who was born in February 2001. We go on holidays together and not a day goes by when I do not speak to Mark. And all this came about through a chance meeting in a radio station.

Another extraordinary day at Radio Trent was when I interviewed Barry Humphries during his tour with *The Dame Edna Experience* in 1982. This show, which was playing at the Theatre Royal, Nottingham, was a complete sell-out. It was the 'must see' that week, and when Barry's Dame Edna is on form there's no one to beat her. The manager of the theatre, Barry Stead, always looked after me because when the theatre's productions were not doing as well as expected, he knew I would support them by mentioning them on air and interviewing the artistes. Then, when there was a major star at the theatre he would do everything in his power to encourage that person to come along and do my radio programme. It really was a mutually beneficial arrangement.

On the day that Barry Humphries was to do my show, we were told that he was coming in wearing his Dame Edna gear because he was going on afterwards to do a television interview for Central News. For some reason the timing of this was changed and I was told that Barry would now be coming in as himself and that I would be interviewing him as Dame Edna without the make-up. 'This', I thought, 'will be a very weird experience.' But when he walked into the studio that morning, wearing a huge fedora, I thought he was a darling fellow and an absolutely wonderful man. He had a minder with him – a crop-haired muscular Australian who, if he had been in TV, would certainly have been cast as a bouncer! Even though I had been initially fazed by the thought of Barry Humphries talking to me as Dame Edna, the interview went incredibly well. The amazing thing was that, although Barry was minus his slap and gear, he went straight into the Dame Edna voice and the chat just flowed. In fact, it was such a *good* interview that it was repeated many times on air and was often fitted into a 'Best of Shows' at Christmas, as was my interview with Kenneth Williams. Barry's *Dame Edna Experience* was already playing to packed houses, so he hadn't needed to come in, but at the very end of the interview he said, 'Thank you so much, Dale, for playing along with me, you're a real gem. Will you come and see the show?'

'Absolutely! I'd love to see the show,' I replied, 'but I haven't got tickets.'

'What night would you like to come?'

I arranged to go two nights later with Sue Ward, my brilliant PA/researcher.

'Come backstage afterwards,' said Barry, 'and say hello.'

When Sue and I watched him perform we thought he was sensational. The show also went down a storm with the audience. To this day it is one of the best shows I've ever seen. I am not somebody who's given to going to the theatre. As my close friends know too well, my arm has to be twisted firmly behind my back before they get me through the doors of any theatre, especially if it's a musical. I love movies and I love DVDs, but I am not a man of the theatre, opera, ballet or classical music, which surprises many. So for me to enjoy a theatre production is very unusual.

Sue and I did go to Barry's dressing room afterwards. Backstage the Theatre Royal has always been corporation green. I found it a very cold, unfriendly place. Sue had brought a book with her that was going to be auctioned on Radio Trent for charity. It was a *Beyond the Fringe* tome about people in the theatre. After this amazingly successful show, done to a full house, we had expected an atmosphere of euphoria but it was all very low-key and quiet. Barry's dresser, a sweet girl, was sitting in the corner and didn't say a word. Mr Aussie Security Man was also sitting there and didn't say a word. Dame Edna – still in all her slap and gear – said, 'Dale, how wonderful to see you. I'm so sorry Barry can't be here himself, but it's lovely to see you, dear.'

'This is a bit weird,' I thought. 'It really is as if he's two people!'

Sue, a very bright girl, was very sensitive to the atmosphere. 'Dame Edna,' she said, 'we *loved* the show. This book, which is being auctioned for charity, features you and it would help enormously if you could sign it.'

'Let me see the book,' Dame Edna replied.

Sue gave it to her.

'I've never seen this,' Dame Edna said. 'Where did you get it from?'

Sue explained.

Still no word from the dresser, still no word from Mr Security Man. Dame Edna then opened the book and proceeded to read it. No one said a word. Sue and I sat there for at least twenty minutes while Dame Edna finished reading the chapter about herself. 'Very interesting,' she then said, snapping the book shut and handing it back to Sue.

'Would Dame Edna mind signing it for charity?' Sue pressed.

'Not a problem – *of course.*' Dame Edna opened the book, signed it, snapped it shut and handed it back to Sue again. 'Thank you so much for coming, Dale,' she said. 'Barry's joining me at the Bird's Nest on Mansfield Road, which I am told is *the* Chinese restaurant to go for dinner. Do you recommend it?'

'Oh, yes,' Sue and I both said, 'it's a great restaurant.'

'I'm so sorry', Dame Edna repeated, 'that Barry couldn't be here to see you himself, but he *will* be joining me shortly at the Bird's Nest.'

Sue and I glanced at each other. 'What do we do now?' we were wondering. 'Is this an invitation to dinner?'

'Is it really a good restaurant?' Dame Edna asked again.

'Yes,' I repeated, 'it's a great place to eat.'

Sue and I were so stunned by Barry's dual-personality approach that when we left the dressing room we didn't say anything to each other for about five minutes. Then Sue said, 'Do you think he really wanted us to join him for dinner?' I had no idea. All I can say is that the man had come straight off stage and, clearly, as an artist, needed time to come down. He's a wonderful entertainer, a consummate professional and a true star. I was *so* pleased to hear later that he'd taken America by storm and was a huge star on Broadway. He deserves his success. And we enjoyed the rest of the evening together.

With Sue's help, in those days I always tried to do the prep for my programmes but, by and large, I winged it. This proved to be cause for regret one day. Vince Hill, the crooner, was in Nottingham for a professional engagement and I was asked if I would like to interview him. I was a big fan of his, so said 'yes' immediately. He arrived really early for the interview and parked his Rolls-Royce somewhat haphazardly in the Radio Trent car park, which wasn't very big. When he wandered into reception, he didn't mention that it was his Rolls-Royce that was now blocking the other vehicles coming in and out. At the time we had a cheeky chappie, who was essentially our odd-job man and, over the tannoy system, he announced, 'Would the owner of the Rolls-Royce in the car park kindly make himself known to reception. The Managing Director would like to introduce him to his daughter!'

I've always loved that kind of comedic quick wit and it made me howl with laughter.

Because Vince was early I hadn't got any of his records from the studio library and when I nipped out to get a couple there was none available. 'Oh, God,' I thought, 'the man's obviously going to expect me to play at least one of his records.' Sue wasn't in that day, so I desperately needed someone else to run out and buy a Vince Hill album. By this time Vince was in the studio, sitting there with a cup of tea and a newspaper. In desperation, I rang one of the girls in accounts. 'Would you come down to the studio, please,' I whispered quietly.

'What do you want?'

'Just come down to the studio – it's important.'

When she came in, I introduced her to Vince, then handed her a piece of paper on which I had written, *Please go and buy a Vince Hill album from a record shop and bring it to me, DISCREETLY.* She opened the note, read it, looked at me, looked at Vince, nodded and walked out of the door. Within a minute she returned. 'If I've got to go and buy a Vince Hill album,' she said, 'I'll need some money.'

I was mortified. Vince Hill, a quiet man, bless him, was reading the newspaper and pretended he hadn't heard.

'I've left my wallet in my car in the car park,' I hissed. 'Go to petty cash, or pay for it yourself and I'll settle with you later.'

'If I've got to get petty cash, I'll have to have it signed for. And John Lockwood, the company accountant, isn't in today, so I have no way of getting the money out.'

I could have smacked her.

At this point, a ten-pound note appeared from behind Vince's newspaper.

'Take the man's money,' I said meekly.

There is a PS to this story.

Off she went, only to return with an Andy Williams album! I was appalled. To his credit, Vince was a very good sport. I, however, still wake up with the sweats when I think about it. It was so embarrassing.

Soon after, I had another run-in, this time with the great actress, Anna Massey, who was on tour and staying at the Albany Hotel, Nottingham. 'You know, she's a really good actress,' Sue said.

'I know – she's marvellous. Can we get her in for an interview?'

'No. She doesn't want to do any. The play's a sell-out and she doesn't need the publicity. Theatre people work nights and they're often reluctant to do morning shows.'

'I know – but let's keep trying.'

Sue did, wouldn't give up, and in the end Anna Massey said she would come in. I've always found that talking to comics and singers is much easier than talking to actors. Actors may be brilliant with other people's words, but they often feel slightly exposed as themselves, unless they're a character in a sitcom or a comedic actor. Even then they *can* be difficult because they feel obliged to be as funny as the character they're known for.

Anna Massey, a very serious, rather intimidating person, arrived at nine forty-five for the interview, which was not due to start until ten fifteen.

'Hello, Anna,' I said. 'I'm *so* glad you decided to come in. I'm a huge fan and I really appreciate it.'

'Not a problem,' she said.

'Would you like a coffee? A sandwich?'

A very posh, plum-in-mouth bird, Anna replied, 'One has already taken breakfast at the Albany. One doesn't require any form of refreshment.'

'Oh,' I said. 'Well, I'm just going to play a Donna Summer record, which will be followed by the horoscopes, the news and another record, then we will come to you.'

'Fine. One will just sit here and do one's *Telegraph* crossword until one is required to speak.'

'Why', I began to wonder, 'did I push for this interview? It's going to be like pulling teeth.'

The news came on, I came out of that and played a record. 'I've just got a couple of dedications to do,' I said to Anna, 'then we will come on air.'

'Fine, one will just sit here until one is required to speak.'

'Anna,' I said, suddenly losing my cool, 'I know that you *very* kindly agreed to come in today, and I know that for theatre people it's especially difficult because it's early in the morning and you have been working late. But it seems to me that this is perhaps a bit *too* early for you. So I will be brief and I won't keep you long.'

'It's not that, Dale,' she said, 'one has a problem.'

'What's that? *What's the matter?*' I asked, bewildered.

'When one has been in the business as long as one has, one has done radio, one has done television, one has done films and one has done theatre. But when one has done wireless work, generally speaking one has been doing plays for the BBC on Radio Four and one has never been interviewed as oneself. And one is sitting here, absolutely terrified of saying *fuck* on the air.'

'*Oh!*' I gasped.

Then she gave me a broad smile.

Once she was on air, she was absolutely fine – lovely, in fact, a true star and very funny with it.

In those days of fewer channels, stars were so much more accessible than they are now and the listeners were really appreciative. During my Radio Trent days, some of the celebs used to do shop appearances in Nottingham on Saturdays. Local businesses would book a star to spend about fifteen to twenty minutes at each venue and the *Nottingham Evening Post* would then advertise and promote the events on radio. If they could get the star to do a radio interview, they would be delighted because the star would then doubtless mention the shops and the newspaper.

Pat Phoenix, who played Elsie Tanner in *Coronation Street*, came up for one of these days, as did Diana Dors. In fact, two of the three occasions when I met Diana Dors were while I was at Radio Trent. Pat Phoenix, though, I had already met several times before, when I took days off from my mid-morning show to spend time in Manchester where *Coronation Street* was filmed. Together with others in the press office, I would then do ten interviews with the various stars, which would give me enough to run two interviews a day for a whole week – '*Coronation Street* on Radio Trent with Dale'.

I also did the same with the stars of *Crossroads* at Central Television, Birmingham. I remember so well going to *Crossroads* for the first time. They were turning around five shows a week and it was just like a production line in a factory. There I was in this extraordinary environment, among all those famous faces, with a tannoy system announcing household names, such as 'Noelle Gordon to set *now*,' 'Sue Hanson to set *now*.' And off they went, breaking off their conversations in mid-flow, because studio time was money. It was run just like a military operation and it *amazed* me. It was the same with *Coronation Street*, although, curiously, it always seemed much more relaxed on that set. I particularly admired Pat Phoenix who was high on life, a marvellous person and actress, and a huge success on that soap.

On the day of her shop appearances she was due to reach

Nottingham early in the morning and I was invited to join her for breakfast at the then-new Royal Hotel in the centre of the city. The last time I had seen her was about two years previously in the snug at the Rover's Return when she was wearing all her *Coronation Street* finery. But by this time she had left the *Street* and was about to star in a sitcom set in a hairdressing salon. What I remember most about that interview was her wonderfully infectious laugh.

'Pat,' I said, 'you look fabulous.'

'You know what, darling,' she replied, 'I believe that when you go out, you must *never* disappoint. You should put on all the slap, do the hair and wear a suit. You should look like a star.'

'Well,' I said, 'you do. You look amazing.'

'Not bad for an old bird, eh?' she replied.

'You're not *that* old,' I said. (I should have known better!)

'How old do you think I am?' she asked.

Pretending to study her a moment, I said tentatively, 'Fifty-six, fifty-seven.'

She let out this huge howl of laughter.

'What are you laughing at?' I asked.

'Thank you for your honesty, Dale,' she replied. 'I'm fifty-eight. But usually when I ask people what I've just asked you, they *never* cross the fifty barrier. They usually play safe and say forty-eight, forty-nine.'

From that moment on we were the best of pals.

It has never surprised me how successful soaps are, as I have always been a huge fan of them. As an enduring reflection of life as we know it – or would like to know it – it always hits the spot, from *Crossroads* to *Dynasty* and *Corrie* to *Dallas*, not forgetting the ultimate, *Prisoner Cell Block H*. I'm a self-confessed soap addict. In many ways *EastEnders* is the perfect soap – but if only they'd give Peggy Mitchell bigger shoulder pads!

I first met Diana Dors when Mum was in *Misleading Cases,* a BBC TV sitcom, with Diana and Alastair Sim. I was only thirteen or fourteen, but I thought Diana was so glamorous. Then later, after her fleeting visit for the shop day, I met her again when she was doing a cabaret night at the Musters Hotel, a large, long, low building, set in the middle of a residential area in West Bridgeford, just to the south of Nottingham. Rex Harvey, who owned the hotel, always tried to book people from pop groups who hadn't been in the charts for two or three years, so he got them at the right price, and he applied the same principle to other artistes who had a cabaret act. The hotel had a small band that seemed to come and go as needed. It was always a good night out for the locals. June, who worked for Rex, was a lovely girl. I knew her quite well and she always kept in touch, letting me know who was appearing: 'We've got Mungo Jerry coming to the Musters, do you want to interview them? We've got Bernard Manning, do you want to come and see the show?' On this occasion she rang and said, 'We've got Diana Dors coming. Do you want to see the show? Will it interest you?'

'Absolutely,' I said. 'When you speak to her agent, tell her that I'm Sheree Winton's son. I'm sure Diana will remember me.'

Sure enough, the agent came back saying, 'We'd love to see you, Dale. Come before the show and Diana will do the interview then and have a chat.'

That night, Diana was going to sing a couple of her 'stock in trade' numbers, the ones she always featured, and then take questions from the audience. Being the quick wit that she was, and given the kind of life that she had led, Diana was never short of a good answer and she always had plenty to say for herself.

As she was due to go on at eleven o'clock, I got to the Musters at nine thirty. June was there and said, 'She'll be here in a minute.'

At twenty to ten, Diana walked through the doors with two of the biggest bouncers I had ever seen in my life. 'Hi, Dale, how are you?' she said. 'I remember your mum well. I haven't seen you since you were a little boy. Nice to see you.'

'Hi, Diana,' I replied, 'this is June who looks after everything at the Musters Hotel.'

Turning instantly to June, Diana said, 'Right, who's paying me?'

'I will,' said June, surprised, 'I'll talk to Rex and see that everything is all right.'

'You know the deal,' Diana replied, 'half up front and half after the show.' Then, turning to me, Diana said, 'I take no nonsense – I get it sorted.'

She was a tour de force standing there, a real glamour girl with platinum-blonde hair, the amazing figure with the boobs out front and every inch the star. She'd done loads of telly and movies in the past, but her career had had its ups and downs of late, which was why she was there. As we made to go to the dressing room, June, clearly shaking by now because she knew this woman was a force to be reckoned with, said, 'Can I get you anything, Miss Dors?'

'I would like a fruit salad and a pot of tea,' Diana answered.

'I'll get it right away,' June replied.

Just as I finished the interview at about ten fifteen there was a knock at the dressing-room door and the bandleader, who also doubled as guitarist, came in. He looked like something out of the TV show, *The Wheeltappers and Shunters Social Club* – club life at its finest!

'Here are my song sheets,' said Diana. 'Those are the numbers I'll be doing.'

'Fine,' he said, 'I'll go and give them to the band.' (He meant his couple of musicians.)

Diana and I continued chatting and, at about ten thirty, the bandleader came back and said, 'Miss Dors, I've given your music to the musicians. You are due to go on at eleven, but we're running a little behind – about ten minutes. Would it be all right if you went on a few minutes later?'

'Fine, no problem,' Diana said, 'however, I have to tell you, I am booked to appear here from eleven to eleven forty-five. And no matter what time I go on stage, I am walking off at eleven forty-five. Please understand that.'

She had obviously been messed around too often by clubs and had reached the stage in her life where she was calling the shots. She was right. A deal is a deal. And audiences do go flat when stars are late coming on. We sat there, watching the minutes go by. It was now eleven fifteen and Diana still had not been called. By eleven twenty I started to twitch a bit because I knew she meant what she had said. She, though, was perfectly calm – serene even. 'These people are idiots,' I thought, 'they obviously don't realize that she means what she said.'

Finally at about eleven twenty-five she went on stage. She sang two numbers, took one question, gave one answer and, at eleven forty-five, she thanked the audience very graciously and left.

I don't think she got her second payment that night. Whether she got it in the end, I don't know, but my bet is that she would have got it. I *hope* so.

A year later she was back in Nottingham to do the shop appearance sponsored by the Nottingham *Evening Post* and I was invited to go along to the Albany Hotel to interview her. Her husband, Alan Lake, was with her on this occasion and they were *so* sweet to me. She had had a lot of health problems that year, had really been very poorly, but she still looked magnificent. The cancer, it seemed, was in remission and she told me she was feeling much better. We did a great interview and I was incredibly sad when I heard that, within a few weeks of her return to London, she was readmitted to hospital because the cancer had spread. When I went to visit her there, I saw Alan coming out. He was clearly distraught. 'She's *really* not well, Dale,' he said, choked. She was not. She was so weak I was only able to stay a couple of minutes. She died very soon afterwards. For me – and others – it was the passing of an era. Diana, like my mum, was from that glamour girl pin-up period and I had really bonded with her. She was a real trouper. To this day, I have nothing but respect for grafters, which is why when I look at someone like my *EastEnders* friend, Barbara Windsor, I have total admiration for her professionalism and the application that she gives to the craft of her job. These are stars who have worked very hard to get to – and maintain – their position and no job is too big or too small for them. They understand the business. I only hope that their talent receives the respect it deserves. It takes a great deal of verve and energy to survive that long in a business that's not renowned for longevity, and I have been so lucky to know a few of them.

People, in fact, have always said how blessed I am with my friends – and I am. When you have no close family to speak of, your friends become everything to you. And what is interesting about my lot is that, apart from my showbiz friends who tend to know each other, I also have many others from different walks of life who don't tend to come across each other. They are all very different – somewhat eccentric – all know about each other, have all met from time to time, but we tend to go out mainly on one to ones. I'm still quite good at picking and choosing new friends, though, because usually I can spot someone with a hidden agenda from fifty paces. It's very rare for me to be wrong about people. My gut instinct is second to none, which is why I have the most wonderful friends whom I love and cherish dearly.

Being part of a community is very much the essence of local radio and, for this reason, Radio Trent always made it very clear to me that they did not like me going home to London at weekends and wanted me to sever my ties there and become localized. By 1982, when Nottingham was changing quickly and becoming quite cosmopolitan, I was ready to oblige. Having attracted a huge number of students, the city was suddenly very buzzy in the evenings at places such as the Lace Market, which still has a village atmosphere, is very pretty, and full of restaurants, bars and charming historic buildings. Stepping out there – a must for locals and visitors – is like going back a few eras to when Nottingham was the centre of the lace industry.

My radio show was still going well and was highly rated, I had a number of friends there, including Mark, and it seemed to me that my lot was good. Mum had left me a certain amount of money but, as I was not brilliantly well paid at Radio Trent, I had got through most of that going up and down between Nottingham and London. When I did my sums I realized that if I sold Hatch End and paid off a few bills, I would still have enough money to buy a house I had spotted up for sale in Nottingham.

I had very mixed feelings about selling the house as it had been my home for so long. However, there are times in your life when, against sentiment, you have to move on. I considered it a new start with more than a knowing nod to the past.

The house I liked in Nottingham was owned by a lawyer and described by the estate agent as a 'Californian villa'. Situated in a row of five equally attractive houses, it was architect designed and had a stucco front. As you looked at the property, there was a huge double garage underneath, with an up-and-over electric door, which I thought was *very* smart. On the first floor was an enormous sitting room with a row of archway windows over a bay front. There were three bedrooms on the next floor, one of them with a dressing room and the biggest bathroom I'd ever seen. It was a stunning house, decorated to perfection and I thought, 'Yes, this will do for me. This is very nice.'

As you looked down from the rear balcony, there was a patio, and beyond this a marvellous rockery made from boulders at least six feet high, backed by the most fabulous views over Nottingham. With the exception of my neighbours, Victor and his wife, Mary, it really was a dream of a house to live in. An elderly couple, Victor and Mary were only problematic because every now and then Mary, poor lady, became, to use my favourite description, tired and emotional, and would have to disappear somewhere for three or four weeks. One day I heard an horrendous noise and, looking out from my balcony, I could see her bashing hell out of a drain with a pitchfork. 'It's the smell,' she was saying to it, 'let the smell go or I'll get the council.'

'Are you all right?' I asked, concerned.

'I've rung the council,' she replied, still bashing away. 'Now I'll *have* to get the police.'

She was clearly very troubled. A short time later, Victor came round to see me and, having apologized for the disturbance, added, 'She'll be going away again for a couple of weeks.'

After these absences, there would be three months of absolute silence, which would then be followed by sheer mayhem. Once, when I had had friends over for dinner and we were saying our goodnights soon after midnight, one of next door's upper windows flew open and some milk bottles came flying down, only missing us and our cars by inches. My friends looked absolutely stunned.

'I'm sorry,' I said. 'But I'm sure she'll be full of remorse tomorrow and will clear up the glass.'

At that moment, however, the window reopened and there she was, standing there in her nightdress, looking like something out of a Hammer horror film. As she beckoned at the moon, all the scene needed was a few flashes of lightning. 'Once again the sounds of a whore awake me at midnight,' she bellowed and promptly closed the window again. The next day the lady went away for another of her rests. 'I've had to have her sectioned again,' Victor told me sadly.

'Oh!' I said, surprised by his sudden honesty. 'I'm so sorry she's not well. I wish her better. If there's anything I can do to help, please let me know.'

Strangely enough, none of this really fazed me. I just felt so sorry for Mary, who was clearly very distressed and in need of help.

My neighbour on the other side of the house was a lovely guy, a bodybuilder called Kevin Farrell who owned a gym. Very much a man about town in his Mercedes convertible, he had the body of an Adonis, and was absolutely adored by women.

Beyond his house were Ingrid and John Glover, and their children, Natasha and Stephen. They were a wonderful family and we all became bosom friends and are still in touch with each other to this day.

Around this time, I was asked if I would like to interview the pop singer, Howard Jones, who had had six top-ten hits. 'Like to Get to Know You Well' was one and he was now promoting his latest album. The suggestion was that I should go and see his show, then go on afterwards to a disco at the Sherwood Rooms to do a raffle draw with him before the interview. A big star name at this time, he was appearing at the Theatre Royal concert hall and the show was a sell-out. By that stage in my career I didn't usually do interviews outside the studio unless it was someone I knew or really liked, but on this occasion I decided to go along to the disco with Mark. I'd been told that Howard Jones would leave the Theatre Royal at elevenish and would then be on stage with me at eleven thirty to do the raffle. Backstage at the Sherwood Rooms, midnight came and went and, at twelve thirty, I was fed up waiting and did the raffle without him. At about twelve forty-five some security men with walkie-talkies suddenly marched in. It was like, 'What's going on here?' Answer: major security – Howard Jones had entered the building. Everybody was pushed aside and flattened against the walls, and I was invited to go into a room to do the interview. If you have ever seen the film *Spinal Tap*, you'll appreciate the scene that greeted me. It was rock'n'roll excess. There, amidst an assortment of pretty girls and the band of security men, was the pop star. Introductions completed, I sat down alongside him, and said, 'We'll be running this interview tomorrow morning and I'll leave some pauses so I can insert tracks from your album.' (All the girls and security guys were listening in.) I began the tape, explaining for the listeners, 'I'm backstage at the Sherwood Rooms with Howard Jones, who has just completed a very successful sell-out night at the concert hall.' I turned to Howard. 'It's *great* to see you. How did the show go, Howard?'

'Fine.' Silence followed.

'This is going to be fun,' I thought.

'Congratulations on your new album, Howard. What I like about you is that you have the wonderful knack of writing catchy pop songs that the whole of Europe has taken to their hearts . . .'

'I do *not* write catchy pop songs,' he interrupted. 'I write melodies to brighten up people's dreary lives.'

By now, I was an old hand at interviewing but I wasn't used to dealing with stroppy pop stars and I didn't back off. 'Well, I think they're very catchy and I really like them,' I said.

'This interview is now terminated,' he replied.

I was so embarrassed. It was not just a simple matter of getting up and leaving. I had to disconnect my tape recorder and put all the gear away. Cut adrift in a sea of sulky silence, I felt harassed and humiliated. Once outside, I was absolutely furious with what I felt were the arrogance and bad manners of the man. But now, with hindsight, I can only assume that, to coin the phrase again, he was tired and emotional.

The interview didn't need editing for the next morning's programme. It was short enough as it was. I just put it on a cartridge, ready for broadcasting. 'I'm going to run this interview as is,' I told the assistant programme controller.

'Are you sure?' he replied.

'*Yes.*'

To this day, I never presume to slag off artistes. There are some I would cheerfully clout out of life and others I never wish to meet again but if I can't say something good about someone, I don't say anything at all. I don't see it as my job to influence audiences by giving a personal opinion. I let the interviews speak for themselves. Where Howard Jones was concerned, I didn't once mention how arrogant he had appeared and how humiliated I had felt and, as usual, after every record I plugged the interview. 'Coming up, Howard Jones as you've never heard him before. *Coming up* an interview you don't want to miss, Howard Jones.'

At five past eleven, after the news, I simply said, 'Here is the interview I've been telling you about all morning. I'm going to play it to you in its entirety. It won't take long!' I ran the tape as it was, then went straight into playing a record. The sympathetic letters and phone calls I received afterwards were phenomenal, and I suddenly realized that to act with dignity and let the man speak for himself was certainly the right approach. You never stop learning. I will only add that he made me feel very small and *all* I was trying to do was my job. Since then, whenever I've heard radio or television interviewers having similar hard times with celebrities I always mutter silently under my breath, 'If you don't want to be there, you shouldn't put yourself in the frame. It's not fair on you, the interviewer or the listener.' I get quite upset about this because that's not playing the game.

Something I have always subscribed to is the quote, 'You can't be *too* rich, *too* thin or *too* suntanned!' At Radio Trent I was *never* rich, *never* thin, but being suntanned became a possibility! I always think I look better with a bit of colour, which was why, in the 1980s, when sunbeds suddenly came into their own and a tanning venue opened up in Nottingham, I was *very* pleased. I know I'm a dark guy, but the darker my skin tones veer towards, the bigger my eyes look, the whiter my teeth look and, mysteriously, I generally look a bit thinner, too. Now I'm on telly, this is even more important because the lights bleach you out. I know people love making jokes about my 'orangey' tones, but I just laugh along with them. Anyway, when the tanning shop opened in Nottingham, I became a regular customer. The following story is *so* Dale! I have the eyes of an eagle when it suits me but, most of the time, I meander through life completely oblivious to my surroundings and the reasons why people might be there.

When I walked into the tanning shop, the gorgeous girl behind the counter, very tanned herself, knew me at once from the radio. 'Come in, Dale,' she said. 'I'll show you around.'

The place was set up like a beauty salon, with various little rooms leading off narrow corridors where I assumed the many girls working there did treatments. I, though, was taken straight through to a high-speed tanning bed, one that is now no longer used because that particular model is so bad for the skin. But no one knew that then and, thanks to my once-a-week visits, I soon turned a wonderful colour. What I could never understand, though, was the staff's incredible attention to detail. I thought I was getting four-star treatment because I was on local radio, but I was still surprised to receive such excellent service. I always had one beautiful girl to accompany me to the sunbed cubicle, and the moment my time was up there was another waiting outside the door to lead me back through to reception and out of the building.

By about my tenth week I had got to know them all by their first names, and I was always telling my friends and colleagues how wonderful they were to take so much pride in their work and appearance. They were always beautifully made up, immaculately groomed and, it has to be said, very sexy.

Usually I drove to the salon but one day I booked a cab. '*Well*,' the driver said as I gave him the name and address, 'I wouldn't have thought you needed to go there, Dale!'

I was a bit surprised and also rather naïve. 'Oh?' I replied, 'I always go there for my tan.'

'It's a *very* nice tan,' he muttered, 'and if that's your excuse, I wish you well with it.'

I honestly thought no more about this and, when the glamour girl on reception that day said, 'Dale, we always listen to you on the radio. Would you play a record for all of us girls at the salon?' I said, 'Of course.'

Next morning, on the radio at 8.50 a.m., I said, 'Here's Harold Melvin and the Bluenotes, and I'm playing this for all the girls I had the pleasure of seeing yesterday at the tanning salon.' I then reeled off the list of their eight names and played the record.

When the news reader, Phil Dixon, came on at nine o'clock, I heard him say, 'And hot news . . . the Nottinghamshire Constabulary has raided a tanning salon and eight girls have been taken away for running a house of disrepute.' My eyebrows shot up – and the penny finally dropped! Ten minutes earlier I had actually *thanked* all the girls for the wonderful time I had had there the day before. Now, minutes later, Radio Trent's listeners knew it was a knocking shop and the girls were all prostitutes. It was only then that I understood why they always showed a bit too much cleavage and escorted me on and off the premises. They were afraid I would discover the hanky-panky that went on there.

There's a postscript to this story, too. About six months later I bumped into the woman who ran the salon (I suppose you'd call her a 'madam'). 'Hi!' I said, somewhat taken aback. 'How are you?'

'I'm fine,' she replied, 'but I've been run ragged, Dale. I've got a delegation coming in and staying at the Savoy, and I need to find ten girls.'

She was still at it – but now freelancing in hotels.

The respectable establishment I subsequently went to for my tan wasn't half so good, but at least I was in safe hands. Feeling safe, though, was soon to be a thing of the past.

For eight stimulating years I was very happy working at Radio Trent and especially happy living in Nottingham after I moved into my luxurious 'Californian villa' house. But in 1985 the recession hit the UK and, for me, like so many other people at that time, there was a very unpleasant surprise on its way to me in the post.

# 5

## 'I just don't know what to do with myself . . .'

WHEN IT CAME TO the signing of my contracts at Radio Trent, I was the *only* presenter who ever refused to become 'staff' and insisted on remaining a freelance. My philosophy then – and now – is: if one door closes, another opens. To this very day, it always makes me smile when I read write-ups in newspapers that say *Dale – an exclusive artist for the BBC* or *Dale – no longer an exclusive artist for the BBC* or *Dale signs an exclusive contract.* The truth is that I have never signed an exclusive contract because I hate feeling under obligation to anybody and, even more important, I would hate any network to feel obliged to keep me on because they have signed a contract. Call it what you will, one of my greatest fears in life is being somewhere I'm no longer wanted. I prefer to think that I can dispense with anybody's services with dignity and they can dispense with mine. I also believe that we should learn from historical precedents. I am a great admirer of the heyday of Hollywood and I think the studio system then worked very well for some of the stars. However, it worked best for Barbara Stanwyck who never ever signed an exclusive contract with

MGM. The studio could then have loaned her out to Paramount in the same way it did with Bette Davis, Joan Crawford, Moira Shearer, Dorothy Lamour (the list is endless). Barbara Stanwyck always remained in control of her own destiny and only ever signed up picture by picture. She also made more money in this way because she upped the ante every time. This non-exclusive approach isn't disloyal, it simply means that if someone gives you the option to work you are lucky, and if you get a radio or telly series that runs for years you're even luckier. Then, if it all comes to an abrupt end, with regular resting periods between contracts, that's show business. Even though I have now been on peak-time television for ten years, there are still times – because I'm very selective – when I wait for the right job to come in. And I still haven't taken up the option of an exclusive contract to keep the wolf from the door.

When I joined Radio Trent in 1977, I only signed a twelve-month contract. Apart from the usual tweaks in pay and other increments, I was still on the same twelve-month contract eight years later in 1985, with the usual one-month's notice clause on either side. For most of those eight years I was the most successful person on mid-morning radio and my share of the audience never went down. In fact, I was rated number one in the marketplace and my contract, which came up for renewal each May, simply rolled on to the following year. By the time the recession hit the UK, I was the most expensive DJ on Radio Trent's payroll and being paid a salary that was considered more commensurate with a London rather than a Midlands radio station. I was still sending off tapes to Capital Radio and Radio One, none of which hit the mark. However, I came close to Radio One a couple of times. That would have been the icing on the cake, as you also got to do *Top of the Pops*! Years later, I was asked to be the guest host a couple of times, which would have to be among the highlights of my career.

During my time at Radio Trent I'd seen many management changes, but the most recent was the appointment of two executives, Ron Coles, who became our Managing Director, and Chris Hughes, who became our new Programme Controller.

In all my years working at the station I had been very lucky. I had never had a day's illness and had never missed a programme. However, just before my next contract was due for renewal, I was taken ill with a dreadful stomach bug and was instructed by the doctor, who came to give me a check-up, that I should take a few days off. I remember lying in bed feeling absolutely wretched as the morning's post arrived. When I eventually collected it between gripes, there was a letter from Ron Coles. It was a letter I had to read over and over before I could fully absorb the shock of its contents. The crucial bit, which I kept returning to, said something like, *I have to write to you today because, under the terms of your contract, I am obliged to give you one month's notice before ending your contract.*

I had *lost* my job! This shattering news had not even been given to me through the courtesy of a one-to-one meeting, but by post. I was, to say the least, *devastated.* Ron Coles was obviously within his contractual rights to give me just one month's notice, but this meant I would have to leave at the end of May, without the chance of looking for – or finding – another job. Like most people in our business, I knew that it's all very well to apply to other radio stations when you're successful and working in a safe haven, but quite another matter when you're out on your ear and unemployed. This immediately begs the question, '*Why* is he in this position? *Why* has he suddenly stopped working after eight years?' Already feeling ill and now in shock, all I could do was to ring my then agent, Jackie Evans, and ask her to deal with the suddenness of it all.

Having spoken to Ron Coles, who apparently explained, 'It's for financial reasons. The station's been hit by the recession,' Jackie got angry and replied, 'But it's *unfair* just to serve a month's notice on Dale in this way. He's given the station eight years' loyal service and the least you can do is give him time to find another job. Or, can we talk about the money? If it's only a money issue, maybe we can somehow make that easier all round?'

What we didn't know until later was that the very same morning Jackie was having this conversation with Ron Coles, there was another extraordinary drama going on at the radio station which

(*Above*) My first photoshoot!

(*Left*) Probably my first trip to the seaside with Mum – summer 1955.

A day out with Mum and Dad, 1957. I had clearly found my love of cars by then.

In the garden with Mum and Nanny Burke
– summer 1956.

Taking my morning walk in
London's West End, just before we
moved to the suburbs – 1958.

Me with Mum, just before the guests
arrived for my third birthday party.

A classic picture of Mum.
I was twelve when this was
taken, and was so proud of her.

The day Mum met Terry-Thomas she was taking part in a sketch for *The Terry-Thomas Hour*. Terry is on Mum's right, Donald Sutherland on her left.

You can see from this photo why Mum was known as 'the English Jayne Mansfield'.

My third birthday party – well, my birthday cake had to be a car, didn't it!

(*Above*) Dad's yellow Zephyr convertible parked behind Mum's powder-blue Ford Popular. Even at the age of five I was desperate to get behind the wheel of a soft top!

(*Right*) Me, age five, in our garden in Edgware, standing on my first swing. You wouldn't catch me wearing horizontal stripes these days!

Age ten, having a cuddle from Mum at home.

(*Left*) On the beach outside the
Martinez Hotel in Cannes.

(*Above*) An early head-and-shoulders
shot of a young Dale.

Grandma comes to stay – summer 1970.

This picture, taken in 1975 when I was twenty-two, was the deciding factor for my first nose job!

At Charlee Brown's in 1976, my favourite gig at the time.

(*Left*) Me and Steve Allen having a mad moment in a photo booth, 1974.

(*Above*) 1976: My resident gig at Charlee Brown's in Tottenham. It's party night, and Steve and I look on as one of the customers impersonates a chicken in a competition.

(*Below*) I do my patter for the crowd.

With my new nose and a job at UBN, I was dispatched to interview Barry Manilow. As you can see, the word 'diet' was yet to become part of my vocabulary.

An early photo of me behind the decks at Radio Trent, which was to be my home for many years.

A live outside broadcast called 'Diet with Dale' – a health and fitness series I did with Radio Trent.

1982, the year Mark and I became friends. Little did I know then that I would become godfather to his three beautiful sons.

Backstage at the Royal Concert Hall with Dame Edna, who had just done a fantastic performance.

(*Left*) Me and Pat Phoenix having breakfast after an interview I did with her for Radio Trent.

(*Below*) One of the last times I met Diana Dors was when she came to Nottingham for a performance. This was taken just six weeks before she lost her life through ill health.

(*Above*) 1986 – my first publicity shot for *Pet Watch*, my first-ever TV show. Little did I know that animals would play such a major role in my later TV series, *Pets Win Prizes*.

1995 – the official *Pets Win Prizes* photo. They say never work with animals, but we had such a laugh making those programmes.

(*Above*) 1994 – this picture says it all – *Supermarket Sweep*! A trolley, lots of groceries and yours truly.

(*Right*) Grandma and Uncle Joe at the studios to see a recording of *Supermarket Sweep*.

(*Above*) Autumn 2001 –
my first Royal Variety
Performance.

(*Right*) Merrill's
birthday bash at
The Belvedere.

(*Left*) Cher and I, backstage at one of the many
shows she has done with me.

Me with Graeme and Karen
Souness in Marbella, 2002.

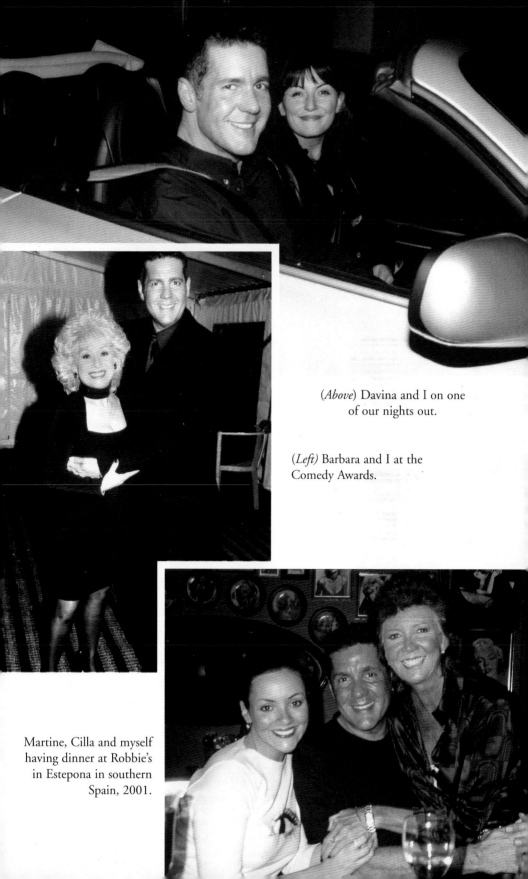

(*Above*) Davina and I on one of our nights out.

(*Left*) Barbara and I at the Comedy Awards.

Martine, Cilla and myself having dinner at Robbie's in Estepona in southern Spain, 2001.

Me with Sarah, Mark's wife, and my three beautiful godsons: Ben, Louis and Joshua.

Mark and I with Ben and Louis, on holiday in Puerto Banus, 2001. (*Inset*) With Joshua, Christmas 200

concerned the rock DJ, Graham Neale, whom Ron Coles had brought in with him to do an evening rock music programme, called *Castle Rock*.

When the police suddenly arrived at Radio Trent to interview Graham, a very surprised Ron Coles had eventually intervened and said to the detective, 'Why are you getting so heavy with Graham Neale?'

'Because,' the detective had replied, 'we believe him to have murdered his girlfriend, Lynn.'

I had always quite liked Graham. I usually saw him on Monday nights when his rock show preceded my soul show, and I knew he had had a steady girlfriend called Lynn for some time. All the DJs knew each other very well and we were all upset for Graham, who was devastated when he and Lynn split up. A few weeks after this, on a Saturday afternoon, I bumped into Lynn, with her new boyfriend, in the Food Hall of Marks and Spencer. 'Hi, Lynn,' I said, feeling a bit awkward. 'How are you?'

'I'm doing great, Dale,' she replied.

A really lovely, smiley girl, she then introduced me to the man at her side. 'He seems a really sweet guy,' I thought.

They were both very into cars, told me they had just ordered a new one and we chatted away about this and that.

'It's been so nice to see you, Lynn,' I said, as we were parting. 'Good luck with your new relationship and new car.'

On the following Monday evening, when I went into Radio Trent to do my soul show, I was very surprised to see Lynn in reception. 'Hi, darling!' I said. 'What are *you* doing here?'

'I'm going to see Paul Young in concert with Graham.'

I must admit, having seen Lynn only a couple of days before with her new boyfriend, I was a bit taken aback.

When Graham was packing up his records and I was waiting to take over the studio for my soul show, I said, 'I've just seen Lynn in reception.'

'Yes,' he replied. 'We're going to the Paul Young concert.'

'Oh! Are you back together, then?' I asked.

'No, not quite,' he said. 'She's just coming to the concert with me.'

I knew that Graham and Lynn knew Paul Young quite well, and that they were huge fans of his, so I thought, 'Maybe it's just a friendship thing.' But I was still surprised. 'Well,' I said, 'it was lovely to see her again. I hope you have a good time.'

'Well,' he replied, 'I hope she's not just come back because I have tickets for the concert.' Then he added something that I will never forget: 'There'll be hell to pay if that's all it is.'

'Don't be like that, Graham,' I said, realizing he was still very upset. 'Just have a lovely evening.'

That was the last time I ever saw Lynn alive.

I saw Graham, though, the next day. He seemed all right, just a bit more distracted than usual. A day or so after this, Lynn was reported missing. The local newspapers covered the story, and we heard that the police had questioned Graham at his home. An appeal for information was then put out on local radio and television. Meanwhile Graham, who had been 'helping the police with their enquiries', was questioned by the police again on the Monday morning just when my agent, Jackie Evans, and Ron Coles were dealing with the termination of my contract. (Timing is everything in my business!)

Graham was eventually taken into custody on the Thursday and, on the Friday, he took the police to where he had buried Lynn. Everybody at Radio Trent, including me, was shocked to the core when we heard that, having attacked her repeatedly with a hammer during the evening of the Paul Young show, he had then rolled her up in a carpet, placed her in his car and buried her later that night near Radcliffe-on-Soar power station. On the Tuesday he had come into Radio Trent to prepare for his next show, then borrowed an industrial cleaning machine to take home and remove all traces of her blood at his house. The police forensic team, however, had found a speck which confirmed his involvement in the crime. The police, we subsequently heard, had suspected from very early on that Lynn's murder was a crime of passion and that Graham was responsible for her death.

Lynn was a truly lovely girl and the incredibly tragic end to her short life was followed by more sadness and grief. Her new boyfriend, whom she had planned to marry, was so distraught that not long after her death he committed suicide. Graham was taken to Leicester to await trial, but he hanged himself in prison before this came up. So in a very short space of time after I had served my month's notice and left Radio Trent, two more people had died. It could not have been a more terrible backdrop to the end of my time at Radio Trent – an unbelievable shock for everyone concerned.

On the professional front, it took me a very long time indeed to get over only being given one month's notice and, during this time, the whole situation became unnecessarily acrimonious and ended in litigation. The fact that it had all become so unpleasant was a nightmare, but it never changed my attitude to signing exclusive contracts!

Two things made matters even worse for me. The first was that when I sold the Hatch End house and moved to Nottingham, nobody had warned me that after you have taken your equity out of the South and put it into the North, it's very hard to buy back into the South. Property values in Nottingham simply hadn't gone up as much as they had in London so, financially, I'd made a very bad move. I was now stuck where I was and unemployed.

The second was that the radio business is a very small world, where news travels at the speed of light. While I had done nothing wrong, people knew that my contract had not been renewed and they also knew about the subsequent litigation. My only plus was that I had extracted a glowing reference from Ron Coles before the unpleasantness really got under way. Ironically, given how hurt and devastated I was, there was never a personal falling out between Ron and me. I accepted that he had made a business decision – and that it was just one of those things. Since then I have met Ron again. He's still very successful in the radio business and, as far as I can tell, he's pleased that I'm doing well.

So, there I was, living in my fancy 'Californian villa' house, with suddenly no income, nothing to do and unable to buy back into London. But just as I was becoming *really* short of money, my good friend, Steve Allen, was instrumental in finding me work in Vienna. I learned that the Austrian network ORF (Östereichischer Rundfunk), had an English-speaking radio station called Blue Danube Radio and, as the government would not allow people, including employees of ORF, to take up naturalization, the station had devised a schedule of three weeks on, three weeks off, for its overseas presenters – and many DJs considered this a three-week annual holiday!

In many ways working for ORF was my salvation. The programme controller, Telia Herold, liked me enormously and being back behind a mike kept me stable. So for the better part of the next twelve months, while my efforts to get back on to British radio were leading nowhere, I went to Vienna for three weeks, returned to Nottingham for three weeks, then went back to Vienna. After my flights and accommodation were paid for, I came home with about £500, just enough to put food in my mouth and pay for my next flight out in three weeks' time. I was losing financial ground big time, though, and getting deeper and deeper into debt, because I hadn't sufficient money left over to pay my gas, electricity, telephone and rates bills and I just couldn't sell the house. I was constantly increasing my overdraft at the bank and eventually I was asked to hand over the deeds of my house as security.

Despite all this, I just *loved* being in Vienna. I had long had a penchant for the Sixties cold war movies: the James Bond and Michael Caine-type thrillers, films such as *Funeral in Berlin* and *The Ipcress File*. In these, there was always a sinister frontier and Russian cars. East Berlin was always portrayed as very dark and West Berlin as very bright. My favourite Hitchcock film then – and now – is *Torn Curtain*, starring Paul Newman and Julie Andrews – and the Berlin Wall! I love European countries. The streets and the shops are so clean, and I just adore the café society and coffee shops, which are so much more civilized than some of our pubs. In fact, if I were a linguist I'm quite sure I'd be very happy living in a European city such as Vienna, Berlin, Frankfurt, Amsterdam or Copenhagen. I love their pastries, climates, the feel of the roads and the cars – especially the long since out-of-production Opel Commodore coupé!

For me, then, Vienna in the mid-Eighties was the perfect combination of East and West. It had real ambience and I thought the majestic architecture, still reflecting the faded glory of the Habsburgs, the trams, the picturesque coffee shops and the all-embracing atmosphere uniquely *fantastic*. I remember being there in December and looking down Kärntnerstrasse – Vienna's Bond Street – and seeing all those glorious women in full-length mink coats. (I know the animal rights people will hate me for mentioning this, but that was the state of play then – animals *were* bred to keep people warm and nobody questioned it. Personally, I wouldn't want this real-fur fashion to come back now because fake fur can look just as good as the real thing – and it's humane.) There is also a wonderfully impressive cathedral at the bottom end of the Kärntnerstrasse, and the Hotel Sacher, where the famous mouth-watering Sachertorte (chocolate cake) comes from, is just at the top of the street. If you like chocolate, this gorgeous cake *and* the Mozart balls are not to be missed.

Blue Danube Radio was an extraordinary operation. It broadcast three shows a day – the breakfast show from 7 to 9 a.m., the midday magazine from 12 to 2 p.m. and the afternoon show from 5 to 7 p.m. There were two British presenters working this rota seven days a week and we stayed in the same little hotel. Having come straight from the cut and thrust of fast-format radio, this was an entirely new dimension to add to my experience. The DJ sat in the studio in front of a microphone with a list of records and a Viennese engineer, who was trained in the art of how to be a radio technician, would be on the other side of the glass. These guys joined ORF when they were twenty and, after being trained, did the same job until they were sixty. As they worked on a rota system, the presenters never quite knew whom they would be working with, but at least a couple of the younger technicians liked and understood modern music. The producers, who also worked on the other side of the studio glass, were English or Americans who spoke perfect German, which was just as well or there would have been even more communication problems with the technicians than there already were. I became quite fluent in German, which is why, on and off, I was able to work for ORF for the best part of a year. My chief problem was that the older engineers were in the habit of waiting for a record to fade out completely before they would switch on the microphone. This used to drive me insane because I had no control whatsoever over my own delivery. I was always sitting there waving my arms about, screaming, '*Put my microphone on – please!*' only to have them raise their hands as if to say, 'In Vienna, *we* do it this way.' In addition to playing records, the DJs also did interviews as well as covering the traffic news. For this reason it was vital for us to learn all the names of the various streets and the areas in which they were situated. To this day, I believe that one of the most insulting things a broadcaster can do is to mispronounce the name of a place that someone, somewhere, is a native of.

I realized quite early on that even if the engineers did speak English, they weren't about to let us know they could. Like mischief makers everywhere, they enjoyed seeing us cock up. This spurred me on, though, and I decided to improve on the German I had learned at school. I was forever carrying a phrase book or a dictionary around and, by my third or fourth visit, even the older engineers, who had been very stubborn to begin with, began to appreciate that I was making a real effort. After that they started to give me the respect they thought I deserved and became altogether more chummy and obliging. Round about then, I also remember trying out my German on a taxi driver who picked me up at the airport. I was staying in the Prince Eugene Hotel, right next door to the Südbahnhoff (train station). I gave him the address, then said, in my newly acquired German lingo, '*Gestern ich war sehr kalt aber heute ich bin warm.*' I thought I was saying 'Yesterday I was cold, but today I am warm.' But instead of just nodding, he gave me a *very* strange look and I sank back in the seat. When I went into the ORF office, I said to our PA, Vicki Gruber, 'I've just had a *very* weird experience with a taxi driver,' and I repeated what I thought I had said. Laughing aloud, she replied, 'I'm not surprised! You've just said, "Yesterday I was cold and today I am gay."' It was a wonderful gaffe.

*

One day, while I was in Vienna, Mark telephoned me to say that his MG Midget had been stolen. Soon after this, back in Nottingham, I went to buy my next lot of travel tickets from a little shop in Arnold, just outside the city. To my astonishment, as I came down over Mapperley Top, I saw Mark's bright-yellow Midget trying to emerge from a side street. Braking hard, I let it out, but when we both had to stop at the next set of traffic lights I leapt out of my car, shot over to the guy who was driving it, pulled open the door and said, '*This* is a stolen car. Get out of the vehicle right now.'

He seemed terrified. 'OK – OK,' he said, 'I'll pull over on the other side of the lights.'

Like a fool, I replied, 'Fine'! But the moment I got back into my car, a very powerful Audi 100, he hightailed it off. The fifteen-minute chase that then commenced took us both all over Nottingham. Dangerous though it was for two fast cars to go screeching around a built-up area, all was well until we arrived at Carlton Hill. Then, to my horror, I saw a group of schoolchildren crossing the road at the bottom. Now, when I think about it, I realize it was the most stupid thing to do, but on I chased after him, my car horn blaring and my hazard lights flashing. Fortunately all the kids got safely across the road, but the driver of the MG, trying to avoid the last of them, braked sharply, went into a skid and crashed into a lamppost. Mark's car was wrecked – a total write-off – but the driver, who was still in one piece, jumped out and legged it.

Later the police told Mark and me that the man who was in the car had burgled a house at Mapperley Top and the house owners, a couple who had just come back from their honeymoon, had now had all their wedding presents restored to them. About an hour after this the police came to my house again, saying that they now had a chap in custody at St Anne's police station, and would I come and assist them with their enquiries and hopefully identify the villain. I was *so* pleased. 'Great – they've got him,' I thought. But when I went to the police station it wasn't the man. I remember the poor guy saying, 'Thanks, mate. God, I've been *so* worried. I haven't done anything wrong and they thought it was me.'

'No,' I said, 'it wasn't you.'

'Cheers, mate – thank you – thank you,' he said, as he was released from custody.

Having only recently left Radio Trent, I was still newsworthy and the story, which was accompanied by a somewhat unflattering picture of Mark and me standing by my Audi, made the front page of the local newspaper. The police were also quoted as saying, 'It was a very dangerous thing that Dale did.' I wasn't at all sure if that was meant to be a compliment! Later, though, I received a very grateful thank you letter from the honeymoon couple and then, about four weeks later, the guy who'd stolen the car turned himself in and asked for countless other charges to be taken into account.

Vienna, where I was never involved in any cops-and-robbers stuff, may have been less exciting, but I was *never* lonely or at a loss for something to do there. The marvellous thing about working for Blue Danube was that the building in which it was housed was rather like the BBC's Broadcasting House on Portland Place in London. It was my first experience of working for an organization that employed loads of broadcasters for its various radio stations, and maintained a huge record library and a big canteen. The DJs who worked on Blue Danube were very sociable and if you wanted to go out every night of your three-week stint there, you could. They always made me feel very welcome, and there was always so much to do and see in Vienna. I loved it. But I was also aware that the job was not really furthering my career and that there was no lasting future in it. I've always been a grafter, with an eye on the next logical progressive step, and I've always needed to feel that I have a sense of purpose in life. When Spencer Tracy, the film star, was asked what he looked for in a good script, he always used to say, 'Days off!' I am the absolute reverse.

For months now my income had been falling alarmingly below my expenditure commitments and at this point, back home in Nottingham, I was now a massive £35,000 in debt. To my horror, one day the bailiffs arrived and I had the devil's own job buying them off with promises that the money was forthcoming. I had no option then – heart-breaking though this was at the time – but to put my lovely 'Californian villa' up for sale to clear my debts. I then remember being absolutely appalled because the property market was thoroughly depressed and try as I might, I just couldn't find a buyer. By then, I felt that my career in Nottingham had come to an end and that it no longer really mattered where I was to live. I was just *so* sad that in looking at the property gap when comparing prices with the South-East, I realised that even when I succeeded in selling the house, the money that would be left after clearing my overdraft and other debts would not be anywhere near enough to relocate me to London.

Eventually, a wonderful woman, Cyd, came to view the house, fell in love with it and I accepted her offer. I then did something which I am ashamed of to this day. Someone came along immediately after I had verbally agreed the sale with her, offered me another £7000 and I was desperate enough to accept. When I went back to Cyd with this news, she was so devastated that she paid the difference to get the house. In time, it did go up in value, so she more than got her money's worth, but I'd still like to say sorry Cyd and I sincerely hope she's been *very* happy in the house.

In moving, I found a very small house in Corsham Gardens, Nottingham. It was just a modern box, with two bedrooms, but it was a roof over my head. I put a deposit on it and, bold as brass, applied for a mortgage. Fortunately, communicating with others has never been a problem for me and the wonderful man at the Abbey National was very sympathetic when I said straight up, 'I have a problem. My bank has been really awful and has made me sell my house to pay off my £35,000 overdraft.'

'Mr Winton,' he interrupted, 'any bank these days that allows an overdraft of £35,000 to help somebody stay afloat is not doing badly. But I *will* look after you.'

To my enormous relief, he did. Although I was very nearly penniless, with no immediate prospects, he gave me the mortgage for the small modern property and I was actually quite happy there. A friend called Peter and two others, Chris and Alex, who had a couple of wonderful menswear shops in the Midlands, subsequently bought houses on the same estate and this sense of 'family' helped to keep me sane.

Writing about those times now, I remember just how desperate I felt when the bailiffs appeared on my doorstep, and how grateful I was to the man from the Abbey National who seemed to understand what I was going through and gave me the mortgage. A few years later, just before I auditioned for *Supermarket Sweep*, I found myself in dire financial straits again. And that's why I am now always so careful about protecting what I have, and why I have done all the right things in terms of pensions and investing for the future. Also, having been deep in the doldrums twice, I never dream of knocking people who are so down that they do desperate things. I prefer to believe that if their circumstances had been different they would not have got themselves into trouble. It's very easy to be pious and judgemental but, when you've been there, when you've actually felt that awful gnawing pain of desperation, you understand how certain things can happen. But I still get frustrated when the not-so-needy justify their behaviour by blaming everything on a dysfunctional start in life. There are millions of people in that situation who work to overcome their problems, pull through and do not end up foul of the law.

In 1985 while, aged thirty, I was still dragging my well-covered bones to and from Radio Danube in Vienna, Mark, thinking he would like to crack radio, was continuing his part-time job on Radio Trent's Care Line, but also working evenings at Brown's Wine Bar – the in-place where all the funky, trendy people went in Nottingham's Lace Market. I was never a great fan of this myself because it was all too studenty and laddish for me, but Mark loved it and had many friends there. As luck would have it, one of these was Maxine Saunders who, at the time, was casting *Girls On Top* for Central Television, a sitcom starring Ruby Wax and Jennifer Saunders, who were still quite new to the biz at this time. Maxine, having met me through Mark, gave me my first job in telly. It was only a bit part, but I was thrilled. I wasn't an actor, had never ever wanted to be one, but I certainly needed the money – all £50 of it – in the bank. I thought (as one does!), 'Who knows? This could be my big break – the moment I've been waiting for!' I had always believed that radio would be my natural course into television. Quite frankly, put me in a box on *Celebrity Squares* and I'd have thought I'd died and gone to heaven! All I had to do for my part as a floor manager was to walk on with a broom when Ruby and Jennifer were supposed to be putting on an amateur production of *Charlie's Aunt*. I had one big comedic moment when Ruby hit me in the goolies with her umbrella, and my name was listed in the closing credits! I loved Ruby's fast-talking American approach to comedy and was very much in awe of her. To this day, supporting artistes and walk-ons rarely have any contact with the main stars, but as I know what it's like to be down as well as up in the business, I always make sure that I talk to absolutely everybody on the set. Barbara Windsor is the same. She knows everybody on *EastEnders* and always talks to the supporting artistes. It's what being a real trouper is all about.

As I dared to believe (one must!) that my bit part in *Girls On Top* would make me a television star, I drove down to London and breezed into the office of Annie Sweetbaum, a theatrical agent, at Arlington Enterprises. Never one to miss a trick, I'd done my research on Annie and discovered that at that time she represented a lot of top TV presenters. She proved to be a larger-than-life character whom I took to immediately. She was full of self-confidence, had a team of lovely girls and (with impeccable good taste!) agreed to be my agent. 'Right,' she said, 'what you need is a hanger. Everybody on television has a hanger these days.'

What she meant by this was that I needed to become an expert in one particular field and, as she had just been asked to help cast a pilot for a new Sunday afternoon show, she had an idea in mind. At that time the BBC, having been very successful with *Crimewatch*, had started to pilot other 'watch' programmes. 'Watch' was *the* buzzword of the moment and, among the ideas being floated, was *Pet Watch*, a magazine programme on pets.

'But I know *nothing* about animals,' I wailed. 'And even *less* about pets!'

Annie was unfazed. 'I've already put up another client, Bruce Vogel, one of England's leading vets, for hosting the show. If I can get you on as the presenter and the pilot programme leads to a series, you could get the job.'

Spurred on by Annie's enthusiasm, I decided to go for it and then took myself off to Harrods' pets department and spent a small fortune, which I could ill afford, on buying props for my two-minute audition piece to camera. Among the things I found was a four-poster bed for a poodle, a remote-control soft toy for a gecko, a portable dog loo, which you buried in the garden and trained your dog to sit on, and some other outrageous novelties. Then off I went to Bristol.

As somebody who had always believed that preparation is everything, I'd done my research, learned my piece by heart (so I didn't need the autocue) and I'd practised playing with the props. So there I was, portable dog loo and all, doing my over-the-top antics and loving every moment of it. And, more to the point, the crew loved it, too. 'Well!' I thought (as one does!), 'this could be *it*!' But, as usual at pilot stage, although the series was being mooted as a cert by now, it was a question of, 'Don't call us, Dale – we'll call you. We'll all just have to wait and see.'

Back at Arlington Enterprises Annie, obviously delighted by the producer's feedback, said, 'I'll try and get you a job on TV AM. I have a gut feeling you could be their gadget man.'

So, once again, off I trotted to Harrods, this time looking for gadgets that I called 'presents for pets'. When I'd found some presents that I thought would be suitable, I dutifully went through my paces, demonstrating all these for the producer of TV AM, the forerunner to GMTV. The guy was obviously amused by my desk-top demonstration and quite liked me, but nothing ever came of it. Then we heard that the BBC had decided not to do the *Pet Watch* series and I was back to square one, with no telly prospects in sight, trotting to and from my work of three weeks on, three weeks off in Vienna. Some months later, however, Annie heard that someone had revisited the pilot and decided that the format could be reworked into a different kind of pets programme for a live series on Sunday afternoons. More important from my point of view, the one element that was liked from the original was my presents-for-pets idea. They were, though, very nervous about me – a totally untried-and-tested TV person – presenting the item. After some negotiation, however, they said, 'OK – Dale can contribute to the first three shows of the first series of seven, and we'll see how it goes.' Once again, I was in with a chance and I was thrilled.

Back in Nottingham my core of loyal friends – Mark, Peter, Chris and Alex – were also very excited. Chris, in particular, because of his menswear shops, was then – and still *is* to this day – a man of great style.

'I need help with my clothes,' I said to him. 'I don't have any money yet, but perhaps you could help me sort things out?'

He was wonderful. He agreed to lend me everything I needed to look the part and to this day it remains a kindness I will never forget. I couldn't have managed without him.

On the first Sunday, while I was doing the live show for the very first time in Bristol, Chris and Peter were glued to a TV in Nottingham. Later they told me that, when I came on after the dancing bear and before the stuffed budgie, to demonstrate my absurd presents for pets, they doubled up in their chairs and cried with laughter because I was *so* camp (and I've never heard the last of this)!

The first series of *Pet Watch* actually did quite well in the ratings but, far from being the launch of my TV career, my life went pear-shaped again because nobody had actually *noticed*, let alone discovered me. It was desperately disappointing and, to add insult to injury, I was always being cut down to size by Peter and Chris teasing me.

'What *are* you doing now?' Peter would ask.

'Well . . . he's no longer working with a dancing bear and a stuffed budgie!' Chris would reply. 'And let's face it, that budgie was the star of the show!'

I have since heard, though, that I *did* have one fan. Ruby Wax taped *Pet Watch* and used to enjoy showing the recording of me with the dancing bear and stuffed budgie. She probably thought *Pet Watch* was one of the BBC's surreal attempts at programming – and it was!

Meanwhile, with no more pets to keep me occupied, I continued to live in my little house, eking out the money I was earning from Radio Danube. Then, all of a sudden (as things do in our business) life turned round and smiled for me. Pete Wagstaffe, a very good radio presenter at Radio Trent, who had since left to start up Beacon Radio in Wolverhampton, offered me a DJ job on the station. Once again, just as I was on the verge of yet another bout of financial ruin, I was back in business and a new era began where I would drive from Nottingham to Wolverhampton to do the morning show. Annie Sweetbaum was absolutely brilliant. She never despaired of me, never ceased trying to get me other jobs and never took any commission from my Beacon Radio work because she knew I couldn't afford it. Even though I now had a reasonably well-paid job, I was still in trouble because, financially strapped as I was, I had not put any tax aside. When the time came for me to go along to the tax office in Nottingham to plead for time to pay, the gentleman behind the counter wasn't having any of my excuses. I had gone in quite boldly, convinced I could sweet-talk my way out of the situation, but it proved to be one of the very rare occasions when I did not succeed. I walked out of that tax office demolished and went to the nearest phone box to ring Annie.

'Whatever's the matter?' she asked.

I explained about the tax bill, then added, 'I thought they'd give me time to pay, Annie. But they're going to render me homeless and take away my car. What can I do?'

'Give me the number,' she said, 'let me talk to the tax inspector.'

'Will you ring me afterwards?' I asked.

Annie is the sweetest of women, but she can be tough when necessary and I was confident she'd get it sorted. But when she rang me back she said, 'You're absolutely right, Dale. He *is* a very difficult man and he will *not* play ball. But don't worry, the agency is going to pay your tax and we will simply knock it off your wages as you get them.' I thought this was absolutely amazing of her. But she really was a wonderful woman then – and is now. Whenever our paths cross these days she invariably acknowledges that she always had confidence in me as an artiste and never doubted that I would break through one day. She honestly couldn't have tried harder for me, but in show business timing is everything and it just wasn't my time. I simply had to wait longer for the right moment. The tax fiasco, though, was a salutary learning curve. These days, I make absolutely sure that I dot all my 'i's and cross all my 't's, have an accountant and always pay my tax on time.

It was thanks to Annie, too, that I met one of my closest lady friends, the television presenter, Merrill Thomas, who was also one of her clients. One day Annie said to me, 'Here's a good one for you, darling – Sunday morning, Battersea Park, "Dog-a-Jog".' This turned out to be a charity fund-raising event in which all of Annie's clients were being asked to take part. I was not exactly keen. It would mean me coming down from Nottingham and being in London at the park by 9 a.m., but Annie can be *very* persuasive and I'm so glad she was.

On the day – it was teeming down with rain, of course – I didn't know a single soul present until Annie introduced me to Merrill, the only person besides me who didn't have a dog! Feeling somewhat inept, we stood around, not quite knowing what a *dogless* couple on a Dog-a-Jog could possibly do. Then suddenly, to our astonishment, we clocked one of the most bizarre sights we had ever seen. Over to our left was a man encased in a *real* iron lung and lying on a hospital bed. After some nervous consultation, between ourselves and then with the willing patient, Merrill and I decided that we would jog around the park, with Merrill pushing the bed along on its wheels, while keeping a very wary eye on the patient's drips and tubes, and I would run obligingly alongside, dangling a bucket into which people could toss coins. Afterwards, deeply relieved that the guy had survived and had actually benefited financially from the experience, and feeling as if I needed a new pair of lungs myself, I said to Merrill, 'That has to be the most *extraordinary* and most frightening thing I've ever had to do!' Then, when we went for a much-needed coffee to calm our post-jog nerves, we began what was to be an enduring friendship. Merrill is now part of my extended family and we speak to each other almost every day. Her children, Saskia and Thomas, are wonderful. One day, I just know that Saskia, who has the talent and the looks, will be a huge film star, and Thomas, who is now a theatrical agent, will continue to go from success to success.

Meanwhile, up at Beacon Radio, *I* was a success. In fact, things were going so well that I was offered a five-days-a-week show. And at that point I decided to sell my house in Nottingham and move up to a rural area as near as reasonably possible to Wolverhampton. I was lucky: I found – and bought – the most perfect little cottage in Bridgnorth, on the Cartway.

The irony of the end of my Blue Danube days in Vienna, which had after all saved my bacon while I was jobless and in the doldrums, was that I acted completely out of character and let Telia, my Programme Controller there, down very badly, not on one, but on *two* occasions. The first was when I decided to sell my house in Nottingham and move to Bridgnorth, and I didn't turn up for duty on my Christmas contract, and the second was when my life went pear-shaped once again, and she forgave me and said I could come back to Vienna. But then, having recently auditioned for *Supermarket Sweep*, I got the job and didn't turn up again. I don't think Telia has ever forgiven me for that second wrongdoing, but I will always remember her as a very kind and totally professional executive who was very good to me. (Sorry, Telia. They are the *only* two occasions in my life when I've broken my word. My behaviour was unforgivable.)

It was while I was at Beacon Radio that I did *the* most embarrassing interview I have ever done. In 1987, A&M Records rang me and said, 'Richard Carpenter has just made a solo album and he's coming to Europe to promote it before he goes on tour in America. Would you like to interview him? If so, we'll pay your expenses from Wolverhampton to London.'

'Fine,' I said. I was *very* pleased. I was a great fan of the Carpenters – and Richard in particular. A&M then told me that they had booked the star into a hotel close to Harrods in Knightsbridge, so that he could use his suite to promote a fabulous album, called *Time*. On this, the tracks that would normally have been sung by his sister, Karen Carpenter, who had tragically died from anorexia nervosa, were sung by other guest vocalists, such as Dionne Warwick and Dusty Springfield. I was thrilled when I heard that Dusty had given her all to the track, 'Something in your eyes', very much a 'Karen song', as a special tribute to Karen. It proved to be a really wonderful record which, although the *Time* album never sold that well, was a huge hit for Dusty on the radio.

When the arrangements were being made for me to go to London, the PR from the record company said, 'Richard's very nervous, Dale. Karen always did the Carpenter interviews in the past and he's still very raw and sensitive about her death. So, please, *don't* mention her.'

'Not a problem,' I said. 'I've listened to the album and I think it's great. Richard's a brilliant musician and songwriter, and I think the album will do really well.'

The next day there was another nervous call from the PR: 'We've given Richard Carpenter to you first,' he said, 'because we know that you will look after him. But remember, if you do decide to mention Karen, in any way, he's likely to get very emotional. So *please* be very careful and treat him very gently. Otherwise, have a nice day in London.'

On the day of the interview Richard, surrounded by what I call 'the ponytail brigade' – this time LA and New York record company execs – greeted me very courteously, but I could see that he was nervous. 'What we'll do', I said in my most reassuring manner, 'is start the interview by talking about the new album. Then, at various points I'll pause you with the words, "Now let's hear a track . . ." and then, when the interview goes out on live radio, we can insert the predetermined tracks there and then.'

I'd done my research and, despite his nervousness, it proved to be a very good and relaxed-sounding interview. At the end, Richard breathed a sigh of relief that it was all over and out of the corner of my eye I could see the execs thinking, 'Phew – we've got away with this.' Richard then turned to me and said, 'Thank you, Dale. I really appreciate you coming down from Wolverhampton for this; and, even more important, for having listened to the album and done your homework.'

'Not a problem,' I said. 'I think the album's sensational and I wish you all the best with it. I really mean that, Richard.'

Much to the surprise of the execs, he then added, 'Would you stay for coffee?'

This was duly brought to the suite and Richard, a gentleman to the last, held out the plate of biscuits to me. 'You have to try one of these cookies,' he said. 'They bake them here in the hotel and I have to tell you they are the *best* cookies I've ever tasted outside the United States of America.'

Without thinking, I replied, 'No, thank you, Richard. At the moment I'm starving myself to death.'

A deadly silence settled over the suite. I realized at once, of course, that I had just made the most awful faux pas and I could see everybody else looking around as if to say. '*Oh God!* Did I just hear what I thought I heard?' I was beside myself. I reached over, grabbed one of the cookies, shoved it whole in my mouth and had crumbs all over my face. 'I'm *so* sorry,' I gabbled, with my mouth full. 'I didn't realize . . . I . . . Oh . . .' My voice trailed off in despair, as I sat there expecting floods of tears from Richard before I was propelled out of the room. But all the record execs were frozen, not quite knowing what to do.

Richard was *so* sweet. 'That's all right,' he said. 'I *do* understand. It's just a turn of phrase, isn't it.'

'Richard,' I said, closer to tears than he was, 'I feel terrible.'

'No need – I quite understand,' he said again generously.

Eventually, I shuffled out of the room in absolute pieces, with crumbs on my shirt and utter embarrassment on my conscience.

In all I worked for Beacon Radio on and off for nearly two years but, frankly, I was becoming *very* bored and I no longer wanted to be a DJ. I guess I had just been doing this kind of repetitive work for too long and my Radio Danube days were its swansong. I remember sitting there one day in the Wolverhampton studio, looking at an Elkie Brooks record going round on the turntable and thinking, 'I don't ever want to play a record like this ever again.' There was nothing wrong with Elkie's record. It was no better or worse than any other record I was playing. It just hit a particular vulnerable spot in me at that moment. I remember finishing that show, going out of the studio and saying to Pete Wagstaffe, 'I want to leave. How soon can I go?'

He was obviously shocked – and concerned. 'But what are you going to do for money?' he asked.

'I've *no* idea,' I said. 'I just know I don't want to do this any more. I'm going to up sticks and sell my cottage.'

'Are you *sure*?' he asked, trying to get me to be sensible.

'Yes,' I almost snapped back. 'How soon can I go? You've been absolutely brilliant giving me this job and I will only leave when you say I can go, but please make it soon.'

One of the problems was that I simply wasn't used to living in the country, and the pleasure of driving along country lanes and passing field after field had worn off after the first few days. 'May I *never* see another tractor again as long as I live', was my attitude. I was actually only in the cottage for three months before I put it back on the market and sold up.

Now here's a very interesting word to the wise: there are times when we all feel that we would like to live the idyllic country life. You know the sort of thing – air you can breathe, freshly cut grass, views as far as the eye can see, rolling hills and the vague murmur of a distant bird cooing to its mate. Having lived in the city all my life I was now convinced that urbanization was in my past for ever. So you can imagine my joy one balmy summer's afternoon in Bridgnorth, when I thought I had found my Shangri La in this village. I bought the cottage immediately, moved in two weeks later on a Tuesday, and for three days tried to kid myself that I enjoyed this rural lifestyle.

Here's where the words of wisdom come in. Always see your potential property at the weekend as well as during the week, because on Friday night that first week, the young farmers hit the town and every bar and restaurant was teeming with lary lads on the booze, on the pull, and on my doorstep. It seemed that between Friday and Sunday nights I was living in a war zone. With hindsight, it probably wasn't that bad – it just seemed that way at the time!

It was then that the truth struck home. In reality, I probably enjoyed the weekends there more than the week! I missed the buzz and rush of city life. I like the idea of being within range of a bar of chocolate or a packet of cigarettes any time of the day or night. As a shopper I need that 24-hour, we-never-close facility available to me. I'm a fidget, which is why people often say to me, 'Just chill out, Dale!' But actually, I am being chilled. I remember announcing to all my friends, with great drama, that I was moving to the country. They gave it a week. But at that time, without a partner in tow, I thought nature and its beauty would be enough to sustain me in a long spell of enforced celibacy.

I was wrong. Three months later, the very moment the sale was completed, I loaded everything I could into the back of my car and put everything else into storage in Shropshire. (Most of it is still there!) Then I waved goodbye to my friends in the Midlands and drove off like the clappers down the motorway. I was facing a jobless future with more financial shenanigans to come, but at least I had £20,000 left from the sale of the cottage. As far as I was concerned *that* would have to see me through for however long it took for me to make it in television. My heart had ruled my head and my wallet, and television or bust was the course I was now set upon!

# 6

## 'Don't let me lose this dream . . .'

ONCE BACK IN London, and urgently needing somewhere to live, I decided to drive straight to Mayford's, an estate agent in North Harrow. Striding in, I said to the nearest guy, 'My belongings are in the car and I need to rent something – *right now*. But I don't have much money.' Unfazed, he came up with the details of an instantly available one-bedroom flat, which proved to be much more suitable for a student than for me. It really was a terrible comedown from what I was accustomed to, but at least I could afford it and there would be no tractors revving up outside.

Having unpacked, the extent of my predicament, stuck in the quicksands of unemployment, was all too apparent. I was now on the wrong side of North Harrow, the wrong side of thirty-three and the wrong side of the bank manager. I had to get a job and a life, and fast. As far as my line of work was concerned, this did not prove easy. With no offers in the pipeline and no opportunities on the horizon, I was happy to take a job in a bar and in a bakery until Mark, bless him, spotted a better job for me in the *Evening Standard*. The job required somebody with the gift of the gab to sell timeshare in Europe. It was not what I had had in mind, but in desperation I took it. It was better paid than the bar and the bakery, and I found I was very good at it. I worked from an office in Central London and did whatever had to be done, and gave of my best to promote the product. Timeshare has a reasonably good reputation nowadays, but in those days adverse publicity made the selling of the idea even harder. Meanwhile, I drew comfort from the thought that Annie Sweetbaum was still trying her damnedest to get me back into show business, and I pinned all my hopes on her. One day when she phoned me, she said, 'Hang in there, Dale, cable TV has just been given the OK and there will be jobs coming up.'

'Ah!' I thought. 'This *is* a boon. More networks, more opportunities, more jobs. And at least there will be some on screen.'

In 1989 Atlantic Visa had one programme that was being piloted for a cable network, *Home Shopping*, an American idea that was being tried out in the UK to see if there was a market for it here. The one-hour programmes, Annie told me, were to consist of four or five different lifestyle items: houseware, furniture, women's fashion, novelty gifts and electrical goods. The producer she had arranged for me to go and see was a wonderful woman called Georgina Vestey. At this time Merrill, who also had Annie as her agent, was doing fashion for TV AM. She didn't really need another job, but as we had decided we wanted to work together she came along for the audition in a Soho studio. Geed up by the thought of working as a team, thankfully we were both successful. I was given the job of hosting the show and demonstrating the final big bargain of the day and Merrill was given the fashion slot. The filming began quickly and, over a two-week period, we featured in ten of the one-hour shows, which were broadcast on cable TV. It was a very hard-sell job, much like QVC is today, but I wasn't complaining. This was my very first on-screen job hosting a show with the help of an autocue and I knew that whatever else happened I would come out of it with a video tape that could be used as a 'demo'.

The job proved to be an extraordinary experience for everybody on the programme. It was virgin territory, all ground-breaking stuff. Merrill would sit there on a makeshift set and a model would come on dressed in some creation that was up for sale at £12.99 in the hope of tempting viewers to ring in with their credit card details – invariably I thought they were frightful! The show was padded out to kill all the available on-air time and, as the host, I would sit alongside Merrill discussing the garments for at least ten minutes. I must say we did have a few twinges of conscience because we had very little confidence in hardly anything we were selling. I remember sitting there one morning as a model came on set in an aquamarine dress and Merrill was doing her usual routine, saying, 'Well . . . you could wear this for daytime with pumps and a shoulder bag, or equally you could dress it up for the evening with a few pearls, maybe tie a glamorous gold belt around it and, perhaps, finish off the whole ensemble with a nice pair of court shoes.'

To keep the conversation flowing I would interject comments like 'What about hair? What sort of hairstyle, Merrill, would you wear with a dress like this?' Then I'd pipe up, 'We've discussed how it can be worn for day or evening, we've discussed hairstyles, but the one thing we haven't touched on is the wonderful colour of this garment. What would you call this colour, Merrill?'

One day Merrill, obviously at the end of her tether with the constant necessity of us having to keep padding out every sequence, replied, 'I'd call it blue, Dale.'

'Yes,' I said, looking at her as if to say, 'Three more minutes to go, Merrill. Help me out here, Merrill . . .' But she just repeated, 'It's blue, Dale – *blue*. What else can I say?'

We howled ourselves into a coma afterwards because she had had no option but to reply in this mode. She'd already used up every shade of blue on the other frocks – aquamarine, delphinium, hyacinth, tinted turquoise, sapphire, cobalt-blue. And, when my push came to shove, she could only sit there exhausted and say, 'It's *blue*, Dale.'

I met a similar problem with a nest of wooden tables that cost the princely sum of £9.99. I'd already discussed on air the merits of the quality of the wood, the beauty of the texture, the subtlety of the colour, the shapeliness of the legs and the remarkability of the price.

I'd also found a reason why this ubiquitous item of furniture should be put in every room in the house, including the bathroom, the loo and the garden shed. At the end of this exhausting diatribe of absolute waffle, I noticed the floor manager giving me the signal to stretch the item for yet another three minutes. So, in disbelief and desperation, I picked up one of the tables, tipped it upside down, turned it back towards me and stood there, with seeming great purpose, examining its screws. Then, inspired, I started counting them aloud, *one by one*, and realized to my intense relief that there were sufficient to keep me going for at least another forty-five seconds of the three minutes. Then, re-inspired, I discovered that the legs were flush with the wood and that the nest had bevelled edges to make them safe for children. God! I absolutely defy anybody to do twelve minutes and thirty seconds on a nest of basic wooden tables. But I did – and I promise you it was an education for the viewers!

Waffling on on the occasions when we unexpectedly needed to fill in time certainly taught me how to sound and look convincing while talking utter bollocks. Like a pair of verbal trapeze artists, Merrill and I honed our interjections to a fine art and sailed through the next two weeks with our hearts in our mouths and our tongues in our cheeks, without once dropping the pass and, more important, without a single cross word. The cable company was *very* happy and we were happy. I had learned to read autocue, work to time, talk to models and work at length with inanimate objects. My only disappointment – and this was a *huge* one! – was when I saw the videotape. I had desperately hoped I could use this as a demo to get me more work, but I was heartbroken. Having been miserable for so long in Shropshire among all those tractors, cows and bullocks, I had ballooned to eighteen stone, and dressed in a double-breasted suit for the show, I looked the size of three of the latter. 'I've *ruined* my one big break,' I wept. 'I've got to do something.' I did. I really went in for losing weight this time. No pills, just a healthy-eating regime, thanks to which I lost the better part of three stone.

Six months later, in early 1990, despite my concerns about the cable TV video, Annie put me up for a job presenting consumer items with David Hamilton for another lifestyle channel. Once again, Merrill came along to the audition and once again we were both successful. Merrill was given fashion and I was awarded the princely sum of £60 to research, produce and present my own choice of consumer items. Emma Forbes, I remember, was chosen for cookery. These were early days for Emma, too, and we all got on very well. David would spend two days in Molinare studios, Soho, recording the links, and then each of us would be filmed demonstrating, commentating and reviewing the various items. I did the music review, which was tantamount to holding up CDs to camera and talking about them. This was great because it gave me an excuse to contact record companies for free CDs. I also did housewares and I remember spending a whole week ringing departments stores to ask if they would lend me products to show on the programme. British Home Stores, I recall, was happy to play ball and they sent along a dozen lamps. The only problem was that some of these were so huge they towered above the plinth behind which David and I sat to demonstrate various bits and pieces. I'm six foot two inches but David, always a joy to work with, is much shorter and some of the lamps completely obliterated him on the screen. Somebody came up with the bright idea of standing him on an orange box but, as I sat there looking up at him and extolling the virtues of the lamps, the viewers must have thought I was a dwarf and he was seven feet tall. After that, I made sure I featured smaller items.

By 1991, now aged thirty-six and only too aware that I was going nowhere fast, I came to a decision that was born more from desperation than desire. Annie Sweetbaum had worked tirelessly trying to get me more work in television, but I decided that the time had come for a radical shake-up in my professional life. It's the hardest thing in the world to say goodbye to an agent who could not have tried harder and who was also such a close friend but, terrible though I felt about this, I told Annie I wanted a new start. Then, after a short time without an agent, I signed up with Peter Plant, a wonderful person, who was very well known throughout the TV industry. Sadly he's no longer with us, but he was a lovely man, a real character.

By this time Mark had left radio for a career in television and, having worked as a researcher on several programmes, he was now working with the executive producer, Judith Holder, at Central Television. One day, when we were having lunch, he mentioned that Central was doing a show for BSkyB called *Anything for Money*.

'It's a fabulous format,' he said, 'Andrew O'Conner's going to be the studio host, but they're looking for an outside reporter who can think on his feet, to go out on the street with a hidden camera and £30 to £40, and coax complete strangers into doing really daft things for money. Why don't you go along for an audition with Judith? If you're lucky you could get the job.'

Ready to give anything a try, I rang Judith and arranged to go for an audition. I'm *so* glad I did because we have become very good friends since those days and in 2001 I did a ninety-minute ITV special for her, called *TV's Best Ever Soap Moments*. Auditions are awful things to do in offices and for *Anything for Money* I was put through a particularly rigorous one by Judith. This involved playing the game with a team of researchers and seeing how far I could push the envelope, and whether or not I could persuade one of them to perform a stunt for me. They had been told to resist my attempts and it was my job to wear them down. In the circumstances I thought I did reasonably well, but I was thrilled when Mark told me that she had said, 'One day that guy's going to be a star.' I was even more thrilled when she booked me for the show.

*Anything for Money* was, as Mark had said, a very good format. It was a very clever and much kinder twist on Jeremy Beadle's *Beadle's About*. One of the stunts, I remember, required me to approach a complete stranger and say with a deadpan expression, 'Excuse me, I've got a rip in my trousers and I've got to go for an important job interview. Will you let me borrow your trousers?'

'*No!*' (Accompanied by fright-flight body language.)

'If I give you £10, will you give me your trousers?'

'*NO!*'

'How much money, then, *would* tempt you to take off your trousers to help me out?' No deal.

Oh well, you can't win them all and our budget obviously wasn't going to rise to the tempting level of any overexposure!

There was also a fake TV commercial that was filmed on a building site. My job this time was to persuade a gang of very butch builders that I was a television presenter who needed extras for a lipstick-for-men commercial. It was hilarious. My timeshare selling techniques served me well, though, and to this day I never take 'no' for an answer.

Once the stunts were filmed, Andrew O'Conner showed the tapes to a celebrity panel who then determined whether I had managed to get the tasks done for love, for money, or not at all. Janet Street Porter was the Executive Producer of the programme and whenever I bump into her these days she always says, '*I* gave you your first break, Dale.' Would I argue? I think back on those shows as some of the most fun I've ever had working in television.

Early fame is a funny thing. You half expect to be recognized as soon as you've done a show, because you think everybody has watched it. I remember standing in a queue in McDonald's and seeing a woman nudging her husband in the next line whispering quite loudly that she recognized me but couldn't think why. Very flattered, because all I had ever done was a bit of satellite and cable TV, I leant across and said helpfully, 'Do you have a satellite dish?' At which point she clasped both her hands together and exclaimed, 'Of course, *now* I recognize you. *You* are the man who put the satellite dish up on our roof!'

As it happened, *Anything for Money* went out on BSkyB, which had only just started up, so nobody *really* noticed me, but the programmes *did* prove to be unexpectedly fortuitous for me. The following year, when Judith moved to the BBC, she revamped *Anything for Money* into *Public Enemy Number 1*, a prime-time Saturday-night show, and invited me to join the team. My heart soared. 'This,' I thought, '*really* could be my big break into prime-time TV.' All I had to do was to make sure that I was the kind of irresistibly persuasive guy whose outrageous requests nobody could refuse, while the hidden cameras whirred. Sadly, though, this show was not recommissioned and it proved to be yet another false start for me.

Fortunately, I had not let my high hopes for the show go to my head. I had kept on the proverbial 'day job' and, as I was still doing occasional items for the lifestyle channel, I did have a regular income, albeit a small one. When one of its producers rang and asked me what I would like to do next, I replied boldly, 'Interview celebrities.' I'd been thinking about this for some time. I wasn't daft, and I realized that top-notch celebrities would not turn out for a no-fee appearance on a cable channel that hardly anyone watched, but I *did* think I was capable of persuading anybody who was 'resting' to let me interview them. 'We could,' I suggested, 'call the slot *Whatever Happened To . . . ?*' How naïve could I be! I had not foreseen that when I rang the stars' various agents, they'd react adversely to any apparent suggestion of their clients being thought of as has-beens. The moment I mentioned the title of the programme, it was a case of 'No, sorry, he/she is *definitely* not available.' When I discussed this problem with Sue Kerr, who later went to work for BBC Worldwide Enterprises, and Andy Rowe, who was then a researcher but later my producer for *The Other Half,* the problem was resolved.

'Let's change the title,' Andy said. 'Instead of *Whatever Happened To . . . ?,* let's call it, *Catching Up With.*

I could have kissed him! From that moment, we got wonderful stars like Petula Clark and Clodagh Rodgers, and an actor I had long admired and wanted to interview. This man, an ex-boxer, had been cast as a bully in *Scum* and had appeared in a one-off special for TVS called *Palmer.* He was not yet the household name that he was to become later for his tough-guy parts in movies and top TV crime series, and his appearance in *The Night Heron* at the Royal Court. But, as I was already a huge fan of his, I rang the studio and asked if I could interview him.

'If you *must,*' the producer replied wearily, and gave me the name of the actor's agent.

'Oh, dear,' the agent said. 'He's *never* done a chat show.'

'I'll look after him,' I said.

'It could be a good learning curve for him,' the agent replied.

That actor was Ray Winstone. He was an absolute sweetheart on the show. He has never forgotten his first chat-show interview and I have never forgotten that he – and others in the series – provided me with wonderful material for yet another demo tape. I still bump into Ray from time to time and we speak on the phone occasionally. I absolutely adore him. He went on to do *Nil by Mouth*, a film part for which he won the Palme d'Or, the films *Sexy Beast* and *Love, Honour and Obey*, and the TV dramas, *Births, Marriages and Deaths* and *Lenny Blue*.

The fees I got for this kind of work were at least keeping body and soul together, and it was *television*. I was devastated when I heard that the channel had been sold to a German sports network. 'What now?' I thought. I knew that Peter Plant was keeping a constant eye out for more work for me, but there was nothing in the pipeline and my ultra lean time was about to return. I just do not know how I would have managed without Mark and Merrill during this period. They were both wonderful – true friends in need – and I've never forgotten their kindness. Without their help I could not have paid for my phone, which was my lifeline, and I would certainly have gone without proper food. (In fact, Merrill's children, Saskia and Thomas, thought I was going to be their next daddy because I arrived in their home every night for dinner.) On another occasion, when a huge, unpayable electricity bill appeared under my door, Merrill responded at once by putting a cheque in the post. She was working on TV AM at the time, but she wasn't by any means making a fortune. It was a remarkable gesture by a true friend.

One day in 1992, while I was still up to my neck in the financial mire, Mark rang and said, 'I've just had a rather unusual proposition. I've been offered the producer's job for the making of a sexy video, and Bob Cousins has agreed to be the director. Would you like to be the presenter?' (Some time later, Bob Cousins, a lovely fella and a dear friend, who directed *Anything for Money*, was also my director on *Supermarket Sweep*.)

'Who's the job for?' I asked, intrigued.

'Kim Turbeville,' Mark replied. 'She's come up with an idea to make a video called *Sexual Olympics – Sporting Girls 1992* for the *Sunday Sport*. It's going to be filmed at the Circus Tavern, Purfleet, and she'd like you to present it.' (Kim, a former girlfriend of Mark's, is now a television executive who puts on the *National Television Awards*.)

'This is a bit dodgy,' I thought, 'but what do I have to lose? Kim's very tenacious about getting things off the ground and there is a much-needed £1500 on offer. Can beggars be choosers?' I took a deep breath and decided to take the job.

At the rehearsal, as I had anticipated, the girls were all busty beauties who had doubtless already exposed their all in the *Sunday Sport* and who were not, therefore, in the least bit shy about giving their all to the randy rigours of the Sexual Olympics.

'Oh, God,' I thought, 'in three hours' time this place will be full of the most boisterous crowd I've ever played to, and all they'll be interested in is the bums and boobs of these gorgeous girls, doing God knows what!'

As I looked out at the room, I was filled with foreboding.

'Oh, God,' I kept muttering to myself, 'what am I doing here?'

I felt like sprinting off at Olympic speed, but I didn't. My job as strictly non-participative presenter was to interview, commentate and eliminate the competitors until we were left with the Sexual Olympic Girl of 1992. The girls' job, backed up by lashings of whipped cream, was to perform near-pornographic sexual acts on stage with a bunch of fruity innocents and accessories, such as bananas and melons. At the end of the first rehearsal, having given my all in a vocal sense, Kim came up to me and said encouragingly, 'You know what, Dale, you did that *really* well. You'll be able to do the real thing with your eyes closed.'

'D'you know what, Kim,' I replied. 'I probably will!'

As the night progressed, the heavily breathing crowd, which had already worked itself up to a baying frenzy, became even more over-stimulated by witnessing the various ways to abuse a fruit and started to show frightening signs of wanting to get at the girls. This was trouble enough, but the final game very nearly proved to be our Waterloo. For this, a huge pool, filled with mud, was erected centre stage and, while two girls were busy wrestling naked in this, my job as referee was to judge the rounds and proclaim the winner. While I was doing this a guy in the audience completely lost the plot and jumped up on the stage and climbed in with them. Then, before he could be evicted, several others decided to follow suit. Meanwhile another guy, either jealous of my pole position or irritated by my presentation, decided to leap up, grab hold of me and throw me in the mud with the other writhing bodies. Mark – ever my hero – then half throttled this chap as he propelled him off stage. It all, needless to say, ended in sheer muddy mayhem.

A couple of days later when I watched the edited video, I sat there, eyes half closed, thinking, 'Oh, my God, I never ever thought I'd end up at the Circus Tavern in Purfleet, rolling around in the mud with the winner of Sexual Olympics 1992.' Then, as the credits rolled, having seen 'Hosted by Dale Winton', I waited for the names of Kim, Mark and Bob to come up on the screen. But no, they'd done the dirty on me and hadn't put their names to the finished product! All that came up was 'This has been a Mucky Beaver Production', which just about summed it up. I remember sinking shamefaced in my seat, eaten up with embarrassment and thinking dismally, 'This really is the most appalling programme that is going to come back and haunt me one day.' How right I was! A couple of years later, just after I had had my big breaks on *Supermarket Sweep* and *The National Lottery* – and was, therefore, newsworthy – a journalist on the *Sport* phoned me saying, 'Guess what? We've rooted out some stills of you doing a porno film in 1992. And we're going to run the story and pics in tomorrow's paper.'

Almost the next moment Peter Plant, my agent, telephoned me, saying, 'Dale – what's happening? What have you done?'

'Nothing recently,' I replied meekly. 'They've got hold of a video of me when I was broke, compèring a ropy talent show at the Circus Tavern, Purfleet.'

As he rang off, seemingly reassured, I thought, 'Oh, God, this is going to look really bad, I'd better alert Richard Holloway [my boss at Central Television for whom I was now recording my second series of *Supermarket Sweep*].'

'Richard,' I said nervously when I managed to get hold of him. 'I'm just ringing to let you know that something stupid I did in 1992 has come back to haunt me. I had absolutely no money at the time and I presented a rather close-to-the-knuckle *Sunday Sport* video. I think there's going to be a few pictures from this in its sister paper, the *Sport*, tomorrow.'

There was a pause at the other end, then Richard said, 'OK, Dale, *not* a problem. Leave it with me. I'm sure everything will be fine.'

I put the phone down, outwardly hoping for the best, but inwardly fearing the worst.

Five minutes later Richard was back, sounding somewhat rattled. 'Dale,' he said, 'you know this video you made in 1992, the one they're going to run the pictures from . . . Were you – I have to ask you this – *naked*?'

'Absolutely not!' I replied, horrified. 'I was fully clothed at all times.'

'Thank God for that,' he said, with a sigh of relief.

Between my call and his, he had obviously thought I was about to be exposed in all my glory, albeit in a pool of mud, with six topless girls. Naked or not, the next day's coverage proved to be sufficiently bad for me to believe that the end of my career was nigh. TELLY LOTTERY KING DALE AT SIX-GIRL SEX PARTY was the front-page headline. This was followed by a lead-in, with accompanying picture, that read: *'TV lottery host Dale Winton was a front man for a sex show where porn stars picked up bananas with their breasts!'* A caption then proclaimed *'See Shock Photos . . . pages, 2,3,4 & 5.'* But despite my fears and forebodings, thankfully, what seemed like an horrific incident that could have done my burgeoning reputation irreparable damage simply faded away, as so often happens, into that day's waste paper bins and the next day's fish'n'chips wrappings. Today's editors and journalists, though, still seem to find it amusing because, every now and again, a picture from that wretched and ill-judged video appears in the press. But I've never yet been tempted to get the tape out and have another look at this raunchy bash urged on by my non-stop patter.

As far as my romantic life was concerned, the lean years of my career were also the lean years of my emotional life. I did date, I did have a couple of 'flings', but these were more mild flirtations than romantic or physical relationships. Financially, I was still struggling and I have always been the kind of guy who, if I go out for a drink or a dinner, has to stand my round and pay my way. While money was so tight, I felt ill equipped to get involved with anybody. My focus was on my career and all my energies were going into getting a proper job in television. If the right person for me had walked into my life back then I would probably have been more distressed than pleased because I felt I had nothing to offer. Later in life I realized that just being yourself can be enough, but I never saw it that way then. It was a low self-esteem period when I thought, 'What would anybody possibly see in me?' To this day, when people flirt or come on to me, I always have a click in the back of my mind that says, 'Are they for *real*? Are they *genuinely* interested in me?' I've never rushed into relationships. Quick-fix, one-night stands never do it for me. I'm the kind of guy who always has to have the 'i's dotted and the 't's crossed – but I will save all that for chapter ten.

What *did* change my life – and not before time! – wasn't one person, but four – Paula Goldstein, Dean Jones, Tony Gruner and Howard Huntridge. This long-awaited break came about when Peter Plant sent my photograph and a demo tape to Talbot Fremantle Television, a company that owned the rights to almost every major game show. As luck would have it, the timing proved perfect. Having just bought *The Price Is Right* from ITV, where Leslie Crowther had been the host, Tony Gruner was about to recast the show for BSkyB. Paula, I was later told, looked at my photo, watched my demo and said to Dean, 'He looks interesting – let's get him in for an interview – and possibly an audition.'

On the day this happened, my hopes were running sky-high, and I was only too aware that this could be the life-changing moment I'd been longing, hoping and working for. I was incredibly nervous. This couldn't have been too obvious, though, because, having formed an immediate bond with Paula and Dean, I was then introduced to Tony Gruner, their managing director – a giant of a man in television who had personally discovered a lot of on-air stars and was renowned for being a true talent spotter. I left Talbot Fremantle feeling that, all in all, it had been a pretty amazing day and that they had liked me.

Once again, though, I was in for a disappointment. Bob Warman, a Midlands presenter, got the job of hosting *The Price Is Right* for BSkyB because he was the main anchor on Central News. I wasn't really surprised. Bob had done much more TV than me and, in addition to this, the series was being filmed at Central. Eventually, of course, the show was returned to ITV, with Bruce Forsyth as the host.

One day Dean, whom I used to meet for coffee, mentioned that Talbot Fremantle had another game show in the offing, called *Personals*. The show was currently being shown on Canadian television, and they were hoping to sell it to a UK network. 'Would you,' he added, 'be prepared to do a pilot for it? There's no money on the table and it might never come to anything, *but . . .*'

With nothing to lose and everything to gain, I replied, 'Thank you, Dean – I will.'

The basic format for the show was very simple: a girl and guy were brought together on screen to see how they would take to each other and, if they did hit it off, there was a chance for them to win a holiday together at the end of the show. Long before I was ever given the chance to present this I had made a point of studying game shows and had decided that the secret of being a successful host was to understand the game inside out. Only then could you truly relax and be yourself. 'This could be *it*,' I kept telling myself. 'I've got to get it right.'

Despite still being a bit low on funds, one of the first things I decided on was a new jacket – and somehow I managed to squeeze enough money from my overdraft to go to Marks and Spencer where, amazingly, I found one that positively screamed game show host. It almost jumped off the coat hanger at me on first sight. It was salmon-pink and I thought it was wonderful. Cut long, it even made me look slimmer. On the grounds of good taste, I realize now that it was not the right colour for me, but at that time, when I wanted so much to make a visual as well as a verbal impact, I felt it was perfect for the role.

The producer of the pilot, Howard Huntridge, turned out to be a wonderful guy who came from Doncaster – a 'Mr Macho' wheeler-dealer who miraculously secured for us the use of the TV AM studio on a Sunday afternoon when it wasn't being used. I was so excited because this was where Anne Diamond and Nick Owen worked on their breakfast programme, and the chance to do some presenting there for people who knew that the golden rule of a game show is for the contestants to be quirky, funny, or sexy, worked wonders for me.

When I walked in that Sunday lunchtime, the place was swarming with some of the sexiest-looking people I'd ever seen, and I remember looking around astonished and saying to Paula and Dean, 'Who are all these gorgeous people dressed in leotards?'

'They're your contestants,' Dean replied.

I was *so* happy to be there. 'It's going to be great,' I thought, as I went off to my dressing room to get changed. 'They all look so right for TV.'

On my way back to the studio, I passed the Green Room where I could hear a number of voices raised in dissent. 'We've been here *three* hours. When are things going to start? When *are* we going to be auditioned?'

Our lovely contestants had obviously thought that it would all be over in half an hour and consequently had made plans for the rest of their Sunday. The reason they all looked so perfect was because Howard had secured them direct from model agencies with the promise of being on TV. He had omitted to mention, of course, that we were only making a pilot that would never be transmitted.

'I'm really worried,' I said to Paula and Dean, 'these people are becoming very restless – and they are *not* happy.'

'It'll be fine, Dale,' they both reassured me, 'don't worry about it.' But I could see they were embarrassed.

But at the very least, the models were about to be given the experience of what it's like to be in a television studio and, who knows, it might have resulted in a demo tape they could use to sell themselves in the future.

Sometimes, as I know, it pays to put up with a bit of inconvenience and to work for free. From the moment I hit the floor I knew I was in my spiritual home, and to this day I love hosting game shows.

Later, when the team and I were having supper in a local restaurant, Howard beamed across the table at me and said, 'That's the *best* pilot I've ever done. You were *brilliant* Dale – thank you so much.'

'I loved every moment of it,' I said. 'When can I have a tape?'

By now I was in dire financial straits, needing a new demo tape like yesterday. I was overdrawn by nearly £7000 at the bank and the branch manager was bombarding me with threatening letters because I had no collateral. I was still living in the little rented flat in North Harrow, had downsized my beautiful Audi car to a Nissan and other than considering the prospect of perhaps selling my vital organs for medical research on the Black Market, there were no money-raising measures I could take.

The moment the tape arrived, it felt like the proverbial answer to the maiden's prayer. I almost flew straight round to NatWest at Hatch End and placed it in my bank manager's hand. 'Please watch this and bear with me just a bit longer,' I pleaded. 'This is a pilot of a show that's going to be a television series. *Please* watch it and you'll see what I mean.'

That took some chutzpah, but it worked. The bank manager phoned me the next day and said, 'You're *very* good! I think this is an interesting show. I hope it works out for you.' He then, on behalf of NatWest, gave me some more time to breathe. But all to no avail. Soon after this, Paula and Dean told me with genuine regret that the show was not going to happen in the UK and that Talbot Fremantle had only managed to recoup its costs by selling the idea to Sweden.

How does one describe such moments, especially when there are so many of them? My battered brain was in a total turmoil. If I were to run cover-to-cover through a thesaurus, I'd settle for words like gutted, thwarted, stymied, foiled, distraught, disappointed. But what I did think, as I put down the phone and avoided looking at my red-coloured bank statement lying menacingly on the kitchen table, was, 'I chose this life. This is not what I had hoped for, but at least I've now had the experience of hosting a game show – and I've actually got a tape to prove it. I also have a colourful new jacket as my sole remaining prop. All I need to do now is go on believing that something *will* happen and I'll be fine.'

How well I know myself professionally. The possibility that, one day, the phone might ring with the offer of a job that I really want to do has always been something that can keep me going. But that doesn't mean I didn't have moments of despair when a show like *Personals* didn't come off. There was no other TV work in the pipeline – and even my bread-and-butter cable channel had gone. It was a case of going back to selling timeshare – and praying for a miracle.

One day in the spring of 1993 I called into Talbot Fremantle's new offices in Camden Town to have a coffee with Dean. As I was about to leave, I saw Howard Huntridge go past the door, clutching a clipboard. Written on it were the words 'Supermarket Sweep'. Now when you are desperate and you see the name of what is obviously a new TV programme, you lose no time in jumping up and putting your head round a door to try to find out what it's all about. 'Howard,' I called after his retreating figure, 'what's 'Supermarket Sweep'?'

'It's a new show,' he called back enigmatically. 'I'll tell you more when the time's right.'

'Dean,' I said, going back into the room, 'what *is* this new show you haven't told me about?'

Using all the persuasive powers I could possibly summon, I

managed to secure a tape and on my little telly back at my flat, I watched the American version of *Supermarket Sweep*. It was a case of love at first sight. I could see immediately that it was a compellingly insane quirky game show, but fabulous, too, and the trolley dash climax was ingenious, one of the best endgames I'd ever seen. 'But,' I thought, 'this will never be made in this country.'

The US has very different attitudes from us when it comes to promoting or showing undue preference to any one product and it was obvious that in America most of the revenue for *Supermarket Sweep* came from sponsorship – sponsorship from companies that wanted their products shown and mentioned on air. For example, 'It begins with a D and ends with a Z. You wash your clothes in it.' Answer: 'Daz'. But that couldn't happen in our country. The format would need to be entirely revamped to avoid unacceptable freebie advertising. For the UK also, everything would have to be generic. For example, 'It begins with an S and ends with a T. It's green, it's small and round, and it's a vegetable.' Answer: 'Sprout' – completely correct but not promotional for any individual product. But despite the obvious problems of adapting it for the UK, I was very excited by the idea and I sat there full of glee thinking, 'If this show ever gets off the ground here, it will be wonderful and I *have* to host it.'

I wanted the show for itself, but I also wanted it for the financial lift-off that it would give me. Having fobbed off my bank manager with my unfulfilled hopes for *Personals*, I was once again in trouble with the bank.

'We can't keep supporting you. We want our money,' was what they were understandably saying.

I could see their point of view, but that didn't make sleep come any easier. If *Supermarket Sweep* came off in the UK, I knew instinctively that it would either be taken to the viewers' hearts instantaneously or rejected out of hand. Either way, it would *not* go without notice and *I* would not be forgotten.

First thing the next day I rang Dean. 'It's a fabulous show,' I said. 'What's happening with it?'

'It's very early days,' Dean replied. 'We know you'd be great for it because you served us so well on *Personals*. But it's complicated. We're doing this as a co-production with Central Television – and that's a first for us.'

I understood at once what he was saying. Normally Talbot Fremantle operated as a format house that licensed shows to broadcasters who then made the programmes themselves. On this occasion, though, it was a fifteen-week, five-days-a-week operation in which Talbot and Central would co-produce five shows a day, making seventy-five shows in all. This really was a major commission for daytime telly and the first run, from September to December, was being scheduled to go out just before *This Morning*, presented by Richard and Judy. There had been various other game shows tried in that slot – *Keynotes, Cross Wits, Runway, Lucky Ladders,* but these had had only relatively short runs and ITV had now decided to invest in a bright new show for a long run.

This was all music to my ears, but I knew that for such a major financial commitment, Central Television would want a big star name in the frame. It's tough enough getting ratings with well-known names attached, but even tougher to pull in viewers without them. Of course, Central wanted an established star and, unluckily for me, it was up to them, *not* Talbot Fremantle, to come up with suggestions for ITV. But at least Dean had let me down gently by saying: 'Everybody at Talbot Fremantle knows you would be great for it,' and I wasn't ready to give up hope yet. 'Who's in charge of it at Central?' I asked.

'Rob Clark,' Dean replied.

As I put the phone down Mark, with whom I had already discussed just how much I wanted *Supermarket Sweep*, rang me. Mark was now Assistant Producer on *You Bet*, hosted by Matthew Kelly, and he said, 'Dale, I have some bad news for you. Rob Clark has just telephoned me regarding Matthew Kelly who he thinks would be great for *Supermarket Sweep*. But as it happens Matthew's already fully committed this autumn, so Rob said OK he'd look for someone else to host the programme.'

'I hope you mentioned me to Rob,' I said.

'No, Dale, I didn't,' Mark replied. 'There was no point – they want a big name.'

As far as I was concerned, Mark had a missed a great opportunity. 'Mark,' I said, 'at the very least you could have said that I would be great for the show. He may not know me from Adam yet, but *you* do and this could have paved the way.'

I can be very persuasive when my blood's up and I begged Mark to ring Rob back at once. As I wrote earlier in this book, Geminis are like bulldozers when it comes to moving obstacles. Although Mark was clearly reluctant, he eventually agreed to do it. When he phoned me back, I made him tell me verbatim what Rob had said. Interlaced with this, there was some good and bad news. The good news was that Rob, who had been a student at Nottingham University, knew my name from Radio Trent and had even seen me at local gigs. The bad news was that he ended the conversation with 'Mmm . . . Well, thanks for the suggestion, Mark, but no thanks. He's too fat – and too camp.'

Having told me this, Mark tried to soften the blow by saying, 'He doesn't know you've lost weight, Dale. Why don't you send him a letter and a tape.'

'Fine – I *will*,' I said and, although I was at my lowest ever emotional ebb, I sat down at once and sent off the *Personals* tape with a covering letter, then went out for a coffee, a cigarette and a sympathetic word with a friend whom I had worked with in lifestyle television. He was younger than me, but we were in the same boat: both desperate for that elusive break in our careers.

'Dale,' he said tentatively, as we sat sharing hopes and dreams in one of my favourite cafés in Soho's Old Compton Street, 'do you ever think that maybe it's becoming a little late for you to make it? Do you ever think you should try something different?'

'No,' I replied, without a moment's hesitation. 'I may never get my own show on TV, but I'll still be happy as long as I can do something in broadcasting.'

That was the truth. By then I might have had more down than up times, but I had never once thought of giving it all up and as for it being late in the day, I'd always taken comfort from the thought that

Larry Grayson was over fifty when he had his first lucky break as a game show host. Once, when I was driving Larry home after he had come in for my mid-morning show at Radio Trent, he said, 'Whatever you do, Dale, *never* give up on yourself. It's the stayers – those who persevere against all odds – who get the breaks in this business.' And he was right. The big breaks may seem elusive and for ever out of reach, but they can and do happen. That's show business – and one of the reasons why I've always loved it.

Of course, I was still hoping to get my own TV show, but if I didn't I wasn't finished yet. I was optimistic enough to know that my glass in life was still half full rather than half empty. I knew that within me I still had the energy and the determination to bash down doors and I was still hopeful that with my personality and persistence one thing could – and would – lead to another. In the past, whenever anything had turned up I had always responded with, 'Well, that's interesting,' and the absolute and unshakeable will to stay in the biz and keep body and soul together had carried me on. Often, that's all you need – a dream, some hope and a little luck, coupled with the confidence and the courage to persevere. Provided these ingredients are in place Larry was right, you *can* survive and you *can* succeed. All I had to do was somehow manage to hang in there and, if Rob Clark let me audition for *Supermarket Sweep*, I might just get the job and my troubles would be over.

Meanwhile, as I waited for Rob's reply I wasn't idle. There was bread to be buttered and timeshares to be sold. Also, in working and waiting for the right chance to come along, Merrill and I had formed our own company called Merridale. Every night, after work, I would go to her home for dinner and we'd sit for hours dreaming up formats for television programmes. Despite all our endeavours we didn't manage to get any projects away then, when we were so desperate to do so, but just recently one of those creative ideas has indeed come good. Watch this space!

When Rob's letter arrived, it was very brief and to the point: *Dear Dale, I can't promise you a network series at the moment, but I watched with great enthusiasm your* Personals *tape.'*

Instead of going into a decline over the loss of *Supermarket Sweep*, I seized upon the words 'at the moment' and 'great enthusiasm', thinking, 'Here's a man, who's in a very powerful position in television and he obviously thinks I do have some talent. I just need to win him over.' Then, just as this door closed, another opened. Thanks to Mark, who knew I could do with the cash, I was asked to do a couple of warm-ups for the *Frost Programme*, a live TV show, presented by David Frost on Carlton, at 10.30 p.m. Normally warm-up guys are comics but, because this was a current affairs programme, they wanted an audience-friendly gift-of-the-gab person. On my second night, as luck would have it, Rob was in the audience and later, as I said hello and thanked him for his letter, he seemed genuinely surprised that I had lost so much weight and was looking good.

A few days afterwards, I decided to back up this chance meeting with a phone call. 'Can we meet up?' I asked. 'Can I take you out to lunch?'

'Yes,' he said, 'I'd love that.'

I was hoping, of course, that having now seen me in action, he would consider me for *Supermarket Sweep*. But a call from Paula at Talbot Fremantle dashed these hopes.

'I know you're still banking on *Supermarket Sweep*,' she said, 'but as your friend, I have to tell you there's no hope of that. It's just gone to Keith Chegwin.'

I was choked. Every fibre of my body knew that I was right for this job – and I not only *wanted* it, I *needed* it, and I had allowed myself to build up my hopes.

When I rang Rob he said, 'I suppose you've heard that we've cast *Supermarket Sweep*.'

'Yes – fine,' I replied, almost dying with the feeling of rejection inside me.

'Does that mean you don't want to have lunch with me now?' he asked.

'No – I'd *love* to have lunch with you,' I said.

My heart was breaking, but I thought, 'Well, if nothing else, I can pitch him one or two Merridale ideas.' But I was gutted. With no other way to get my career sorted, I rang Telia Herold in Vienna and asked her if, despite having let her down before, I could do another Radio Danube contract.

'OK,' she said kindly, having forgiven me. 'I'll give you two dates, Dale. But don't let me down this time.'

'I won't,' I promised sincerely, contrite and very appreciative.

My plan was to have lunch with Rob, go to Vienna to make a few quid, then come back to North Harrow to reassess my whole existence, then maybe go away and live abroad. With all other doors seemingly closed to me my thinking was, 'I may as well be miserable somewhere in the sunshine as in England.'

I have to say that this was the only time in my life where I considered giving up on my chosen career. I began to think, 'Well, I'm good at selling timeshare, why don't I go and live in Spain or Portugal and sell timeshares to the Brits on holiday?' At least that way I would have a permanent tan and the social life had to be better than the one I was experiencing.

The only other hope in the pipeline at that time was a game show that Merrill and I had dreamt up for Merridale, called *Seven Deadly Signs*, which we had pitched to Buena Vista just before my lunch with Rob was planned. Buena Vista, knowing that the BBC was looking for a new game show for Terry Wogan to host, had taken up a short option on this but, as I was still hoping to host it myself, I decided there and then to pull it before it went any further and offer it to Rob instead.

When I did this, during our memorable lunch in a restaurant in St Christopher's Place, to my absolute joy and almost uncontainable relief, Rob simply loved it. 'Dale,' he said, 'it's *brilliant*. Let's give it a go. What I'd like you to do is sell the idea to my boss, Richard Holloway, in the same way that you've just sold it to me.'

Over coffee, when Rob and I were talking seriously about the format for this game show, I couldn't help remembering that he had told Mark that I was 'too camp'. You don't really think I'm gay, do you, Rob?' I asked him quite directly. 'I only asked,' I said mischievously, 'because people are always astounded when they find out I'm married with two kids.'

'You're what?' spluttered Rob, spilling his coffee. Then, reading my expression, he said, 'You *are* kidding, aren't you?'

'Yes,' I said, 'just kidding.'

I was more than satisfied that I had got one over him as a repayment for his 'too fat, too camp' comment. And years later, by which time we were great friends, we both recalled this moment.

As I left the lunch that Friday I felt quite elated. I was still deeply disappointed about *Supermarket Sweep*, but at least Rob had liked *Seven Deadly Signs* and I was feeling more hopeful about my future.

On the Sunday morning, too early for any of my friends to risk ringing me, the phone rang in my little flat in Harrow. 'Hello?' I said sleepily.

'Hi, Dale, it's Tony Gruner here,' the voice said. 'I'm sorry to trouble you on a Sunday morning, but it's about *Supermarket Sweep*.'

Oh, that's sweet, I thought. The Managing Director of Talbot Fremantle is ringing to tell me that the show has gone to another artiste. I know that. But what a gentleman to tell me himself.

'As you know, Dale,' Tony was saying, 'we originally wanted Ross King and then we wanted Keith Chegwin . . .'

I suddenly sat bolt upright. He had said 'wanted' and that was past tense. Hadn't Chegwin got the job?

'And there were other people we wanted,' Tony was now saying.

My mind was going stir-crazy. I had lived with this dream for weeks and all I could think now was, 'Perhaps there's still hope.' '*Shut up and listen!*' I told myself.

'The upshot of it all, Dale,' Tony was now saying, 'is that we are still without a host for the show and I want to talk to you tomorrow. Could you be in my office at nine o'clock?'

'Absolutely,' I said. I was so stunned that several minutes passed before I replaced the phone on the handset.

That was the longest Sunday I had ever known. I've never been a clock watcher, but that day I was worse than the rabbit in *Alice's Adventures in Wonderland*. I just couldn't stop looking at my watch.

First thing Monday morning, clutching a composite videotape showing me doing bits of serious journalism as well as the usual camp things, I went to see Tony Gruner. The meeting did not open well.

'We've got a real problem with you,' Tony said bluntly. 'Howard and I think you would be wonderful for *Supermarket Sweep*, but you are *not* a name and quite frankly we think you are *too* camp.'

'OK, Tony,' I said, 'point taken. But before we go any further, why don't you have a look at this demo tape.'

As he sat there watching it, I said, 'Producers produce, directors direct, presenters present. I'm a professional. If you tell me the tempo and the style you want for a performance, this will not be a problem for me.'

'It's not us you have to convince, Dale,' he replied. 'It's the people at Central Television. And even if you do that, they then have to convince Marcus Plantin, who's Head of Network, and Dawn Airie who's Head of Daytime. I'm not kidding you,' he added, 'we've done all we can. We want you, but it's not our call. The rest is up to you. Come to Central Television's London offices on Wednesday morning and do your best.'

'Thank you, Tony,' I said.


On Wednesday morning, the first thing I heard when I woke up was a letter plopping ominously on to my doormat. There, awaiting me, was the dreaded next missive from NatWest, informing me it was curtains and they were sending in the bailiffs. By this time I was with another agent, Nick Ranceford-Hadley at Noel Gay, but I knew there was no point in ringing him because there was no outstanding money for him to chase up. Instead of panicking, I placed the letter on the kitchen table and set about putting on my very best, newly revised game show image – a navy-blue suit, crisp pale-blue shirt and a really smart tie. 'If nothing else,' I thought, 'I'll go down like the *Titanic*, with a bit of style.'

My heart was in my mouth as I arrived at Central Television's offices in Portman Square, but I managed a confident smile as I entered the room and greeted Tony Gruner, Howard Huntridge and Rob Clark, and was then introduced to Richard Holloway, the Controller of Entertainment at Central Television. 'The others are already on my side,' I thought. '*This* is the one executive I have to sell myself to.'

Before the meeting, as part of my prep, I'd watched every tape of *Supermarket Sweep* that I could lay my hands on and was gratified when Richard acknowledged this in the middle of the discussions by saying, 'Well, it's quite obvious that you *know* and *like* the show, Dale. That's a good beginning.'

Howard (a typical shoot-from-the-hip guy) then added, 'But what Richard wants you to know is he doesn't want a *camp* host in a Lurex boob tube for this show.'

I looked at him in disbelief, but simply said again, 'Producers produce, directors direct and presenters present. I will set the tempo and the style to whatever is required. I can be as camp or as non-camp as you want me to be. I'm not Joan Crawford, but I'm not Arnold Schwarzenegger either. Between you and me, I'd quite like to be Diana Ross, but that's another story.'

As the laughter died down, we exchanged a few pleasantries, but I was left feeling that the meeting had been far too superficial. Richard smiled and said, 'Lovely to meet you, Dale, thank you for coming in.'

There I was, about to leave the room, but I knew in my heart that I hadn't clinched the job. As I stood up, I paused. I don't know where one gets the strength in such moments, but I suddenly found myself doing what Richard now calls 'my piece to camera'. The words just flowed. 'Richard,' I said, 'I've not quite finished yet. There's something else I'd like to say.'

Leaning back in their chairs, they all looked up at me as if to say, 'What on earth is this man about to do now?'

'You *should* give me *Supermarket Sweep*,' I said, 'because I am the best presenter that you'll ever find for this show. But if you don't give me this job, you should give it to someone new anyway. The industry is crying out for new talent – and this is a perfect opportunity. The biggest success in television during the last eighteen months is Chris

Evans on the *Big Breakfast*. He came from nowhere, but he's delivered an audience. The public wants *new*. They're sick and tired of seeing the same old faces. You must give me this job, do you understand what I'm saying?'

'Yes,' Richard said, looking stunned.

'There's more I'd like to say,' I continued, inspired with almost superhuman fervour. 'You *should* give me *Supermarket Sweep* because you'll find Lord Lucan and Salman Rushdie sooner than you will find a better host for this show. I'm the best presenter you will ever find for it. What's more, Richard,' I added, 'don't be afraid of camp. Women love a bit of camp. It *will* work. Do you hear what I'm saying?'

'Yes,' he murmured.

Now in my stride, I found I was using all my well-proven timeshare techniques, littering my sales pitch with 'Do you *understand*?' – 'Do you *hear* what I'm saying?' This might not be a property deal in Europe, but I was trying to get a closure from him. I needed to. I felt that I was fighting, literally, for my life in show business.

'I'm almost done,' I said. 'I don't want to alienate or offend you, Richard. I'm not an arrogant man, but I want you to know that I *am* the best man for this job – and that you have to give me this job. And I promise you I will *not* let you down. Do you understand?'

'I *hear* what you're saying and I do *understand*,' he replied patiently.

I could hardly believe my ears when he then said to the others, 'Well, I suppose a *bit* of camp won't go amiss.'

This set me off again. 'Richard,' I said, as he turned back to me, 'please give me this job. I promise I will not let you down. *Trust me. Just trust me.*'

The whole room fell silent for a moment, then Richard said again, 'I hear what you're saying, Dale, and I do understand.'

By now I was a quivering wreck and I very nearly blew it with one more unnecessary thrust: 'I know it's not my place to say this, Richard, because I never tell a man I respect how to do his job, but . . .' Suddenly realizing what I was doing, I abruptly stopped myself, closed my eyes and fell silent. The impact this had within the room was dramatic. But I wasn't play-acting. The seeming eternity of silence was then broken by someone – God knows who – mumbling, 'Has anyone else got anything to add?'

'I think Dale has said enough for all of us,' Richard replied. 'Who's your agent, Dale?'

'Nick Ranceford-Hadley at Noel Gay,' I answered.

'Dale, let me take you to the lift,' Rob said.

As I backed obediently out of the room, quietly expressing my thanks and shaking hands respectfully with everyone, I was thinking, 'Oh God! What *have* I done?'

I glanced at Rob, expecting a ticking-off but, to my astonishment, as we closed the door, he suddenly punched the air with his fist. '*That* was *marvellous, bloody marvellous,*' he said, with a broad, supportive grin. 'I've never seen anybody do that before.'

'Are you serious?' I said. 'I've just shouted at your boss – *bellowed* at him to give me the job. That's no way to behave, surely.'

'It was brilliant – marvellous,' Rob replied. '*Well done!*'

As I walked out of the building and crossed Portman Square, I was shell-shocked – a danger to myself. I'd never behaved like that before. I'd always done what was expected – just answered questions and listened to what was said. It's simply not acceptable for artistes to lecture heads of entertainment. But since then, Richard has always referred to that event as my piece to camera and moments that reminded him of the film, *Chorus Line,* when the dancer pleads, *'Please give me that job – I need this job!'*

Still in a daze, I found myself in the Food Hall of Selfridges, thinking, 'I should check to see if there are any messages on my answerphone at home.'

There were two: one from my agent, Nick, saying, 'Dale, ring me as soon as you pick up this message.' The other was from Dean at Talbot Fremantle, saying, '*Ring me, re Supermarket Sweep,* as soon as you pick up this message.' I didn't know whom to ring first. I decided on Nick but, as he was engaged I rang Dean. 'You have to know,' I said, in an effort to pre-empt him, 'I behaved appallingly in the interview. I . . .'

'*No*,' Dean interrupted, 'you were brilliant. Richard absolutely loved you and we'll be getting back to you.'

Shell-shocked again, I rang Nick.

'Richard loved you,' he confirmed. 'And if they can get it past the network, you've got the job.'

Oblivious to all the customers milling around the Food Hall, I sank forward on to a cheese counter. 'Say that again – *several times*,' I said to Nick.

And, just to please me, he did. He also, as I regained my senses, reminded me that there were more hurdles ahead; that the most difficult part now would be to get ITV, which had commissioned the series on the strength of a major-name presenter, to agree.

Still on cloud nine, I then went to see Nick, just to celebrate the moment. I then went to do the same with Dean. By the time I got to Talbot Fremantle, Tony, Richard and Howard had composed a letter to Marcus Plantin at the Network Centre, saying that they had found the right host for *Supermarket Sweep*.

When I returned home, I pushed the letter from the bank to the opposite side of the kitchen table, put my head in my hands and wept. Tears of joy. Tears of relief. Tears of almost disbelief. I knew I shouldn't get too excited yet, but . . .

When Marcus Plantin received the letter, he answered it saying that he had passed it on to Dawn Airie, Controller of Daytime TV. We then had to wait an agonizing three weeks for a formal reply because there was so much going on at ITV, including the possible rescheduling of *News at Ten*, which actually didn't happen until much later. During that stage of general upheaval, daytime shows were a low priority. It was the longest three weeks of my life. In the meantime I took a copy of Marcus's letter to the bank. Handing it to the manager, I said, 'You've waited this long, just give me a little more time. This will solve all my problems.'

'OK,' he said, with a patient smile beneath eyes of steel. 'Fine.' I fled before he could change his mind.

But the waiting was not my only problem. The time for my Radio Danube contract was coming closer and closer, but I didn't dare ring Telia to cancel it in case *Supermarket Sweep* slipped through my fingers again. All I could do was look at the phone and will it to ring. When, at last, it did, Nick said that Marcus Plantin and Dawn Airie had said, 'OK – we'll give Dale a chance.'

It was one of those moments when you feel like rushing into the street to kiss everybody in the universe.

# 7

## 'I want to stay here . . .'

THE MOMENT I got the contract for *Supermarket Sweep*, my life changed. A self-confessed shopaholic, I couldn't have dreamt up a more suitable game show for me if I had spent a lifetime trying. Any afternoon spent shopping, anticipating that glorious rush at the point of sale, and then trotting home with bulging carrier bags was my idea of heaven – to combine this with the achievement of my own game show on telly was sheer bliss. My friends, of course, had known for years that shopping till I dropped – and flirting – were the two loves of my life and they fell about laughing when they heard I was going to host a show set in a supermarket. I, though, was unrepentant. When the *Guardian* asked, 'How would you most like to die?' I was *not* joking when I replied, 'Loading one too many shopping bags into the back of a red Aston Martin Virage.'

As it happened, thrilled though I was about my big break on ITV's new five-times-a-week game show, I wasn't being paid the kind of fees that would fund that kind of shopping spree. But a fifteen-week run, totalling seventy-five shows in all, was excitement enough for somebody who had been scared witless about picking up the post, or answering the phone, lest it was the bank threatening me with bailiffs again. At least I could now keep my long-suffering bank manager sweet by paying off my overdraft. If any further consolation was needed, it came in the form of a small clothing budget from the show's co-producers, Central Television and Talbot Fremantle, and the appointment of a designer, called Stuart, to take me shopping. This time, instead of purchasing one jacket from M&S – paid for with my bank's money – I bought ten, some in pink, some in bright green, all in high fashion. I was actually spoiled for choice when it came to deciding which one to wear for my photo shoot. All I then had to do was to enjoy myself and prove that I was right up everybody's aisle. However, I was absolutely in no doubt that this would be easier said than done. Against all odds, I'd got the job, but I knew the powers that be were still *very* twitchy about me doing the show. The first of any series comes under intense scrutiny and it was made very clear to me, both before and during the London rehearsals, that *Supermarket Sweep* was seen as more than a one-series show, and that its ultimate success or failure was resting on my shoulders. I didn't need to be a mind reader to know that they were all thinking, 'Can he do it? Has he got the stamina to stand up to the pressures of recording five shows a day, five days a week so that, in three weeks' time, we'll have seventy-five shows in the bag? Or will he go off his trolley?'

With no time for self-doubt, I decided the only way I could hit the ground running and become king of the aisles was to put all these questions aside and focus on nailing the games into my head and getting to know the other members of the team. It was an impressive line-up. I had already met Tony Gruner and Richard Holloway, the Executive Producers, Howard Huntridge, the Producer, and Dean Jones, Associate Producer, but there were at least thirty-two other off-screen people to become acquainted with – cameramen, sound and lighting directors, floor managers, production assistants and secretaries, make-up, wardrobe, costume, and audience and contestant researchers. Just remembering everybody's names was a feat in itself. Then there were my three lovely on-screen hostesses, Caroline Tearell, Justine King and Samantha Jayne Williamson, and our warm-up man, Bobby Bragg. A very talented comic and an excellent presenter in his own right, Bobby, one of the tops at warming up audiences to just the right level, was to be the disembodied voice that the viewers would hear giving the commentary when the contestants were doing their trolley dashes around the supermarket. Finally, there was Ken Morley who, renowned for his part as the supermarket supremo, Reg Holdsworth, in *Coronation Street,* had agreed to cut the ribbon into our shoppers' paradise and declare it officially open.

During the run-up to the first recordings my bedtime reading was the Bible – not the Holy one – but the *UK Supermarket Sweep Bible.* Running to fifteen tightly packed A4 pages, this detailed the game and the rules. I was very conscientious about reading this document ahead of the London rehearsals and our decamp to Central Studios in Nottingham.

Meanwhile there was also the order of the jackets to be decided. For a show going out every weekday morning, I really needed to wear a different outfit every day, but the clothing budget had not quite stretched to this. Some mental arithmetic was called for – and achieved. It was like one of those awful mathematical teasers you are set at school. If I wore one outfit each day, all day, for the recording of that day's five shows, then the twenty-five shows from that week's filming could be screened out of sequence, so that the same outfit would only be seen five times throughout the entire run of seventy-five shows. Having been marked ten out of ten for that problem solved, I returned to concentrating on the format and the rules of the game. My job, as quiz master, included posing questions, such as:

*Bonbon* is the German name for sweet. *True or false?*
What is the missing word: Raspberry . . . doughnut?
Which product did Sir Walter Raleigh bring back from America?
Which of the following groups had a hit with 'Brown Sugar'? (The Archies/The Platters/Hot Chocolate/The Rolling Stones/The Beatles/Bob Marley and the Wailers?)

I am yellow, I am soon dirty, I go smoothly, I am nice to touch, I make things shine. What am I?
What am I? ORDIHESHSRA ACSUE?

And so on and so forth.

(I trust you knew the answers because, in the heat of the moment, our contestants often didn't!)

Having been given the chance to prove they were masterminds of supermarket shelves, the contestants were then awarded points, which were turned into 'sweep time'. For this, the countdown clock was started up and off they went on a high-speed trolley dash along the shelves, piling as many goods as they could into their trolleys. The couple who then returned to me with the highest value of goodies earned the chance to proceed to the 'Super Sweep', an even more manic dash through the supermarket, following coded clues to try to locate the £2000 jackpot.

From the moment I'd first seen the American version of *Supermarket Sweep* I'd thought it was a terrific show and couldn't wait to get on the set. Studios, with their floors criss-crossed with wires, their walls forever being shifted or repainted, their ceilings sagging with overhead lights and their cameras corralled in corners, are commando courses for the unwary. But, empty or full, half built or half dismantled, I love them. Our set, constructed with the help of consultants from the Asda chain, was a huge replica supermarket, fitted out with shelves and freezer cabinets packed to the gills with all the provisions to be found in any major food store. Even before the audience arrived, the child in me couldn't resist a few practice runs up and down its aisles, pushing a trolley with all the high-speed artistry of a Formula One racing driver!

When we are recording five shows a day, we do three in the afternoon and two in the evening. Because of the way *Supermarket Sweep* was constructed, we did three part ones, which consisted of questions and answers, followed by three Sweeps and then the Super Sweep during the afternoons. This was followed by two questions and answers, two Sweeps and two Super Sweeps during the evenings. So it was all *very* stop-start, and members of the team had to keep reloading everything back on to the shelves and reorganizing the studio. It was a very long day for everybody, and I always felt for the audience. Quite frankly the novelty of being in a studio and watching a show being made has long since passed for members of the public, and securing a good, lively participative audience is now one of the most thankless tasks in television. Although *Supermarket Sweep* was run like a military operation, by five thirty in the afternoon the audience had often had enough. We were also shooting the programmes in July and August, during the height of the summer, which meant that it was boiling hot outside but, to keep me cool and the audience awake, the air-conditioning was always full on and the studio was like an iceberg. The afternoon audiences would arrive in their light summer clothes, but by the time we had finished they would be sitting there with their headscarves on because it was so cold in the studio. Whenever I watch reruns of *Supermarket Sweep* I can always tell which shows were recorded in the afternoons and which in the evenings. This is because the audience for the afternoon shows, when most people are working, were elderly people whom we used to bus in on coaches from their residential homes, and the audience for the evening shows were much younger, including lots of students.

Day one of recording any series is jumpy enough but, looking back, I don't know how I survived that first day. I was a bag of nerves, and winging it was not the word! Each time I moved a muscle or my lips, Howard stopped me in my tracks: '*Don't* wave your arms about . . .', '*Don't* walk like that . . .', '*Don't* talk camp . . .', '*Act* butch . . .', '*Talk* butch . . .' were the mantras of the day.

The only thing that gave me the necessary life force to keep going and do what I was told, even though it all felt *so* wrong, was the memory of Tony Gruner saying to me in the dressing room, 'Think of your Mum, Dale . . . Do it for her.' I was very grateful for that piece of advice, but not so sure about his next instruction: 'You're tall, dark and good-looking, so when you're presenting, think Ronald Colman.'

Suave and sophisticated though I knew that 1930s matinée idol to be, he had never, to my knowledge, done a quiz show and he couldn't have been further from my idea of a game show host.

'Yes – right – Ronald Colman!' I mumbled obediently. But really I was thinking, 'Oh, God, Tony, can't I just be myself? Can't I be Dale Winton?'

I soon discovered, though, that I was not the only person coming in for this kind of instruction. On the first day a bewildered Bobby Bragg crept up to me, shaking his head in disbelief and whispering, 'I've just had the weirdest conversation with Tony Gruner. He wants me to think Charles Boyer when I'm warming up the audience.'

'Well, aren't *you* the lucky one,' I said. 'He told me to behave like Ronald Colman!'

With two of MGM's most bankable stars on the show, Tony obviously thought we couldn't go wrong.


Apart from working very hard on the series, I was also working *very* hard trying to keep my weight under control. If, during this time, someone had looked at me and said, 'Dale, you have the look of a man possessed!' (which I do sometimes when I'm hungry), or even 'Dale, you're the worst person ever to be allowed in front of a camera', *that* would have been OK. But if they had dared to say, 'Dale, you're looking fat,' I would probably have strangled them. During the first series of *Supermarket Sweep* I remember thinking, 'This is a dangerous time for me. It's always when you're under pressure or stressed that you're tempted to comfort-eat.' And I *was* stressed. It was my first network show for ITV and a lot was riding on it. Needing nourishment to get through the recording of five shows a day, I used to order a continental breakfast in the hotel, which included mouth-watering croissants, a Danish pastry with custard and a Danish pastry with fruit. I managed to resist the Danish pastries in the mornings but, because they looked *so* delicious, I didn't have the heart to let them go out of the room. Instead, I used to put them in a drawer in case I needed a midnight feast or suffered from night starvation. I realized that this was very silly and that, if I gave in, I would be eating all the wrong kinds of food at the wrong time of day, but . . .

On one occasion at about ten at night, I was so determined *not* to eat a Danish pastry that I threw it in the waste-paper bin and went to bed. At about three o'clock in the morning, though, I woke up wanting that pastry. As I stood over the bin, I checked myself, saying, 'Dale, *what* are you doing? You're thinking of fishing a Danish pastry out of a waste-paper bin. *Stop it!*' Then, to make absolutely sure I wouldn't weaken, I emptied all the cigarette butts from the ashtray on top of it.

People who know me well are only too aware that I'm a chocoholic and that whenever I'm stressed or unhappy I'll go to desperate measures to get hold of some. I've even been known to send a taxi driver to an all-night filling station to buy me a few bars. For a whole year it was Milky Way, for six months it was Bounty; right now – and this has been the case for some years – it's Chocolate Caramel bars, which I find absolutely irresistible. Having had a couple of man-size bites, though, I sit in the car and I actually talk to it. Talking to chocolate may sound like disturbing behaviour, but trust me, on the rare occasions I've done this it has come very easily to me. It probably says a lot about my love-hate relationship with food, and my passion for forbidden fruit. I know I'm not supposed to eat it and there I am, loving every naughty but nice moment. Eventually, I fish the piece of chocolate out of my mouth and say, '*Dirty. Nasty. Naughty,* Dale,' and I throw the remainder out of the window. If I'm ever done for being a litter-bug, it will be this action that causes my downfall.

I get so annoyed with myself. I know that if I put on weight my trousers will feel tight and I will feel unhappy. But if I feel unhappy, only chocolate makes me happy. It's an infuriating vicious circle because I have to watch my weight all the time. These days the diet that really works for me is a protein-only regime of oak-smoked Scottish salmon or chicken cooked in lemon. If I have time, I also buy bran sticks and soya milk from the health food shop, and top this up with a fresh fruit salad with no sugar added. I love Italian restaurants, but I've educated myself to order only plain penne with a bit of tomato sauce.

Exercise is important, too, and I now go to the gym regularly. All the way there, I say to myself, 'I'll go on the running machine, nothing else.' There was a time when I had a personal trainer but, as I was afraid I'd end up looking like a Muscle Mary, I gave that up. I always used to pooh-pooh people who were obsessed with going to the gym and working out, and I used to resent the fact that this ruled their life. 'Do you want to meet for a coffee?' I'd say. 'No, no, I have to go to the gym . . .' they'd reply. Or, when planning a dinner-date it would be, 'Can we meet later? I want to go to the gym . . .' I used to think this was so rude, but I understand it now. While I grumble to myself all the way to my club and hate every minute of it while I'm there, I feel fabulous afterwards.

When I have a job coming up, I keep a pair of jeans in the cupboard as my weight marker. At the moment, for the first time in my life, I can actually buy clothes off the peg and feel comfortable in them. My only problem now is that my legs are so long that I have trouble finding the right length trousers, but I can live with that. I've also just discovered Timberland for casual wear. I saw Samuel L. Jackson wearing a pair of fantastic blue boots and I went to a great deal of trouble to find out what they were. I then acquired pairs in navy and mid-blue. I had no idea until then that Timberland were so cool. I also suffer from a serious sunglasses habit: I've now got over thirty pairs. A typical Gemini, I always buy two of everything.

Being only too aware that *Supermarket Sweep* was my one shot at fame and that it would be curtains for me if the show failed, I was absolutely determined that people would remember my name. Having seen an American show in which the host's name was always mentioned in the answers, I set about drilling this approach into my contestants. 'When you give me an answer,' I reminded them, day in, day out, '*say* my name. *Say* "Pizza, *Dale*", "Ham, *Dale*", "Spinach,

*Dale".' The only time this nearly backfired was when the answer to a cheese question proved to be 'Wensleydale, *Dale*!'

Some people might think this self-promotion shameless, but to this day Howard says it was an inspired move on my part. Along with 'go wild in the aisles' and 'check it out, check it out', it was destined to become a kind of nationwide catchphrase and the students loved it. By series three, the popularity of *Supermarket Sweep* was legendary on university campuses and was even being blamed for youngsters missing their first lecture of the day!

As the days turned into the final weeks of recording series one, Central's PRs were working tirelessly to acquire us some advance publicity for the show, but all to no avail. Daytime TV wasn't the force then that it is today and I wasn't a household name who justified column inches. So, with no back-up from the national papers and magazines to guide the viewers our way, the first of our shows – which we had only started to record in August – hit the screens in September 1993. I was thirty-seven years old and if, as I so hoped, this proved to be make rather than break time for me, I'd be three years ahead of the 'life begins at forty' syndrome.

Suffering from a curious mix of elation and trepidation, I settled down to watch the first transmission in my hotel room. I was in for a shock – the biggest disappointment of my life so far. I hardly recognized myself on the small screen. 'Oh, God,' I kept muttering, mortified. 'Oh, God!' I had hoped my dark days were over, but now I was not so sure.

I'd been so brainwashed into not making a single camp move or lisping a word that I'd overdone the machismo and ended up with the most butch presentation known to man. My performance might have done me proud in a John Wayne movie, but it did nothing for me on *Supermarket Sweep*. I looked like somebody who'd just had a charismectomy and a personality bypass. To be a success as a game show host, I knew you had to come across as yourself, but there was none of me in that show. It really was a very odd performance and I knew any viewer worth their salt would see right through me. Every single frame revealed that I wasn't being true to myself. As far as I was concerned it was a disaster and nothing that any of my friends said could make me feel otherwise. I was inconsolable and all their 'It's good, Dale. It's great, Dale' just made me feel worse.

The only comfort was that when the reviews started to come in I was probably more prepared than most people to discover that the show was being hammered. It was described by the pundits as crass and tacky, full of unrepentant consumerism, and summed up as trash TV at its worst. But – and it was a big but – there was a surprise in store. The viewers did not agree with the critics and were turning on in droves. They loved the show, appreciated it for what it was, a trolley full of fun, and were spontaneously combusting in their armchairs. And regardless of anything the media wrote, the series continued to rate really well.

That was an enormous relief, of course, for Central, Talbot Fremantle and ITV. But for me, far from my troubles being over, they were only just beginning. When TV companies commission big-budget programmes, they organize market research to analyse what focus groups consider good or bad and, as far as *Supermarket Sweep* was concerned, the general consensus was that although they loved the show they were not at all sure about the host. Given that I had come over as a very strange hybrid of Dale-meets-John Wayne, I wasn't at all surprised. I thought they'd hit the nail right on the head. But this was small comfort. At a time when I should have been over the moon on what was obviously going to be a hit show, I was utterly miserable. There were, however, two crumbs of comfort about to break for me, and both proved to be fortuitous.

Making guest appearances on other people's shows is part and parcel of hosting one's own, and I was given an instant lift out of the doldrums when I was told that Cilla Black, one of showbiz's true professionals, loved *Supermarket Sweep* and wanted me to come on her *Christmas Surprise Surprise! Special* pushing a trolley. I had first met Cilla in about 1978, at Radio Trent, and liked her so much that I could easily have been one of the first to forecast that she'd become a national treasure. When she came into my studio that day for one of her on-tour interviews, we hit it off straight away. I now know that she doesn't even remember this occasion, but who could blame her?

Throughout the Sixties and Seventies she was doing wall-to-wall chat show interviews, and one radio station and one DJ is much like another. What I remember best, though, is that, having covered her musical career, I said, 'Cilla, we have something in common.' I meant that we were both Geminis, but Cilla, studying my face very closely for a moment, replied, 'Yes! We've both had nose jobs by Percy Jay.' It was true. I'd had mine done when I was working at UBN in 1977, but there's more on that in chapter eight.

By the end of that interview I knew Cilla was a very special gifted person, with a phenomenal love of life and an energy second to none, but I had no way of knowing then that, not far off in the scheme of things, she and Bobby Willis (truly one of show business's happiest married couples) would take me to their hearts and become two of my closest friends; and that after Bobby tragically died of cancer in 1999, Cilla and I would become so close that we are now part of the fabric of each other's life.

The Bee Gees were her star guests on *Surprise Surprise!* that night, but she thanked me so warmly for appearing on the show and was so complimentary about *Supermarket Sweep*, which she told me she had watched from the moment it started. High praise indeed!

My first guest appearance, then, proved to be fortuitous, but the gods must have been looking favourably upon me, because so did my second – this time on *Celebrity Family Fortunes*. The reason this turned into such a special occasion for me was that I met Shane Richie, also a guest on that night's show, and we travelled back to London together. This should just have been a companionable drive down the M1 in a car that had been hired for us, but our travels came to an abrupt end when the car suddenly coughed and spluttered to a halt by a motorway service station. The lady driver was mortified and very embarrassed, poor thing, but while she set about organizing a replacement car to come to our rescue, Shane and I took refuge in the cafeteria. He had just had a huge success with *Win, Lose or Draw* and I was hosting a show that was reaching the 3 million mark in the ratings, but there we were, beginning to think we might end up thumbing it home.

'Just look at us,' Shane said as we carried two none-too-clean plastic trays of eggs, sausages and bacon to a grubby table, 'the *king* and *queen* of daytime television, now stranded miles from nowhere in a service station at three o'clock in the morning.'

Far from feeling depressed, we both thought this was outrageously funny.

'When do you do the second series of *Sweep?*' Shane asked a moment later.

'I doubt that there'll be a second series for me,' I replied, brought suddenly down to earth.

'That would be a shame,' he said, his voice full of sympathy. 'Having met you, I can see that you've got what it takes for TV. If you could only relax on camera and be yourself, you'd be great, Dale.'

I nodded dismally, not wanting to bore him with too many details, but he suddenly said, 'Why don't you let me help you? Why don't you come round to my house and, if you like, I'll go through the show's tapes with you and tell you where I think you're going wrong.'

I could hardly believe my ears. A second independent opinion was just what I needed at that moment and here was a man who, despite the pressures of his own career, was prepared to help me with mine. 'Are you for real?' I asked, overcome by his generosity.

'Let's make a date now,' he replied.

When I went round to his house, there was another treat in store. Shane introduced me to his then wife, Colleen Nolan, one of the amazingly successful Nolan Sisters. When he took me into his study, the first thing he said was, 'You know the Nolans are *very big* in Japan . . .' I had to smile. Having spent so much of my life in the DJ world, the phrase 'You must play this band's record – they're *very big* in Japan' was daily fodder and, as I stood looking around a room lined with gold and platinum discs from the Nolans' Japanese record sales, those words actually meant something.

Shane was just great that day and I have never forgotten his kindness. He really was a friend in need and, despite all his own pressures, nothing was too much trouble for him. We sat there for ages playing, pausing and replaying the videotapes while he gave me endless tips on how to polish my performance. Even more important, he confirmed what I so needed to hear: that the best moments in the show were when I came closest to being myself. It really was a timely reminder of what Will Shakespeare meant when he wrote, '*This above all, to thine own self be true . . .*' By the time I left Shane that day, my confidence in my own judgement had been restored and I was utterly determined that if there was to be a second series of *Supermarket Sweep* I'd do it my way this time.

Meanwhile, feeling more light-hearted than I had for weeks, I decided to treat myself to a more decent-looking car, a new Nissan 200 SX. Foolhardy maybe, given that I was still living in a rented flat, but this bit of retail therapy did wonders for my spirits.

What I didn't know then – and amazingly didn't know until two years later – was that ITV had already commissioned the second series of *Supermarket Sweep*, but had instructed Central and Talbot Fremantle to 'get rid of Dale' and recast the job of host. Meanwhile – because nobody on the production team had breathed a word of this to me – I was left in the dark about what was to be or not to be . . . Then one day, by which time I had almost given up hope, Howard said, 'The show probably is coming back for a second series, Dale. But, before we go back into full production, we need to try out a different tempo with you.' He then had the grace to add, 'You were right, we were wrong. We need to let you loosen up a bit and be more camp. This time we really do want you to be yourself.'

This, of course, was music to my ears. But not for long.

At the first run-through, for which the production team used pretend contestants and an ad hoc audience, I was very Dale and allowed, without any interruptions this time, to do what came naturally to me. But then Howard, getting completely carried away and going over the top, said, 'That was very good, Dale, but crank it up even more.'

Dubious though I was, I once again put my own judgement on hold and, wearing an horrendous *Hawaii Five-O* shirt, really let rip. I must have looked like Julian Clary on speed but, as the audience and the team clearly loved this approach and were cheering me on, I tossed all caution to the wind and was more outrageously camp than Frankie Howerd, John Inman and Julian Clary all rolled into one. I just thought we were all letting our hair down and having a bit of fun, but I was shocked to the core when I discovered that the production team were saying, 'The second tape – definitely the second tape. It's absolutely fantastic!'

'You're out of your minds,' I said, dumbfounded. 'It's too much – much too much. I was over-compensating – just having a bit of fun. I couldn't possibly sustain that kind of performance over seventy-five shows. It would drive me and everybody else insane.'

'No,' they kept contradicting me. 'It's great, Dale. It's exactly what we want.'

'It's outrageous!' I said. 'If you play that tape to ITV they'll have a pink fit. They won't want me, you, or the show. Please,' I begged them, 'don't do this to me. Don't show them this tape.'

After a short deadlock, a compromise was reached. 'OK,' they said. 'Just to please you, we'll record it one more time.'

So, amid cries of, '*Keep it camp, Dale . . .*', '*Camp it up, Dale . . .*', I returned to the set. I could hardly believe what was happening. I had arrived absolutely determined to do it my way and be as camp as I liked, but now they couldn't get enough of it. This had to be one of the most extraordinary U-turns in television production. I took a deep breath, muttered to myself 'break a leg' and bounced back into action. This time, however, it proved to be a case of third time lucky. They were happy and I was happy. If Professor Higgins had been present, we would all doubtless have sung one of my favourite numbers from *My Fair Lady:* 'I think she's got it. By Jove, she's got it . . .'

What I didn't know that day (because I was *that* stupid and trusting then) was that I was not doing try-outs for the new series – I was being *re-auditioned* for my own show. Outrageous! But this had come about from the best of intentions. When word had come down from on high, saying, 'get rid of Dale' Richard, Tony and Howard had all stood shoulder-to-shoulder together and stuck by me, saying, 'No. It was our fault. We told Dale how to perform and we must give him a second chance.'

My performance was not the only thing that was changed for the second series. I had always thought that the start of the show lacked vitality and vigour, and that it was impossible for me to be my usual tactile, friendly self and build up a feeling of intimacy while I was made to stand behind a lectern at least twenty yards from the contestants. This time, though, I was permitted to make a livelier entrance by running rather than walking down the stairs on to the set and allowed to move freely among the contestants. The overall effect was a totally different feel and a much more intimate show. I also looked much better on screen. Having noted a review by Margaret Forward that said, '*When Dale's standing there in a green jacket against a backdrop of fruit and veg, it's hard to distinguish him from the fruit and vegetables,*' I abandoned the acid-drop jackets and went in for a more sober and much more trendy image.

Meanwhile, behind the scenes, unbeknown to me, the powers that be at ITV were obviously happy with the changes – and with me – because Central and Talbot Fremantle asked me to sign on the dotted line for the second series. Life, I felt, was now definitely on the up. I still wasn't earning enough money to exchange my Harrow flat for a house, but I didn't let that dampen my spirits. At least I could now afford a two-bedroomed maisonette I'd spotted. In estate agent speak, this was described as, 'situated in Hampstead', but, in reality, it was in the livelier, but not so grand, Kentish Town.

When the second series of *Supermarket Sweep* hit the screens, it was as if nobody had really noticed or discovered me until then. 'What's happened to Dale?' everybody, including the media, seemed to be asking, astonished. 'He's *so* different.'

I really couldn't have asked for a better affirmation that, in showbiz like in most walks of life, it pays to be yourself. During the first series, I'd always noticed that people looked at me in a rather quizzical way as if they were not quite sure who or what I was or where I was coming from, but now colleagues, contestants and members of the public were much more at ease with me. I realized I'd gone up a notch in everybody's perception and that they now found me approachable, which is something I treasure. As the show continued to gain ratings,

Central's Press Officer rang me and said she was finding it much easier to generate publicity and she could now, if I wished, get me some column inches. 'Would you like to do a bit more press?' she asked. '*TV Times* has already been on to us today, saying they'd love to do an interview with you.'

Having had an uphill struggle for so long, I was only too pleased to oblige. At least this meant people were sitting up and taking notice of me. But even as I said, 'Yes, of course,' I was also aware that, although any publicity is considered good publicity, this could prove to be a double-edged sword for me. Most performers are sitting ducks where media journalists are concerned, but some are more so than others. In showbiz, carefree remarks are renowned for producing the proverbial 'storm in a teacup' or 'mountains out of molehills'. But fear of the unknown has never stood in my way and I had already made up my mind that I would never be the kind of artiste who refuses to give press interviews. From time to time – then and now – I might say, 'Now's not a good moment, can we do it in six weeks time . . .' but only on very rare occasions would I say 'no' – and only then if there was a very good reason for doing so. Since those early days on *Supermarket Sweep*, I've attracted more than my fair share of the usual personal-life probes that are the lifeblood of today's tabloids, but by and large the press has treated me reasonably well. As far as I'm concerned we all have a job to do and it's not playing the game to court publicity early on, only to say later, when their need is greater than yours, 'Thank you – but goodbye.'

Something else it's never wise to do is bite the hand that feeds you. But, curiously, that was the position I found myself in with Howard Huntridge who'd been so instrumental in helping me to get *Supermarket Sweep*. Central's Press Officer rang me one day, saying, 'Dale, some journalists have been ringing us wanting to talk to you about your new record.'

'What record?' I asked, baffled. 'I haven't made a record.'

'But I've got it in front of me,' she replied. 'It's a single called "*Supermarket Sweep – Will you Dance with Me*" and it's coming out this Christmas.'

It was all news to me.

The first person I rang was my agent. 'Nick, do you know anything about a *Supermarket Sweep* record?' I asked.

'No,' he said, mystified. 'Nobody's said anything to me.'

I was *not* a happy man. And I was even less happy when I discovered that it *did* exist and that Howard was responsible for its creation. I was even more unhappy when I listened to it and discovered that its lead singer – singing the theme music from *Supermarket Sweep* to a disco beat – was a well-known topless model who was chiefly renowned for her work for X-rated magazines, and that, without my permission, I was featured along with her and a group called the Bar Codes, doing my catchphrases such as 'Go wild in the aisles – check it out, check it out', lifted from a video of the show. I'd already had more than enough trouble with the topless model scenario at the Circus Tavern and the last thing I needed now, just as my career was taking off, was more of the same.

'I'm not happy about this, Howard,' I said.

'But the labels have already been printed,' he replied, obviously panicked by my reaction, 'and the record company's banking on your support.'

'I don't care,' I said. 'Nobody's asked my permission, my voice is featured without a fee or a credit and I don't want anything to do with it. You'll just have to pull it.'

In the end, after much persuasion, I agreed to a deal that would help to promote the record and get Howard out of deep water with the record company. But it was very much a case of making the best of a bad job. A video was recorded with me doing my links and catchphrases to camera, and a new sticker, giving me the necessary credit, was designed to place on the single. And thanks to the record selling much, much better than anyone had ever expected, I was invited to put in a guest appearance on two highly rated TV programmes. The first was *The Word*, a very trendy teenage pop show, hosted by Terry Christien, and the second was *This Morning* with Richard Madeley and Judy Finnigan. For me, these were the first two occasions when I was being interviewed as a personality with

something to promote, and when I stepped on to the set of *The Word*
I was absolutely bowled over by the warmth of the young audience's
rapturous applause. It was a magical moment – my very first
confirmation that I had succeeded in reaching a very wide audience
that included all age groups, and that my career was now beginning
to exceed my own wildest expectations.

Another event that confirmed this was when I was asked to put in
a guest appearance at a gig at the Forum in Kentish Town to introduce
St Etienne, the pop band which had a huge cult following among
students. Once again, when I walked on, I experienced an incredible
wave of affection from the audience. It was all *so* new, *so* momentous,
that I couldn't quite grasp what was happening. There I was, a game
show host on daytime TV aimed primarily at housewives, but being
embraced by pop fans. It was only then that I realized that my public
persona had gained a momentum of its own and, from then on, each
day seemed to bring new surprises. Even the press, which had so
relished having pops at me and *Sweep* during the first series, was
suddenly singing a different tune and giving us both good reviews. But
no one was more surprised than me when a really big accolade came
our way from a most unlikely source: the prestigious Arts page of the
*Observer Review.* Under the heading, SUPERMARKET SWEEP IS A
TREAT, Andy Medhurst wrote, *It's crass, it's tacky but I can't start my
day without it . . .* Sweep *has mushroomed into British television's most
unlikely cult: its unrepentant consumerist vulgarity has been celebrated in
the style monthlies and the music press, and its host, the bouncing,
flouncing Dale Winton, received a hero's welcome on* The Word.

Oh, how things had changed! I couldn't believe it.

After all my previous crash landings, it was like touching down on
terra firma. I could hardly believe my luck when Nick first mentioned
that my profile was now rising so fast that more series of *Supermarket
Sweep* were definitely in the bag and that I was en route for in-
between job offers as well.

Meanwhile, the fame thing was growing apace and I was now
being recognized by passers-by. The only thing that puzzled me
about this was that as I became increasingly well known, people

invariably said the same thing when they stopped in their tracks to say a friendly 'hello', or to shake my hand, or to give me a peck on the cheek. Having finished their initial greetings they always added, 'Well . . . You're not at all what we expected. You're just the same *off* as *on*!' I never quite had the cheek to question this by replying, 'Really? I'd love to know what you were expecting,' but I wish I had. Quite clearly, having met me, they were pleasantly surprised by the fact that I am very much 'what you see is what you get' and I loved the bonhomie. I certainly didn't want to be a stand-offish person, who walked about with my nose in the air and who just elicited shy murmurs of 'You know who that was . . .' as people walked past. On the contrary, I always wanted to be the kind of person whom people felt they could approach and say hello to, or ask for an autograph. The only time this nearly ended in disaster was in 1998 when we were in Nottingham recording a series of *Supermarket Sweep*. Saturday was a beautiful day and, needing a bit of lunchtime retail therapy, I decided to go to the city's Broadmarsh Shopping Centre. As I turned into it, though, so many people rushed up to greet me that I found myself unable to move and I very nearly had a panic attack. 'Perhaps,' I thought, 'I *do* need to be a bit more careful now about going out on my own.' But by and large, I never let being on television change my life. Even now, when I move in professional circles where people are always saying 'If you come along to this, we'll send a car for you,' I always take my own car if there's parking at the location or nearby. I love doing my own thing and this even includes going to the dry cleaners and doing my own supermarket shopping. In short, I refuse to let the job curtail my activities. The person's more important than the fame.

One totally unexpected perk that came from my being on *Supermarket Sweep* was an out-of-the-blue reunion with Mum's side of the family. After Mum died in 1976, I'd continued to speak to Grandma on the phone from time to time and had visited her in Sheffield whenever I could, but some years had passed since I'd last seen her or

Uncle Norman, Uncle Joe and Lorraine. Then one day I had a telephone call from Lorraine, saying in her usual bubbly way, 'Dale, we're going to hire a minibus and come and see you doing *Supermarket Sweep*.' I was delighted. When they arrived at Central Studios, Grandma looked a million dollars. She was very smartly dressed and instantly drew my attention to her new set of teeth. Rightly so – they made her look twenty years younger. During that day's recording I couldn't resist bringing her up on the stage and introducing her to the audience. She was completely unfazed by all the fuss and just stood there graciously, saying, 'My grandson – my grandson.' It was a very special moment for both of us.

Afterwards, when we were chatting in my dressing room, she suddenly came over all serious and said, 'Dale, what will you do when you've finished this series?'

'Well,' I replied, 'I don't know yet, Grandma. There will be other work, but nothing's for sure yet.'

'When do you finish work on this?' she asked.

'In about ten days' time,' I said.

'*Then* what?'

'I'm going to take a break, Grandma.'

'Then what?'

'Well, I might have some more time off, Grandma.'

There I was, presenting this hugely successful daytime television programme, recording the usual seventy-five shows in three and a half weeks (which actually represented over four months of screen time of *Supermarket Sweep*), with the promise from Nick of a good career to follow, but there was Grandma having an anxiety attack that I would have no immediate work at the end of the series. 'Showbiz is very stop-start work,' I added reassuringly, 'but . . .'

'*Right!*' she interrupted. 'So what you're really saying, Dale, is that at the end of next week you'll have finished – and you'll be out of work.'

'Yes. But my work isn't like a nine-to-five job, Grandma. The programmes I'm recording now will be on the telly for months.'

'But what you're really saying,' she fired back, her north-country spirit to the fore, 'is that you have no work. And if you have no work, how are you going manage and how are you going to pay your mortgage?'

I knew I was losing this argument. I tried coming back from various angles to help her understand that I was actually being paid very handsomely for what I was doing and I really had no worries about paying the mortgage, but she couldn't get it out of her head that, by the end of the following week, I was going to be out of work. I then tried to remind her of something I'd said earlier: that there was just a chance I'd be hosting a TV programme for Anglia the following year.

'But that's not until next year!' she said, appalled.

'Grandma.' I sighed. 'That's the way my business works. And although it must sound very strange to you, I'm actually more successful than I've ever been before.'

'OK, Dale,' she said, obviously not at all reassured, but deciding our conversation wasn't going anywhere, 'it's been nice to see you.' Then, as she made ready to leave the dressing room, she started to fumble in her handbag. 'I haven't got much money,' she said, 'but I'm sure that will help. . .' And without giving me a chance to absorb what she was doing and respond, she swept out of the door.

As I stood there, looking at the ten-pound note she had pressed into my hand, I was reduced to tears. It was such a sweet gesture and it totally floored me.

The following day, just as I was about to ring Grandma, she rang me: 'It was very nice to see you, Dale – and I'm *so* proud of you. But I've been thinking. What you really need is a steady job. Why don't you get on *Coronation Street* or *Emmerdale*. It's soaps that'll make you *really* popular with the audience.'

I tried to explain that actors acted and presenters presented, but as far as Grandma was concerned she'd got the answer to my problems and she wouldn't let it go. 'I'm not so keen on you being in *Neighbours,*' she added several times, 'because that would mean you'd have to leave the country. But then again, if push came to shove, you'd just have to do that and go to Australia. Just promise me you'll think about it.'

'OK, Grandma,' I said, knowing that nothing else would ease her mind, 'I promise.'

As I put down the phone, I picked up the ten-pound note she had pressed so lovingly in my hand and placed it inside the jacket I'd worn that day on *Supermarket Sweep*. It's changed homes a few times since then, but I've never had to spend it.

By then I'd done five series of *Supermarket Sweep* – 375 shows in all – with still more coming along, and Grandma had become one of my most avid fans. She'd also tuned in for several of my guest appearances on shows such as *Just a Minute, The Upper Hand, You Bet, Celebrity Squares, Win, Lose or Draw* and *Noel's House Party*. I'd always known how proud Grandma was of Mum – and her greatest parting gift to me was when she said, 'If I'm *this* proud of you, Dale, just think how proud your mum would have been.' Grandma died peacefully in 1997. She was then in her eighties, but she honestly didn't look a day over sixty. I bless her memory.

# 8

## 'I've got a good thing . . .'

By THE YEAR 1995, life was feeling good. *Supermarket Sweep* was now firmly established as one of daytime TV's most popular shows and thanks to this, other job offers were coming in. These may not have been quite what I was hoping for, which was the next step up the ladder that would lead to a prime-time evening show for the BBC or ITV, but at least they would keep me busy for longer than three weeks of the year. Being in demand was a new experience for me and each time Nick, my agent, rang to tell me something new had come along, I was thrilled. I never had a career strategy then (or now). Working in television and being a high-profile professional presenter was (and still is) an adventure. In the meantime, each new offering enhanced my life's rich pageant and topped up my earnings on *Supermarket Sweep*.

Garry Bushell, a gutsy TV critic whom I had always admired for writing what so many others would think twice about before putting pen to paper, had never mentioned *Supermarket Sweep* in his columns but, when he wrote his piece 'Day Crime Television' listing the top ten worst daytime shows he had ever seen, he placed our show in the number one spot. Friends and colleagues, thinking I would be distraught, kept ringing up and saying, 'Are you all right, Dale?' But, surprising though this may seem, I took it all with good heart. 'Well,' I thought, 'everybody – including Garry – is entitled to their own opinion and if I've got to be in the shit list rather than the hit list, I'd rather be number one.' Those close to me, however, became even more concerned when they heard that the very next day after the list had been published both Garry and I were appearing on Bob Monkhouse's *Celebrity Squares*. Even Bob's wife, Jackie, phoned and said, 'Dale, we've just read Garry Bushell's review. Are you all right?'

'*Darling*,' I said, 'that's so sweet of you, but I couldn't be better. I'm really looking forward to being on the show.'

That was true. I'd always been a huge fan of Bob's, who is one of showbiz's real gentlemen, and for me this was a family moment. Mum had appeared in his 1959 movie, *Dentist in the Chair*, and in the past, when journalists had asked me, 'What would be your personal mark of success?' I'd replied, 'Being in the box on *Celebrity Squares*. Once I've done that I'll die a happy man.'

When I arrived at Central Television in Nottingham, I discovered that *Celebrity Squares* was filmed in the same studio, by the same crew, as *Supermarket Sweep*, so I felt very much at home when I was introduced to the other competitors, Ross King and Lionel Blair, and Cheryl Baker, who'd recently had a huge success with Bucks Fizz. When I came face to face with a somewhat embarrassed-looking Garry Bushell in a corridor, I thought, '*Right*, I'll deal with this, as I do most things – head on.' Holding out my hand, I said with a smile, 'Garry Bushell – Dale Winton. It's so nice to meet you. How are you? I need to talk to you about your column in yesterday's paper, but now's not the time, so I'll deal with you later.'

'Oh! OK,' he replied, obviously very ill at ease.

'On second thoughts,' I added, looking him straight in the eye, 'I'll deal with you right now. I read every word in your column and have memorized most of it. I'm very aware of your opinion of me, but I'm left wondering one thing. Does this mean a bonk is now out of the question?'

It was the last thing he had expected me to say. He beamed from ear to ear. That moment was the beginning of a friendship that has lasted to this day. I still admire his uncompromising approach to his work and I couldn't have been more pleased when he asked me to be godfather to his lovely daughter, Jenna.

Once, while I was doing *Supermarket Sweep*, I went up to Newcastle to be a guest on a pilot that Tyne Tees TV was making about psychics. When I'm working, I don't usually socialize in the evenings. I go straight back to my hotel, call room service and have a quiet night. On this particular evening, though, I thought, 'This is silly. I don't know Newcastle and this is an opportunity to explore it.' Once outside on the street, only too aware that Newcastle men are renowned for their tough, macho, no-nonsense approach to life, I began to wonder if I'd done the right thing. By then my face was well known and I had a very camp image that might not go down a bundle with the local lads. Feeling quite nervous on my own out there, I thought, 'Is this wise? If I bump into any of them, I might attract the wrong kind of attention and end up getting a real pasting.' I was about to turn back when I saw a guy with a bag of chips walking towards me. The smell coming from the bag was irresistible. 'Where did you get those?' I asked, my smile disguising the trepidation I was feeling at simply approaching him.

'Down there,' he mumbled, his mouth otherwise occupied.

Having bought myself a portion, I remained inside the chippy eating them. As I was the only customer in the shop, I was relaxed and happy, enjoying standing by the window, looking at the cranes outlined against the night sky of the dock. But just as I was nearing the end of the bag, all hell suddenly erupted outside. The club next door had obviously just turned out and forty or so of the toughest-looking guys I'd ever seen were surging into the chippy. 'Oh, God!' I thought, as I was trapped in the corner and immediately recognized by some of the lads, 'I'm in for it now. I'll be lucky to get out of here alive.'

I couldn't have been more wrong. Far from being sneered at and jostled for being camp, or at the receiving end of knuckledusters and boots, they were delighted to see me on their home turf and greeted me with friendly whoops and pats on the back. Just as I relaxed and thought I'd got away with it, and was saying my goodbyes, one really tough geezer stepped out of the crowd and said, 'Hold on, Dale. Hold on. There's something I've always wanted to ask you – something I've always wanted to know about you . . .'

'Here we go,' I thought, dreading the all too familiar are-you, aren't-you? question, followed by it all suddenly turning very nasty. Still ringed around by a group of the lads, I replied, 'OK.'

'You know those three lovely hostesses on *Supermarket Sweep*,' he said, almost salivating. 'Do you *shag* 'em?'

My relief was phenomenal. 'No,' I replied with a wink that projected every ounce of masculinity I could muster. 'I've always made it a rule in life *never* to mix business with pleasure.'

Then, to disbelieving snorts and jeers of, 'Go on with ya, lad!' I was allowed to go on my way.


*Weekend Plus*, the first of my new shows, which began in January 1995 and ran concurrently with the next series of *Supermarket Sweep*, was a Friday-evening round-up of the week for Anglia Television. I co-hosted this with Samantha Norman – Barry Norman's daughter – and although it was exhausting having to tear around all the different locations with only one cameraman in tow, it was great fun. And while I was doing it I chalked up a couple of memorable 'firsts' for its viewers when I interviewed Boyzone just prior to the release of their first record, 'Love me for a reason'.

This happy time, though, was soon eclipsed by what proved to be my best paid to date, but worst-ever experience on TV. This programme, which Nick, my agent, thought promised so much, was a prime-time show being produced by Planet 24, a company which had had a great hit with *The Word* and was now having an even greater success with Chris Evans's *The Big Breakfast*. Keen though I was to be given my first chance to host a new prime-time programme commissioned by the Beeb, the moment I watched the pilot of *The Weekend Show* I thought it was a disaster waiting to happen. Steve Wright, one of my broadcasting heroes, had hosted the pilot, but he had had the good sense to turn down the series.

From day one onwards, having been persuaded by Nick and his boss, Alex Armitage, that I'd be crazy to reject an opportunity to work with the production company of the moment, I was in despair. The studios at Bow, in the East End of London, were just one up from a Portakabin, not at all the kind of set-up where you would expect a prime-time show for the BBC to be filmed. Nobody, from top to bottom of the team, seemed to know who was supposed to be doing what or where. The whole thing was a catalogue of un-mitigated disasters from start to finish. It was a case of 'busy-busy-busy, working the whole day through', but never really getting anywhere. I've always liked to do my prep, but I was getting scripts at the very last moment because people were always frantically rewriting them. Three weeks before the first show was due to be transmitted, I asked if they could recast the job because I didn't have a good feeling about it. But try as I might, I didn't succeed in leaving the show. The BBC was also quite nervous about it going out live, so it was recorded late in the afternoon for a six o'clock transmission in order to allow for any necessary nips and tucks to be made.

The whole production was so shambolic that on one occasion someone even forgot to book the audience. Given everything else that had gone wrong and the fact that nobody seemed to be able to make up their mind about anything, even that fundamental faux pas seemed almost a minor oversight by comparison. 'Where's the audience?' I asked. 'Surely they should be here, seated by now?'

'Oh, my God!' was the reassuring reply.

The next thing I heard was that somebody had been despatched to a nearby bingo hall to coax the people from there to be our bums on seats. Then, because they had been promised a game of bingo and a £100 raffle during one of the breaks, we had to stop in the middle of recording the show to do this. I couldn't believe what I was doing. Even the raffle went wrong. When I drew the winning ticket, two people stood up, waving the same number. 'Well,' I said amidst the wild confusion, 'we'll just have to give you both £100.'

'No!' some cheapskate hissed from behind. 'Tell 'em we'll split it and give them £50 each.'

'For goodness sake! This couple could probably have picked up better winnings, yelling "housey-housey" in the local bingo hall,' I replied.

Under some sufferance, both were given £100. And I was given an abject lesson on the fallibility of a poor production under pressure.

One joy I did get from hosting *The Weekend Show* was working with its two presenters, Liza Tarbuck and Daley Thompson. To this day Liza and I have remained the closest of friends and I love her dearly. The only other pleasure was interviewing stars like Marti Caine, Joan Collins, Barbara Windsor, David Seaman and *Coronation Street*'s Liz Dawn. It was not, though, a happy time for me and, as I drove away from the last of the series, I vowed never again to do another show for Planet 24. Since then, however, I've learned that in general terms no TV production company is better or worse than another. It all comes down to personal chemistry, which is nigh on impossible to define. Some years later when the lovely Richard Woolf, Planet 24's then Head of Entertainment, invited me to host Barbara Windsor's *Hall of Fame*, I broke that promise to myself and I'm so glad I did. It was a totally different ball game, a really happy Planet 24 time and a wonderful tribute to Barbara.

But back in those days, greatly in need of a pick-me-up after *The Weekend Show*, I went straight to a car showroom and blew the money I'd just earned on a brand-new Audi convertible. This time I wasn't being foolhardy. My immediate future was already financially secure. Two weeks into recording *The Weekend Show*, my best friend, Mark, had telephoned me to say that he had been asked to produce the second series of *Pets Win Prizes* and that, as Danny Baker, its first brilliant presenter, was already committed to another contract, the BBC had suggested that I might be just the right person to take over the show.

I was thrilled. *Pets Win Prizes* was kitsch and different and this time, instead of thinking 'maybe . . .' I felt, 'Yes, definitely!' Show business is not renowned for giving performers second chances but, thanks to the Beeb having retained its faith in me, I was living proof that when you have a grief encounter and touch rock-bottom in the ratings, the only place to go is up. To this day I'm convinced that if *Pets Win Prizes* had not come along at just that moment, nobody else would have given me another prime-time show. As it was, I did thirteen programmes for the second series of *Pets Win Prizes* and was booked to do another series in 1996.

What I remember most about that show was the smell. I like to think that my studios are fragrant places, but try telling that to sheep, geese and llamas. And slippery floors were not the only challenge. Our health and safety might have been at risk, but the well-being of the animals was paramount. The gecko, for instance, proved to be more demanding than any Hollywood star. He had to be brought to the studio in an air-conditioned limo, the temperature in the dressing room had to be absolutely perfect and his tipple of specially brewed water had to be prepared in advance. When it came to the lizard's turn, we had to wait around for absolutely ages while the studio was air-conditioned to just the right temperature and, by the time I'd come on and gone off the set a dozen times, I'd developed a need for some TLC myself. And that was before we faced up to the tricky business of getting the animals to perform on camera.

Terry Nutkins was our animal expert. In the normal course of events I couldn't have asked for a more charming presenter, but there was a definite blip in our relationship the day we had a tarantula on the show. 'Look, darling,' I said, going into instant panic mode, 'spiders, even small ones, give me the creeps. I don't mind what *you* do with this tarantula, but don't bring it anywhere near me. And don't you dare ask me to hold it. If you do, I can't answer for my actions.'

'This', he replied soothingly, 'is a fear I can help you overcome.'

'Not now and not on air,' I said. 'I don't want anything to do with a hairy monster that bites.'

'They hardly ever do that,' he replied.

'Maybe not,' I said, 'but I'm not in a hurry to find out!'

A bit later in the dress rehearsal Terry, having completely underestimated my fear, said, 'Come on, Dale, just hold the spider?'

'Absolutely not,' I said, ready to take immediate flight.

'Trust me,' he said, 'it'll be fine.'

'I *do* trust you,' I replied. 'But the answer's still no.'

'OK,' Terry said. 'When we do the recording, I will hold the tarantula myself and just stand next to you while I'm talking about it.'

'Not too close,' I said. 'If it moves, I'm out of there.'

Come the show, already sweating with fear at the thought of Terry standing next to me with a deadly poisonous tarantula in his hand, I couldn't believe my ears when he said to the audience, 'You *want* to see Dale hold the spider, don't you?'

And as I stood there in a blind panic, saying, 'No, no, no!' the audience, thinking this was all part of the game, started yelling pantomime style, 'Yes, yes, yes!'

I have no idea what stops you from doing a quick exodus at a time like that but, somehow, dripping with sweat and gabbling in terror, my inborn professionalism forced me to remain in front of the camera. Even now as I write about this experience my hands are clammy and my heart's running a marathon. When Terry put the spider on my hand and it started to crawl up my arm, I was shaking so much I nearly passed out. By the time he realized that perhaps this hadn't been such a good idea and took the spider off me, there was a pool of sweat in the palm of my hand and the whites of my eyes had never looked so white. Until that moment I'd thought a round of applause was worth anything, but *not* that day. I left the stage half dead from fear, knowing I'd sacrifice ten standing ovations – and my career – rather than go through that ordeal again.

When it came to the naming of one of the games, though, I had some off-screen fun with the producers. A recurring theme throughout the series was an identification game which we called 'That's My Goldfish', 'That's My Spider', 'That's My Gecko'. On this particular occasion, though, we had twelve cockerels placed in twelve separate boxes so that our celebrity guest could only identify his bird by its legs or feet. So, to follow the same pattern as all the other games, we were going to call that particular game 'That's My Cock'. The producers, however, ever mindful of the BBC's rules about not exceeding the limits of good taste, decided that we couldn't possibly call it *that*.

'Well, maybe you're right,' I said. Then I added, 'OK. Why don't we call it "My Cock's Two Feet"?' Believe it or not, that's how it went out on prime-time TV!

With 6 million viewers welcoming *Pets Win Prizes* into their living rooms, that show proved to be the long-awaited watershed for me and a very satisfactory commission for the BBC. But, sadly, as there were only a limited number of games we could play with furry friends, reptiles and insects, we all knew it would have to come to an end with the third series. By the time that happened, however, I'd made nonsense of the old showbiz adage 'Never work with animals or children.'

Being a household name brings many surprises in its wake. Nobody could have been more astonished than me when I was asked to play a game show host, wearing a pink lamé suit, in the film, *Trainspotting*. I *so* enjoyed being on location in Glasgow and queuing up with its stars, James Cosmo and Ewan McGregor, to get a bacon buttie from the refreshment trailer. When the film came out it proved to be 'the must-see movie of the Nineties' and, as I sat there watching myself on the big screen, I counted my blessings to have had a part in it.

Having achieved the seemingly impossible and become a household name, I was enjoying the attention I was getting in the papers and I liked being recognized when I was in restaurants or out and about collecting my dry cleaning, but I always knew it wouldn't be a laugh a minute. Happy though I was to set aside time for the press and to stop and give the paparazzi the pictures they wanted, I wasn't daft. Like most people in our business, I knew it was the story we didn't want told – or the picture we didn't want shown – that the tabloids were most looking forward to publishing. What they really wanted from me was copy that would lend itself to clever-Dick titles, such as '*Rising Camp*' and '*The Darker Shade of Dale*'.

In October 1995, a very good showbiz friend, Alistair Divall, an excellent broadcaster who was then on *Keynotes*, rang me and said he was coming up to London from St Albans, could we meet at Brent Cross, the huge shopping complex in north London, have lunch and then do some shopping? When we met I greeted Alistair, as I do everybody, with a friendly kiss but, as luck would have it, this moment was caught on a paparazzo's camera and sold as a picture exclusive to the *News of the World*. Under the headline, SUPERMARKET SWEETIE, the lead-in read, '*Checkout this – it's TV's Supermarket Sweep host smooching a bloke in Tesco's!*' And this was then followed by a caption that said, '*Cheeky Dale is caught sneaking a checkout kiss*'. It was hilarious. The paparazzo would have been hard pushed to alight on a more heterosexual man than Alistair. But, strangely enough, just one month later there was another exposé concerning me and Alistair, this time in the *People*. This came about on a Saturday afternoon, very soon after I had exchanged my Kentish Town maisonette for a house I had fallen in love with – and could now afford – in South End Green, Hampstead. This house, which was located in a mews, complete with cobblestones, bollards, decorative railings and Victorian-style street lanterns, was protected by electronically controlled wrought-iron gates, but as these sprang obligingly open to let residents drive in and out, it was not exactly safe or secure. Everyone in the public eye knows that the worst time you can be phoned – or doorstepped – by the press is on a Saturday afternoon because that means one of the Sunday papers is going to run a story about you. And the reason *why* they doorstep you so late is to ensure you don't have the chance to do a damage limitation exercise by giving your side of the story to another newspaper.

On this particular Saturday when I opened my door there, waiting for me, camera poised, were a photographer and a journalist. As a flash went off in my face, I slammed the door shut. Then, as the doorbell rang again, I said, through the letter box, 'What do you want?'

'We have a picture of you in a compromising situation,' was the reply. 'And we'd like to talk to you about it.'

Having stood a moment, allowing all the recent events of my life to flash before my eyes, I decided it was safe for me to open the door. 'What on earth are you talking about?' I asked.

'We have a photograph of you with a man – on a bed.'

'Really?' My immediate concern was that I never look my best when I'm lying down. 'Does my face look fat in the picture?' I asked.

This was not the response the journalist had expected. 'Is that *all* you're worried about?' he said.

'Well, yes, actually,' I replied.

'Well, it's a very telling picture,' he growled.

'Then show it to me,' I said.

'*No!* Well, certainly not before you've talked to us about the man you're in bed with.'

'I haven't a clue who that could be,' I said, genuinely nonplussed. 'And if you're not going to show me the picture, go away. Shoo.'

'All right. I'll tell you what it's about,' the journalist said. 'It's a picture of you on a bed with a man, in a shop, in Tottenham Court Road.'

Having done a quick recap, I suddenly realized what he was on about. The day before when I was walking up Tottenham Court Road with Alistair, I'd spotted a bed in the window of a shop called Dreams. 'That's just what I need for the new house,' I'd said. 'Come on, Alistair, let's go and try it out for size.' Once inside, completely oblivious that we were being photographed by a paparazzo positioned across the road, we did what everybody does when buying a bed – we lay down on it and bounced up and down on the mattress.

'You can print *that* photograph,' I said to the journalist. 'The man's Alistair Divall, a really good friend of mine. He's not gay and I'm sure he *and* his girlfriend will be delighted to give you a quote.'

The story they'd obviously hoped to print was, 'Dale has a new house; this is Dale's friend. They're trying out the bed together; they must be going to share it.' However, they went ahead anyway. The next day, the heading alongside the photographs of Alistair and me fully clothed on the bed, read DALE AND MATE TRY SUPER BED, followed by, *Dale Winton, the camp host of TV's* Supermarket Sweep, *set bedsprings rocking when he shared a mattress with fellow game show host and self-confessed sex stud Alistair Divall. Bachelor boy Dale and Alistair were spotted bouncing on the bed fit for a queen in a London shop but walked out without buying it.*

I think the *People's* readers saw through that one!

Within the last six months there have been odd occasions when I've been doorstepped and photographed. This usually happens when there isn't much news going on and all they want is an unusual picture of someone off the TV, perhaps not looking their best or, even better, with someone they shouldn't be with. It doesn't seem to matter where in the world you are either. In January of this year I was holidaying in Barbados with my friend, Merrill, and on one of the days her daughter, Saskia, and I walked along the beach together. Unbeknown to us we were being photographed and within three days the *Daily Mirror* published the photos with the caption, DALE WITH WOMAN! It did make me laugh, as did my agent, Jan, when, on another occasion I was being followed by a furtive-looking photographer with a zoom lens. This went on for days and in the end curiosity got the better of me and Jan rang the paper in question to ask why I was being followed around. They replied that they had heard that a woman had moved in with me and that we were having a raging affair. Lord only knows where these rumours come from.

When, after so many years of wishin' and hopin', you suddenly find yourself in demand, part of you is still afraid that it's a ten-day wonder, a flash in the pan, and that any moment now your number won't come up any more. But overnight in January 1996, my column inches in the press turned into column yards when I won the lottery – not the pound-a-dream millions, but the wonderful job of hosting *The National Lottery*. Anthea Turner, the Lotto Queen, who'd achieved super-star status since she left *Blue Peter* to take over the show, was off for two weeks, working downunder in Australia for GMTV, and I'd been asked to stand in for her on a night when the roll-over jackpot was a whopping £23 million. The celebrity guest, who was going to release the balls, was American rocker, Meatloaf. With lottery fever gripping the country as millions of punters went wild in the aisles for their record-breaking 'It-could-be-*you*' tickets, there could not have been a better time for it to be *me* hosting the show. My lottery-winsome face was everywhere. I couldn't pick up a paper or magazine without reading about my big win in the job stakes. By then I was used to seeing snippets about me in the tabloids, but imagine my astonishment when I saw a write-up by Nigel Farndale in the *Sunday Telegraph* magazine of all things, being very supportive and calling me a cult hero. I found such high praise in a quality broadsheet quite extraordinary.

*The National Lottery* was a dream come true. Having hosted the show when ticket sales reached a record-breaking £86.7 million the first week, and the £23 million jackpot rolled over again to a £45 million whopper the second, I was invited back to host the show again. Then, when Anthea signed an exclusive deal with ITV, I was lucky enough to get her job. Since then I've hosted the show more times than I can remember on both Wednesdays and Saturdays. I love doing it so much that if I'd been asked to choose between winning the lottery itself or the job of hosting it, I'd have chosen the job. And I wouldn't for the world have missed meeting Lynda Wood, the costume designer, who had worked for Anthea Turner, Michael Parkinson, Esther Rantzen and Clive James. Since those days Lynda has become such a close friend that I almost share her with her husband and her children. She's very dear to me and has seen me through many highs and lows.

One of our most surreal times together was when we found ourselves shopping for clothes in the very stylish Thierry Mugler shop in London's Bond Street. This was a first for me because I'm usually a Hugo Boss or Kenzo kind of guy who wears nothing too tight or fitted, but because I was unhappy in love at the time, weight had fallen off me and I was pencil-thin and able to get into Thierry

Mugler's trendy clothes. The downside was that physically I was feeling very weak, and while we were in the shop I suddenly started to feel very giddy and had a terrible nosebleed. While I was standing there dabbing myself with tissues, the assistants began to exchange knowing looks. I remember wanting to say to them, 'Stop looking at me as if I've got some sort of substance problem! *Nothing* could be further from the truth. The reality is that my heart's just been broken, I haven't been able to force any food down me for days, and if I don't leave this shop and get some fresh air I think I'll pass out.'

Lynda was brilliant and immediately propelled me through the door. So there we were, standing in the middle of Bond Street, with her saying, 'Right, Dale! No arguments. You're going to eat something and, what's more, you are going to eat it right now.'

What *is* bizarre is that I then found myself sitting in Fenwick's department store being force-fed a cheese-and-ham toasted sandwich while the cream of Bond Street shoppers kept stopping by my table to say how fit I was looking and complimenting me on my weight loss. Since then, whenever I've gained a few pounds, I think what I really need to sort out my waistline is a good dollop of emotional heartbreak. That works for me every time.

Where image is concerned, the press then turned its hawk-eyed attention to why, aged forty, I was *so* wrinkle-free. Far from denying I was the kind of bloke who enjoyed being plucked and tweezed for the sake of my looks, I was only too happy to lift the lid on my beauty tips. Here I was, forty years old and new to a business in which 'young, young, young' is all you ever hear. This, believe me, is an industry that eats its elders. I would have loved to have been born with chiselled good looks and be the kind of guy who could leap out of bed in the morning, tousle-haired, and look amazing, but I wasn't, so I was prepared to work harder at looking my best. When in the mid-Nineties, I found myself listed alongside stars such as Barbara Windsor, Anthea Turner, Mandy Smith and Princess Diana, who, like me, went in for regular CACIs – non-surgical facelifts – I wasn't in the least put out. I've always been perfectly happy to be open about my non-surgical facelifts which I've had done at a clinic in

Hampstead for the last five years. The computer-aided cosmetology instrument, which lifts muscles, was originally developed to aid people with sports injuries when they were unable to exercise, but the practitioners realized that if you could use this system for rebuilding injured muscles, you could also use it cosmetically. When I had my first treatment they did half my face and then handed me a mirror so that I could see the change. The difference was extraordinary. I then had about eight sessions, followed by a maintenance course, and it really did tighten the muscles of my face. Having said that, I always knew that nothing beats the knife and that, in addition to the nose job I'd had done when I was twenty-two (the very one that Cilla had outed on radio when she spotted Percy Jay's handiwork), I would have some more cosmetic surgery done when the time was right.

I appreciate that some people say you shouldn't change what God has given you – that you're meant to be that way – but my answer is, 'He didn't give us clothes either, but we don't walk about naked!' Cosmetic surgery is extreme, but I embrace the science whole-heartedly. If you turn on the TV any day of the week, you'll find more than one programme talking about make-up, diets and ways to improve your looks. Fascinated as the press are by this, it only seems to be a reflection of the public's obsession. Whether reading magazines or watching a well-known face on the TV, the eye sees everything and we're all very quick to comment on whether this person's looking younger, or that person's let themselves go. Most people seem to have a preoccupation with self-image and I'm not alone in this. I come from an old show business tradition which adheres to the sentiment that if you're in the public eye, it's your duty to give the public what they want and present yourself as best you can. As far as I'm concerned I'm a product and it's up to me to present this package in its most palatable form. I really believe that looking smart, clean and well turned-out is what the public expect and is part of the job.

Age has no fear for me, but it seems to me that if an artiste is to prolong his time in the light, it doesn't half help if, whichever way you can, you hold back a few years. We've all seen how American stars have been nipped, tucked and pulled to within an inch of looking like someone from another planet. This is not good, but if a little help – whether it's an electronically non-surgical facelift, or going under the knife – can help to boost your confidence, improve your appearance and keep you looking young, that's fine by me.

The most extraordinary thing about my two experiences under the surgeon's knife – the nose job in 1977 and the face lift in 2001 – is that both nearly resulted in post-operative disasters that could have ended my career on screen. The first, the nose job, came about because when I was a DJ, working for UBN and on the club circuit, I often had to have photographs taken to accompany articles about me in UBN's *Biscuit Weekly* and for posters promoting the clubs. And whenever I looked at these pics, I was aware that my nose, which I had inherited from Dad, presented a problem. It was too big and it dominated every shot of me. Mum, who had had a nose job herself in 1962, was always very aware of this and often said to me, 'One day, Dale, you should have your nose done, too.' A typical guy, though, I was always laissez-faire about this. But, about a year before Mum died, she asked me to go with her when she was having a facelift consultation with Percy Jay, the Harley Street cosmetic surgeon who had given her such a perfect nose that nobody but Dad and I had ever realized that she'd had it done. Whether her consultation was a ruse to get me to see Percy Jay I will never know. Mum certainly didn't need a facelift and, while I was waiting for her in reception, Percy Jay apparently said, 'Sheree, you don't need anything doing at the moment. You're far too young. Come back and see me in about fifteen years' time.'

'Fair enough,' Mum replied, 'but while I'm here, Percy, will you have a look at my boy? He's waiting for me in your reception and he *really* does need a nose job.'

So, unexpectedly, I found myself being taken in to see Percy Jay, who was known as the nose man because his nose jobs were second to none. A very distinguished, silver-haired man, he looked like a slimmed-down version of the actor, James Robertson Justice, who was so brilliant in the *Doctor* films in the late 1950s and early 1960s. Having looked at my nose, he said, 'Oh, yes! We can certainly improve on this. We can make this a lot better.'

As we came out of his consulting room Mum said, 'What do you think, Dale?'

'Well . . . yes, fine,' I mumbled.

'When you feel ready, you can have that done,' she said, obviously pleased.

I resisted it at that time and no more was said. But a year after Mum died, by which time I had had some more photos taken, I saw my nose again and thought, 'D'you know, Mum was right.' Then, on the spur of the moment, I telephoned Percy Jay. He remembered Mum, was so sorry to hear that she had died and said he would be delighted to perform my operation. The only drawback was that he was very busy and had a six-month waiting list. I was *so* disappointed. These are the kind of decisions you need to act upon at once and, having psyched myself up to have it done, I wanted the operation there and then.

About two weeks later, though, I got lucky. I had a phone call from Percy Jay's office, saying he had had a cancellation. 'If you can come in this evening,' his secretary said, 'Mr Jay will do the operation tomorrow.'

'Yes!' I said. (Great thing to be decisive!)

I rang United Biscuits and said to Alan King, my boss, 'Alan, can I have a couple of weeks off? I've got to have a nose job.'

He was so stunned, he just said, 'Yes.'

So in I went to the London Clinic, where I was told that the bed I was about to occupy had been vacated by someone very famous who had decided not to go ahead with the operation. Once settled into my room, silently having hysterics that I could come out with a little *retroussé* Faye Dunaway nose, I pinned photos on my pyjama jacket of famous stars who had noses I admired. Included among these were Dirk Bogarde, Paul Newman and Sean Connery. 'I'm a big guy with a big face,' I kept thinking, 'he's got to get this right the first time because once the bone of your nose is broken, the operation is irreversible. You can't just change your mind and go back to what you had before.'

The next day I remember feeling very happy after I was given my pre-med and I kept pointing at all the faces on my pyjamas, muttering one of Mum's favourite expressions, 'Less is more, less is more . . .' The surgeon must have taken one look at me lying on the table, and thought, 'I'm a surgeon *not* a magician.' But in my state of pre-med, I just thought I was going to emerge from it all looking like Adonis.

When I came to I had this enormous plaster cast on my nose, which I was told I would have to live with for ten days before attending the clinic to have the plaster removed. It was *so* frustrating because I was absolutely desperate to find out what the nose would look like. Once home, I thought, 'What I will need after the clinic visit is time to recuperate.' So I got on to my old schoolfriend, Lawrence Moore, a close friend to this day, and said, 'Lawrence, d'you fancy two weeks in Majorca?'

His usual obliging self, he replied, 'Absolutely, Dale.' He was up for it, I was up for it, so off I went and booked it.

On the appointed day, I drove with great glee to the London Clinic. I felt the plaster come off, felt Percy Jay dab the nose with spirit to remove all the residue, then heard him say with a sigh of satisfaction, 'You look very handsome, Dale. I'm *very* pleased with the nose. You may look at it now in the mirror on the wall.'

When I did I was horrified. I hadn't anticipated quite so much swelling and, that aside, I wasn't at all sure that I liked the shape of my new nose. My previous one had somehow defined the character of my face and I didn't recognize the new visage that was looking back at me. Rendered speechless, I felt really emotional. All I remember is backing out of the door saying, 'Thank you, thank you' to Percy Jay and then sitting in my car outside weeping for an hour, and muttering, 'What have I *done* to myself?'

It was just as well that I didn't know then that it would be at least six months before my face settled down and I would feel the benefit of Percy's handiwork. But by then I realized it was the best thing I could have done. Percy had done me proud and had given me exactly what I wanted.

After the clinic visit, Lawrence and I had a great holiday in Palma. The sun was shining, my spirits lifted and we decided to rent two scooters to explore the island. In those days there was no legislation about wearing crash helmets and some of the scooters were not very roadworthy. Having seen a sign for Andraix, a delightful harbour town on the other side of the island, we set off. I've always been a bit of a boy racer – cars, motorbikes, I love them. But as I was flying along on this particular scooter down the motorway, its throttle suddenly jammed and I couldn't stop the wretched thing.

As I overtook Lawrence he waved, thinking I was just being a daredevil, but I was panicking like crazy. 'I'm going to crash,' I kept telling myself, 'I've just spent a small fortune on nasal reconstruction and now Percy Jay's handiwork is going to hit a chalk wall and be ruined!'

With one hand still desperately trying to release the throttle, I used my other to clutch on to my nose for dear life. 'If I'm going to be smashed to bits and put in the ground,' I was thinking, 'at least they'll say, "the nose was sensational".' Fortunately, just before this became a reality, I managed to release the throttle and slow the scooter down. When it finally came to a halt and I met up with Lawrence again, I said, 'I'm not getting back on that thing. I'm going to get a cab back.' I really was in a terrible state.

You would think after this experience I would have opted for recuperating at home after my second experience under the surgeon's knife but no, I did not! At the beginning of 2001, when I was having coffee with my dear friend, Merrill Thomas, we began to talk about cosmetic surgery and how in order for this to be really successful it was necessary to have a little done often. Although I was worried about making any drastic changes to my appearance, I was also aware that my face was beginning to look a bit heavy and my eyes were a bit baggy. Anybody who has worked with me on a show knows that I need to have the cameras way up high because I've always thought that I had a bit of a turkey neck and a double chin. Friends constantly reassure me that this isn't so – but I'm not convinced. Television reveals everything and I was just at the stage where if I had waited longer for the operation I would have needed to have a lot done, whereas if I did it now I would probably get another five to ten years out of it before I needed to go again. Given a different career, I would much rather have grown old gracefully but, as I was in a young man's industry, I decided the time had now come. Merrill, ever her supportive lovely self, then told me that she had heard about a world-eminent cosmetic surgeon in Switzerland. Named Dr Michel Pfulg, he had a clinic in Fribourg, Switzerland. (These days his clinic is in Montreux.) 'I've seen his work,' Merrill said, 'and he's a really great cosmetic surgeon. In fact, I'd quite like to have my lower eyelids done by him.'

'Oh?' I said. 'Well, I'd like to get my double chin done and my face lifted.'

So there and then, we both decided that when I finished recording *The Other Half* in the early summer, we would take the plunge. When Merrill then mentioned she'd heard that Dr Pfulg was going to be in London the following week at No. 1 Aldwych, I said, 'OK, let's go for it. Let's book our consultations.'

Keeping young and looking good, without looking ridiculous, was what was on my mind, and I considered that a facelift would be a good investment in myself and in my future. Reassured by what Merrill had said, I felt that Dr Pfulg was the right man for the job and I couldn't be in safer hands. The fact that his clinic was in Switzerland was a plus. I didn't want to have the work done in England and risk being photographed coming out of a clinic when I was not looking my best.

The following week, Merrill and I went to see Dr Michel Pfulg at his London hotel. When I went up to his room he looked at me, tugged at my face here and there, and then said he would be happy to do the operation.

'I don't want my eyes done,' I said, 'just my face and my double chin lifted.'

'Dale,' he responded, 'I think your upper eyes need doing as well.'

Convinced by then that he was a man I could trust, I said, 'OK, I'll have my eyes done as well.'

The plan that was hatched then was that Merrill would have her eyes done on 10 July and I would have my surgery done on 12 July. (But, luckily from a professional point of view, I was able to change my appointment to 5 July.) After the operations Merrill and I would then convalesce by spending a few days at Vevey on Lake Geneva and stay at Le Mirador for a further two weeks until our stitches were due to come out. So off I flew to Switzerland, knowing that the only people who knew what I was up to were Merrill, my agent and my dear friend Mark.

'This is *so* you, Dale,' Mark said. 'Something's bound to happen. I wonder what it'll be?'

How well Mark knew me! Something extraordinary was in store, but my only concern as I flew off to Geneva was that I would be OK in time for the filming of *TV's Best Ever Soap Moments*. From Geneva I took the train to Fribourg, where I checked into the pension, and by five o'clock that day I was sitting in Michel's office, beginning to feel very nervous.

'No food, cigarettes or alcohol after eight o'clock tonight,' he said. 'But you can have tea, coffee and water.'

Although the no-alcohol rule wasn't a problem for me, the ban on cigarettes certainly was. '*Please* don't make me look taut and pulled. Just a *little* lift,' I asked demurely.

'Trust me, it'll be fine,' he replied. 'I'll see you tomorrow morning at eight o'clock for the surgery.'

So there I was, alone, in this small Swiss town of Fribourg on a lovely summer's evening. Having walked through the town, I stopped for coffee at a café. My mobile phone was on the table in front of me and I kept looking at it wistfully. With the exception of the few who knew what I was doing, I couldn't call anyone for a chat, because they'd ask where I was. Being a true Gemini, I was having second thoughts, wondering if I was doing the right thing and I wanted to ask everybody's opinion a dozen times, but there was no turning back now. Then, just at that moment, would you believe it, Dr Pfulg walked by on his way home and caught me red-handed with a cigarette *and* a cup of coffee. My acute embarrassment and feelings of guilt were only exceeded by my growing fear and apprehension about going ahead with the operation at all.

'Michel,' I said nervously, as he sat down beside me, 'do people ever change their minds and chicken out at the last minute?' (I was obviously feeling very vulnerable at this point, especially as Merrill was not due to arrive for another week.)

'No,' he said, 'it's very rare for people to do that.'

'What's the main reason they do?' I pressed.

'Fear of the anaesthetic,' he replied.

'Oh, God!' I thought, 'I haven't even thought about that. Now there's something else for me to worry about.' 'Why the anaesthetic?' I asked.

'Well, sometimes they worry that they will not come round afterwards.'

'Oh, God!' I thought again. 'That's never even occurred to me.'

But Dr Pfulg was so laid back. He had a beer, I had another cigarette. Promising that this would be my last and fearful that it might be, I took myself back to my hotel.

Next morning I took a taxi up to the clinic where I was introduced to the anaesthetist and prepared for the operation. The next thing I knew was that I was being told that the operation was over and I could go back to my bedroom. Once in there, I was told to lie very still, not to move my head too much, and *not* to talk on the mobile phone. One of my problems, though, is that anything that's put into my system has an immediate and strong effect on me, and on this occasion the anaesthetic had sent me into the depths of depression and my mind was not quite functioning as it should have been. I have often used the term 'tired and emotional' about other people, but this time it was me who was tired and emotional and who needed to let off steam. In spite of what I'd been told, I rang a very close friend in England and for no reason whatsoever blasted him out of the water. I was absolutely vile to him, then, having got all the vitriol off my chest, I was filled with remorse and started to sob uncontrollably. Within fifteen minutes, I'd run the whole gamut of emotions from bolshy aggressor to a vulnerable weeping mess. My friend was a diamond, took it all on the chin and didn't say anything unkind. Then I zonked out. Five hours later I came to, filled with the horror of this dreadful phone conversation. At this point I didn't care that I had just had a major operation and had stitches running from under my chin to my ear – stitches everywhere. All I wanted to do was to put right my earlier phone call. I rang my friend again and said, 'I'm so sorry I was so venomous and rude to you. Please understand I didn't mean a word of it.'

'I don't know what you're talking about,' he said, making it clear that he understood that anaesthetics can play strange tricks on the mind. 'You must have dreamt the conversation, Dale.'

I knew there and then that he was just being kind and thoughtful, and I will always be grateful to him for that.

The next morning, Merrill rang the clinic to check that I was all right and, after a conversation with her, I was driven to Le Mirador Hotel on Lake Geneva, a beautiful, forty-minute journey from Fribourg. Having asked the driver of the car to stop at a chemist just outside Vevey, I went in to get everything on the surgeon's prescription. My face was stitched, plastered, swollen and looked very strange, but I felt great and wasn't in any pain. As I gave the prescription for the ointment, plasters and ice packs to the chemist, he looked at me very sympathetically and said, 'Car crash, was it?'

Looking at him aghast, I thought, 'How bad must I look?' There I was, in the middle of nowhere, in a little Swiss village, with a pharmacist who obviously thought I'd been in a head-on collision with a lorry. 'Maybe,' I thought, 'this wasn't such a great idea after all.'

Le Mirador, a very large hotel, is cut into the mountainside overlooking Vevey and Lake Geneva, with stunning panoramic views of the lake, the Alps and the Swiss Riviera. In the distance I could see Montreux. It also had a superb restaurant and all the facilities one could possibly need, and I spent the next five days there enjoying room service and watching television and DVDs. When I went back to Fribourg to have some of the very fine stitches taken out (the others had to remain in place for another two weeks) I collected

Merrill who, in the meantime, had had her lower eyelids done, and we then went back to Le Mirador together. Merrill was in one wing of the hotel, I was in the other. We both had very swollen faces and spent a lot of time looking in mirrors, waiting for the swelling to go down and wondering what the effect was going to be.

Initially, because of the stitches, which ran from underneath my chin, around the back of my ears and above my eyes, I found it very difficult to sleep, but at least the cool mountain air was soothing. But one morning, at about four thirty, I was suddenly awakened from my sleep by a loud crashing sound. Sitting up in bed, I looked out of the window expecting to see the night sky, stars and the mountains. But instead I saw a very ominous, bright-orange glow.

Leaping out of bed, I went over to the balcony door and, to my horror, saw that the awning over my balcony and the one next door had caught fire and the whole area was alight. The heat of the fire was so intense that it had caused the metal frame, which supported the awning, to crash down on to the balcony and it was this that had awakened me. I had never been so terrified in all my life. Sparks from the balcony fire had come into my room, and suddenly the place was a mass of flames and, coughing from the smoke, I rushed out, still in my T-shirt and boxers, and started banging on the adjoining doors, yelling, '*Fire, fire! Wake up, wake up!*' I then rang the fire alarm and members of staff started to appear with fire extinguishers, directing the guests away from the corridor. Within minutes, the local firemen arrived with hoses, traipsed through my room and extinguished the flames. I was in shock, realizing that if the awning had not crashed down with such a loud bang, I could have died from smoke inhalation.

Picture the scene: just off the operating table and into convalescence, and now staggering about the hotel in the middle of the night, my face full of stitches and dressed only in my T-shirt and boxers. It was too surreal for words. 'If I *had* had to go to hospital,' I thought, 'and the press had heard about it and photographed me with all the stitches around my face, I would never have heard the last of it.'

Fortunately, the fire, which had started on the balcony next to my room, then spread to my awning and two adjoining ones, was put out before it caused any more damage. But everything in my room was blackened by smoke and soot, and I had to be relocated to another room in the hotel. To this day, I can recall the smell of burning. When I showed Merrill my fire-blackened room the next morning, she burst into tears. Apart from her obvious concern for me, it was a particularly traumatic moment for her. In 1990 she had been involved in a hotel fire while on a press junket to Cairo; and, by extraordinary coincidence, the flames that had spread through the Egyptian hotel had also started when an awning had caught fire. Merrill, who was in the hotel's restaurant at the time, had managed to crawl on all fours to the nearest exit but, tragically, three of the press party had died. When she telephoned me from a Cairo hospital to tell me that the accident would be reported on the news and asked me to let her children know that she was OK, her voice had sounded dreadfully hoarse and she was obviously suffering from serious smoke inhalation. The whole incident, I later heard, had been made so much worse because, although the fire brigade had been called at once, their fire engines were too large to pass down the tree-lined avenue to the hotel's entrance.

As a result of this traumatic experience, whenever Merrill checks into a hotel room these days, she always looks for a fire exit before she goes to bed and keeps a large handkerchief on the bedside table so that, if there is a fire, she can dampen it and cover her face with it. Now, after the Switzerland incident, I, too, check out fire exits in hotels and I always try to get a room on one of the lower floors.

When I'm being interviewed, I'm often asked what my most treasured possessions are. All I can say is that on the night of the hotel fire in Switzerland, the only things I picked up were my mobile phone, so that I could keep cherished text messages, and three rings that had been given to me by someone very special in my life.

There are two postscripts to the Swiss idyll . . .

About four days after our surgery Merrill's daughter, Saskia, flew out to join us for a few days' holiday. By this stage, although Merrill and I were still very swollen, we thought we were looking *tons* better.

In reality, though, we were just psyching each other up and trying to think positively. So when, wearing dark glasses and baseball caps, we went to collect Saskia, we made a flamboyant entrance, saying, 'Don't we look fabulous, don't we look great!' Saskia, though, took one look at us, her chin started to quiver and she said, 'You both look *horrible!*' and burst into tears. Months later she also said, 'There you were, both so pleased with yourselves, and you had no idea of the state you were in!'

On my arrival back in London I wanted to go and support Martine McCutcheon on the opening night of *My Fair Lady*, but I knew it was a bit too early for me to be doing this. My face was still swollen and my eyes hadn't settled down yet. When I think about it now, I realize it wasn't the most sensible thing for me to do. Two days after the *My Fair Lady* outing, the *Sun* carried a big before-and-after picture of me headlined, WHO'S HAD A SUPERMARKET TWEAK, DALE? These days I don't mind that sort of coverage, but at that time, just a couple of weeks before I was due to start filming *TV's Best Ever Soap Moments*, I kept very quiet on the whole issue.

The second PS to the Swiss idyll concerns yet another drama. I'd literally only just returned to London when I had a call from Saskia in Switzerland. Merrill, who had stayed on in Geneva to spend a few days' holiday with her parents, had slipped and fallen on the day she was to collect them from the airport and she was now back in hospital with a huge gash on her head. Poor Merrill, having just shed one lot of stitches around her eyes, now had a second lot to contend with on her head. I wanted to fly back to her side straight away, but she insisted she was fine and would be home as soon as she was mended.

Despite all the dramas, I'm proud of the fact that I had the nerve to go through with the cosmetic surgery. Michel Pfulg did a good job and I was pleased with the results. For me, it's not just a vanity thing. I consider it part of my job to look as good as I can for as long as I can on TV, and if that means a little help along the way, then why not? The secret is to get it done before other people start saying, 'Oh! Isn't Dale looking old.'

*

Now I will return to the mid-Nineties. While, thanks to my non-surgical facelift, the eyes of the press were trained on my missing wrinkles and on the hope that one day they'd catch me out with my other half, I was preoccupied with *The Other Half*, a new prime-time TV series for me. This came about because, halfway through recording the second series of *Pets Win Prizes*, I was taken out to lunch by Mike Leggo, the BBC's Head of Entertainment, who had a new idea up his sleeve. In my view, any format that you can explain in a couple of sentences, such as 'Here's Jane and here are four guys, which one's her other half?' is excellent. And that's what this idea proved to be. I thoroughly enjoyed hosting these shows, but I was very glad I wasn't one of the contestants who had to use their powers of observation and deduction to guess the identity of their opponents' partners. I get people's relationships wrong every time. Once when I was in a bar with some friends, I spent ages talking to what I thought was a couple, only to find out at the end of the evening that they were brother and sister!

Among the key questions to help our contestants get it right were: 'What secret from your partner's past would they hate to have revealed? What does your partner think is their greatest talent? If your partner could have a day out with someone famous, who would it be? What's the most embarrassing thing your partner has ever said or done in front of your parents? If you compared your partner to a wild animal, what would it be and why?' There was also a kissing round when one man was kissed by four girls to establish whether body language would give the game away, or whether a quick peck on the cheek was more a sign of true partnership than a passionate kiss. And sometimes we did celebrity specials, which tended to be transmitted at Christmas or Bank Holidays, when the contestants had to guess the famous couples' other half. For the show I was also filmed touring the houses that the real-life couple shared, so that the contestants could pick up some more helpful clues. These journeys took me the length and breadth of the UK from Dundee to Devon and also the jet resort of Puerto Banus, near Marbella. What more could I ask?

From my point of view, the beauty of *The Other Half* was that it was a really good, simple show that served me brilliantly well over five series and never let me down as a ratings winner. To get two series out of a show is wonderful, to get three is a blessing, but to get five is an absolute bonus. There are, of course, classic game shows that run for ever, but new shows only tend to get two or three series. We had five, which made me a very happy man and it is still a show that could – and probably will – be revisited.

The TV critics weren't sure about *The Other Half*, but it proved to be another hit with the viewers and, as an unexpected plus, it brought Cilla back into my life. This occurred because, in between recording the shows, I found myself sitting in for Lorraine Kelly for a week on *GMTV*. 'Great,' I thought, 'I'll ask Cilla to be on the show.' When I rang her office, though, I was in for a disappointment. Robert, her son, told me that Cilla and Bobby were in Spain for a couple of weeks, staying at their villa in Marbella, and that Cilla wouldn't be back in time to do the show.

'Oh, that's extraordinary,' I said, 'I'm going to be in Marbella next week filming a British couple for my series, *The Other Half*.'

'Well, if you have any spare time, why don't you get together there?' Robert said.

When I rang Cilla and Bobby, they couldn't have been more friendly and pleased to hear from me. 'Come and have lunch with us,' Cilla said, sounding very relaxed and on great form.

And, no sooner said than done, she and Bobby came to collect me from my hotel and took me to their gorgeous villa just outside Marbella.

I *adored* being with them. I couldn't have felt more at home sitting on their patio, chatting to Bobby while Cilla rustled up the most fantastic lunch and, from that moment, we all became friends who went out as a threesome. These days, along with Paul O'Grady, aka Lily Savage, and Christopher Biggins, I'm proud to be a member of what the press loves to call 'The Cilla Mafia'. She really is a very special person and, since Bobby died in 1999, we speak all the time on the phone and go out together at least once a week. She was so brave when she lost Bobby. It would have been so easy for her to go to pieces and withdraw behind closed doors but, heartbroken though she was, she said, 'I may have lost the love of my life, but I haven't lost my love of life.' That's so Cilla – and, along with all her other friends, I'm really looking forward to celebrating her four decades in showbiz in 2003.

One Cilla story I can't resist writing up now is the time she phoned me and said, 'When you get to the end of your work schedule, Dale, why don't you come and join me in Marbella for a week, then we can fly back together?'

On this occasion she was there with Paul O'Grady and they had both received an invitation to attend Cliff Richard's sixtieth birthday party on board a yacht in Nice. In order to do that, they discovered, they would have to fly from Malaga to Nice. As that journey involved two flight changes, they decided to go by helicopter. On the day, however, the weather conditions were so bad and the visibility was so poor that Cilla decided it was too dangerous and sent a telegram to Cliff, saying that she and Paul were very disappointed but they were unable to get to Nice. That should have been the end of that sad story but, as it involved Cilla, there was a surprise surprise ending in store. As we walked into the VIP lounge at Malaga airport for our return journey to London, we suddenly came face to face with Cliff, plus some of his birthday party guests – former members of The Shadows, Gloria Hunniford, Bobby Davro, Olivia Newton-John – all of whom were also returning to London or going on to other destinations.

'*Cilla*!' Cliff said. 'Why didn't you come to my birthday party? I had a stateroom on the yacht all ready for you. What happened? Where were you?'

Poor Cilla could not have been more embarrassed when she learned that her telegram had never reached its destination and that her stateroom had been left unoccupied. As I stood watching Cliff talking to her in the VIP lounge, while Cilla was eating the piece of birthday cake he had given her, I thought, 'No wonder these two people are stars. They both have that indefinable X factor that, even when they're not on stage, just makes them stand out in a crowd.' I have to say, too, that I could only marvel at Cliff's eternal youth. He looked absolutely incredible that day.

Fortunately, when we celebrated Barbara Windsor's sixtieth birthday in 1997, there were no transport problems or adverse weather conditions to contend with. It was held at the Belvedere restaurant, Holland Park. One of the lovely things about Barbara, whom I call Bar but Cilla and many others call Babs, is that she is never judgemental and doesn't have a snobbish bone in her body. Both her past life and present life friends were at the party. I had a great time meeting almost the entire cast of *EastEnders*, then found myself in the midst of some true East Enders, with names that had been made household legends by crime-writers in the 1960s. At one moment I was grabbed by Tony Lambrianou, who said in exactly the kind of gruff voice I'd expected him to have, 'Hello, Dale. I'm taking you to meet the Governor.'

'Who's the Governor?' I asked. (As far as I was concerned *that* was my hostess, Barbara!)

'Freddie Foreman,' he replied, adding, 'Don't forget, Dale, he's the Governor. *Respect.*'

As he propelled me through the room packed full of Barbara's family and her friends from all walks of life, I didn't know quite what to expect. But there and then, I tuned into the fascination that exists between the East End fraternity and show business people. Say what you will, and I always speak as I find, Freddie Foreman and Tony Lambrianou could not have been more charming to me, and on subsequent occasions when I've bumped into them this has remained true.


Leaving an agent, as I mentioned once before, is the most difficult thing for an artiste to do. I had had a very successful run with Nick Ranceford-Hadley at Noel Gay Artists but by 1997, as one of the first people on Nick's list to break through into prime-time television, a number of highly respected people in the business kept saying, 'Dale, you should think about being with a different agent now,' and the name that kept cropping up was Jan Kennedy of Billy Marsh Associates, who had a number of top prime-time performers on her books, including Bruce Forsyth, Rolf Harris and even the ongoing estates of the legendary Morcambe and Wise. For a Gemini, who loves to procrastinate, this was not an easy decision for me to make. Nick and I had always got on very well, and I had even introduced him to the lady who became his wife – Pamela Spur, a beautiful blonde Californian psychologist, who was a good friend of mine. Nothing specific had happened to make me want to leave Nick but, in my heart of hearts, I sort of agreed that I needed a fresh pair of eyes on my career, and the more Jan Kennedy's name was mentioned, the more I began to feel that perhaps it was time for a change. One day in the middle of recording another series of *Supermarket Sweep*, someone at Central suggested that I should give Jan a call and introduce myself. By this time, series three, I was doing five shows a day, equalling eighty-five shows in all, over a fourteen-week period. My regular routine was to leave Nottingham on Friday nights at nine to return to London, and then spend Saturdays and Sundays recouping my energies for the next week's onslaught of twenty-five more shows for *Supermarket Sweep*.

When I got hold of Jan and said I would like to meet up, she replied, 'Right. Why don't I take you out to lunch on Sunday?'

The moment I met her I thought, 'She's fabulous.' She was totally on my wavelength and I could see that, as well as being a very chic and tenacious businesswoman, she had a big heart and, even more important, having been on the stage as a singer and dancer working in her early years with all the major names of her time before becoming an agent, she clearly understood artistes.

'The first thing you will need to do if you *do* decide that you want to come to me,' she said, 'is to ask your lawyer to check your contract with the Noel Gay agency.'

'I must have it somewhere,' I replied. 'But, to be honest, Jan, I haven't seen it since I signed it.'

'Well, you will need to find it,' she said with all the finely tuned persistence of someone obviously well used to dealing with powerful people.

I left the restaurant thinking, 'That lady is sensational, a one-woman tour de force, and I'd love to have her as my agent.'

When I telephoned Dean Jones at Talbot Fremantle, he confirmed my decision. 'Jan Kennedy is one of the best agents in the business,' he said. 'And even though I know it will now cost our production company much more next time we negotiate *Supermarket Sweep*, I have to admit she'd be perfect for you.'

By the time Mark came to see me later that afternoon, the finding of my contract with the Noel Gay agency had become an obsession. Having helped me to hunt high and low for it without any success, Mark, bless him, then volunteered to go up into the loft. Five minutes later I heard a shout of glee. He'd found it. Like most contracts, though, it proved almost impossible for us to make head or tail of it. What did become clear, however, as we sat poring over it was that, according to the dates, it was actually due to expire in two days' time and, unless I gave notice at once, it would automatically run on for another three years.

'God,' I thought, 'what incredible timing! If I'd postponed my lunch with Jan until after I finished the current series of *Supermarket Sweep*, it would have been too late for me to make a change.'

That evening I sent the contract by taxi to my lawyer.

First thing the next morning, just before I was due to leave for Nottingham, he phoned me and said, 'If you want Jan Kennedy to represent you, Dale, you will have to give notice to your present agent right now. You are within twenty-four hours of being locked in.'

That was difficult.

'What am I doing?' I kept thinking. 'This is the last thing I need just before recording another twenty-five shows for *Supermarket Sweep*. And Nick's been brilliant . . . How can I fire him just like that without any warning?' But if I wanted Jan to represent me I *had* to do it.

What I hated most was when the lawyer then told me that I must do it by letter, because this was a decision that had to be confirmed in writing. This seemed an awful thing to do to a person who was my friend, as well as my agent, but I just had to bite the bullet and get on with it. Only time will tell if I can ever repair my lost friendship with Nick and Pam.

Meanwhile, Jan has proved to be a brilliant agent for me. I love her like a sister. She's the perfect diplomat, a wonderful negotiator and an absolute master of her craft when it comes to the setting up of contracts. Brinkmanship, which plays a very large part in any business deal, has never been one of my strong points. I can't bear to think about the money side of a proposal. It's the job rather than the cash that matters to me. '*Don't* blow it, Jan,' I mutter under my breath. '*Don't* blow it. I *want* this one!'

But I have no need to worry. Brinkmanship is one of Jan's greatest talents, and I'm always the first to agree when she finally puts her head round the door and says to me, '*Thank God, Dale, you're not my agent!*'

People often ask me how I manage my diary so well. The reality is I *don't*. I'm forever jotting things down on bits of paper which I promptly lose. I'm very good about remembering dates, though. If I have to be somewhere, even if it's three months down the line, that date will stick in my mind. I'm also good at remembering phone numbers. Being a Gemini I can never make up my mind until the last moment when requests come in that should really go in the diary. Lisa Ratcliffe, who works for Jan, always succeeds in getting me to do more than I ever could if I were organizing my diary myself. She knows exactly when to ask and when *not* to ask me a question. I am probably her worst nightmare, but I do love her. Everybody needs a Lisa in their life and I'm very lucky to have her in mine. It's one of those rare relationships in business where someone you work with has become a really dear and trusted friend.

By the end of 1997 I was thinking of moving home again. The house I'd bought in Hampstead's Southend Green was lovely but, as it faced a main road and people were forever knocking at my door, I was feeling somewhat exposed and vulnerable. I was also being driven insane by the constant clanging of the electronically operated wrought-iron gates just below my bedroom window. Then, when some of my neighbours took it upon themselves to keep telling me that my car wasn't perfectly parked in the allotted space, I decided that the time had come for me to run wild in the aisles of estate agents.

Despite the dramatic change for the better in my financial fortunes, I soon discovered that most of the desirable properties in central London were still out of my league. But the Force, as they say, was with me. One morning in January 1998, an estate agent called Neville Serlui rang and said, 'I have a house that's just right for you in an area you will love.'

'If it's in the West End or central London,' I said, convinced he'd overestimated my earnings because he thought I was always on the box, 'you can forget it. I can't afford anything in that area.'

'Just come and have a look at it,' he replied. 'It really is exactly what you want.'

When I did go to see it, I was instantly tempted. The location was just perfect. Although badly in need of refurbishment, it was magnificent and the idea of living in that elegant three-storey house in that particular street, so close to the glorious tree-lined vistas of a park, seemed very attractive – and somehow very grown-up.

'It's an absolute bargain,' Neville kept saying. 'The lady who's selling it has just been let down by her previous buyer and all she's interested in now is an immediate exchange of contracts so that she can go ahead with the purchase of the house she wants to buy.'

That evening I happened to be having dinner with Barbara Windsor, who lived very close to the house that I was now considering buying. 'Come and have a look at the outside of it,' I said.

When we drove past the owner, who was just going in, recognized us and said, 'Come and have a look around.'

Once back in the car, Barbara said, 'It's fabulous, Dale. If you don't buy it, *I will*!'

That was all the confirmation I needed, and even when a very good friend, Chris Jay, said, 'Given all the refurbishment you want done, you probably won't be able to move into the house until October, Dale,' I still decided to go ahead with the May exchange.

The original configuration of the house was hall, kitchen, sitting room and loo on the ground floor; two bedrooms and a bathroom on the first; two bedrooms and one bathroom on the second. But by the time I'd finished weighing up my needs, a chunk had been nipped off the sitting-room to allow for a really spacious kitchen, the downstairs loo had been demolished to increase the size of the hall; the first-floor bedrooms had been converted into dressing rooms, housing floor-to-ceiling cherrywood wardrobes for all my clothes (!), and the top floor was transformed into a den which could house all my toys – my collection of classic cars, an elaborate sound system and cinema. My bedroom, linked to my bathroom by a spiral staircase, was built on to a raised platform above the den. In other words the whole interior of the house was rebuilt.

While the house was being gutted and rendered to a shell – and the bath for my black-and-white bathroom was changed three times because I kept deciding on a more luxurious one – there wasn't a single girlfriend of mine – Barbara, Cilla, Martine, Davina McCall, Liza and Lynda – who wasn't invited along to give an opinion. One night Cilla, on her way to meet Bobby for dinner, arrived wearing a beautiful pastel-coloured Escada suit and matching shoes with three-inch heels. I was terrified when she insisted on me giving her a guided tour. Every interior wall of the house was demolished or half demolished, all the floors were littered with builders' rubble, boards were missing everywhere and there were no banisters or handrails on the now wobbly stairs. Oblivious of all this – and the knee-high dust – Cilla just continued tripping – and I do mean *tripping* – around.

When it came to decorating the house, simple being my middle name, I was thinking clean white walls and beige carpets but Chris was adamant that, as the house was quite grand, it should be decorated in a much more opulent way. A Gemini through and through, the worst thing anybody can do is give me a choice. I always thought Henry Ford had the right idea when he said, of the original T Ford, 'You can have it any colour you like as long as it's black.' Well, I'm kind of like that when it comes to decorating. 'You can have any wallpaper you like,' I kept saying, 'as long as it's white!' But I was dragged screaming into colour, which included a striking shade of blue, and ancient Roman-themed panels and borders. At least I was allowed beige on some of the walls and for the carpets, and a matching wall-hanging and throw, featuring my hero, Alexander the Great, on my huge Gothic iron bed.

I was hoping to move into the house in October, but it wasn't ready until December. Finally, with Chris's help, I moved in on Christmas Eve. He then hung the pictures, including my favourite of the opening of the Great Exhibition in 1851, and supervised the placing of the antique furniture. We then found ourselves up against a dreadful problem with a magnificent mahogany cabinet that I had bought to house the television in the corner of the sitting room. 'The only way the TV will fit into that,' Chris said, 'is to take the back off the cabinet.'

I was horrified. We were not talking MFI here. He despatched me to the kitchen and told me not to come out until he'd finished! There I sat, head in hands, while Chris hammered merrily away. It was the most horrendous sound I'd ever heard but, amazingly, he succeeded in getting the television inside the cabinet without damaging it. The back of the cabinet is now stored in my loft, so if I ever do decide to sell it, at least it can be nailed back on again.

Slowly but surely, the house was transformed into the kind of home I'd only ever expected to dream or read about. To this day, I still wake up and cannot believe that Dale Winton, a jobbing presenter who once found himself living in a minute North Harrow flat on income support, lives there.

By Christmas 1998 those far-off days when I arrived in London jobless and in debt up to what the press called 'my big brown eyes', seemed to me something that had happened to another guy in a previous lifetime. With *Supermarket Sweep, Pets Win Prizes, The Other Half* and *The National Lottery* under my belt, I was now being described in *TV Choice* listings as 'The game show host they love the most.' Then, as if this was not joy enough, another of my dreams came true. I was given my own BBC prime-time show, *Winton's Wonderland*, which was billed as a nostalgic voyage through three decades of the TV age, from the Swinging Sixties to the Naughty Nineties. With a cracker in one hand and a glass of bubbly in the other, there was no better icing I could have wished for on my Christmas cake.

Set in a magnificent penthouse apartment, with stunning views of the skyline from the BBC's Television Centre, *Winton's Wonderland* was a star-studded hour-long extravaganza, full of guests, such as my mates Barbara, Martine and Davina, from my own wish list. On what proved to be just the first of three annual hostings of this show, 'the showbiz bash of the year', I had bags of festive fun viewing favourite commercials, recalling the fads that created the dedicated followers of fashion, and welcoming on to the show stars such as The Drifters, Jimmy Tarbuck, Suggs from Madness, June Whitfield, Billie Piper, Jimmy Nail and Boy George. One wit from the media couldn't resist saying my interview with Boy George gave a new meaning to the expression 'camp as Christmas'. But did I mind? No. I was having the time of my life going through archive after archive of amusing footage of stars, music and commercials, and playing zany panel games such as, 'Icon in a Sack'. For this, our celebrity panel had to guess whom we'd bagged up. To help them Geoff Hearst tried to bat his way out, Angela Rippon tried to high-kick her way out, and Henry Cooper tried to punch his way out. Other delights included Anthea Redfern as a special surprise for Noddy Holder of Slade who was a great fan of hers, and music from Culture Club, the Foundations and Georgie Fame.

One of my personal favourites on *Winton's Wonderland* was Jimmy Nail whom I had first met when I interviewed him for Beacon Radio about his record 'Love Don't Live Here Any More', and again later when he made a guest appearance on *The National Lottery*. When I first heard that he was coming on to *The Lottery*, it crossed my mind that, since he was renowned as a tough guy who was always being cast in 'hard man' roles on TV, I might not be his cup of tea. But far from it, he couldn't have been more friendly and even greeted me with a luvvy kiss on telly. I was in for a bigger surprise when he knocked on my dressing-room door after the show and said, 'I just wanted to thank you for tonight, Dale. I'm *so* pleased we chatted in the way we did. It's very good for audiences to realize that, while I may have a very tough Newcastle image, I feel perfectly OK about being so familiar with a gay person on TV.'

I was rendered speechless. My sexuality had always been left an open question, but Jimmy had assumed I was gay. He'd done it so charmingly, though, that the moment I recovered I said in the campest voice I could muster, 'Oh, Jimmy, that's so sweet. Thank you!'

After his guest appearance on *Winton's Wonderland*, he surprised me yet again. 'I've got a great idea, Dale,' he said. 'You and I should do a TV sitcom together, something along the lines of *The Odd Couple*.'

He wasn't joking! Since then we've made several attempts to get this idea under way. It's gone through many gestations and hasn't happened yet, but we're really hoping that one day it will. Jimmy Nail and I in a sitcom together would be inspired TV!

Another occasion I remember so well on *The National Lottery* was when I walked into the BBC reception area and was confronted by a line-up of huge hampers from Harrods. 'My God!' I said. 'Who are those for?'

'Mr Julio Iglesias,' the receptionist informed me. Julio was to be one of my guests on the show.

When I went down to the studio floor, I mentioned the hampers to one of Julio's entourage from Sony in Los Angeles, New York, Miami and London. Well, he is one of their top-three selling artistes worldwide.

'Yes,' the London Sony person replied, 'Julio's very partial to

Harrods' hampers and, as he's flown over for the show in his own jet, we've ordered those hampers for him to take back to Miami.'

'Well,' I thought. 'This *is* star treatment!'

But nobody deserved it more than Julio. I always know when we have a true pro on the show. They don't just take refuge in their dressing rooms until they're called. They take an interest in everything from camera angles to lighting and always watch the rehearsals for the whole show. Julio is very much this kind of artiste. On this occasion he had a new record out with a very strong Latin-American feel, and he was going to sing this, backed by two dancers.

At the very end of *The Lottery*, after the main draw, when everybody assembles with me on the centre stage, I plug the next week's show. Then, as we all wave goodbye, I sometimes do a little dance while the music is playing. When we were rehearsing this bit of the show, Julio suddenly whispered in my ear, 'Dale, let's have a bit of fun at the end. After you've said your goodbye to the viewers, let's do a little dance together and then, pretending we've made a terrible mistake, we can turn round and dance with the girls.'

Even as I agreed that would be fun, I was thinking, 'What will his entourage make of that?' Having watched me going through my camp routine, I guessed they'd already made up their minds as to the kind of person I was and I couldn't believe they'd be too pleased with that finale. Anyway . . . come the dress rehearsal, I said my goodbyes, thanked my guest, the music started to play, Julio grabbed me and we started to dance. At this point, as I'd anticipated, all hell broke loose among his flotilla. Down they all flew from the audience rostrum on to the stage, flapping and squawking, '*Stop, stop, STOP! NO, NO, NO*! Julio no dance with a man – especially *that* man. *Wrong* signal!'

'It's all right,' was Julio's firm riposte. 'We separate in just a momenta and we dance witha girls. This is part of the gag.'

At the mention of *girls*, the Sony people breathed a huge sigh of relief and calmed down. But I will never forget the panic on their faces as they envisaged all their record sales plummeting because Julio Iglesias danced with a man! Julio, I have to say, is one of life's special people, a true gentleman and a wonderful artiste. I would gladly work – and dance – with him again *any* time.

Another highlight of my professional life came in January 1999 when the BBC recognized that, although I was now established as a game show host and for presenting *The National Lottery*, I was also a versatile guy who could be trusted to bring a light-hearted spin to one of its more serious factually based programmes. As somebody who had battled with weight problems all my life and who had succeeded in dumping five stones of excess baggage, I was invited to spearhead the Beeb's biggest-ever health campaign, *Fighting Fat, Fighting Fit*. With an hour-long programme aimed at getting the nation fitter and healthier through diet and exercise, I kicked off the event with *Weight of the Nation*. For this, I looked at what we eat, how we exercise, and why so many of us Brits were getting fatter and fatter. Then, hopefully having helped the viewers to slim down, I invited them, in March 2000, to *Kick it with Dale*. This campaign to help people stop smoking proved to be a huge personal challenge for me. Everyone knew I was a heavy smoker, so cheating was out of the question. At the time when I said, 'Yes – I'll do it' I immediately put it on a back burner and reached for another ciggy. But as the day came nearer and nearer for me to quit the demon weed, I realized that the pressure was on and I *really* did have to do it.

Sally Dixon, the producer of the programme, had lined up all the alternative therapies, including Nicorette tablets, chewing gum and patches, and a cigarette holder which gave you a quick fix without damaging your health. But my personal favourite was the patches. The main reason I enjoyed these, though, was because, being me, I broke all the rules. Instead of starting off on low-strength patches and building up to full strength, I went straight on to the strongest ones. I also forgot to take them off, as directed, when I went to bed at night. The upshot was that I had the most amazing dreams – and nightmares – known to man. Every night when I fell asleep it was a voyage of discovery. I either woke up smiling like a Cheshire cat from the sexiest dreams I'd ever had, or shaking with terror.

I did manage to fulfil my part of the bargain for a couple of months after the programme, but then I had a double 'outing' in the press. One for being caught smoking like a chimney at a BBC function, the other when journalist, Andrew Collins, couldn't resist a tease in the *Observer*.

'Dale *never could*,' he quipped, 'resist a nice fag!'

# 9

## 'Will you still love me tomorrow . . .'

COME 1999 I was full of optimism. *The National Lottery* was doing great business and securing big-star names, and I was told that Paul Jackson, who was Controller of Entertainment at the BBC, was very keen for me to host six fifty-minute chat shows that would include some music and be combined with the Wednesday night lottery draws. In this way the Beeb would be able to offer its viewers a really good alternative to the football that was being shown on ITV. I've always admired Paul Jackson professionally, always felt safe in his hands and he has always been very supportive of me. That aside, he's a really nice guy and his wife is an absolute darling. When I say 'chat show', I use the word lightly because there were then – and are now – many people who are established at doing these kind of shows and, although I had proved I could be trusted with more in-depth programmes, such as *Weight of the Nation*, I was still better known in the business as somebody who presented the fluffier side of television. I was therefore considered more suited to entertainment than chat shows. Paul Jackson, however, knew the exact direction in which he wanted both me and the new lottery show to go, and I will always be grateful to him for recognizing that I could deliver a chat show type of programme.

When someone like Paul has confidence in you, it shores you up, makes you feel good about yourself. You might appear to be a very confident individual when you're up in front of the cameras, but you can't do it all alone and you do need support. At the end of the day, people don't sit around after a programme saying, 'Oh, the editing wasn't very good on that' or 'I didn't like the set much'. What they say is 'Oh, I *did* like Dale's show' or 'I *didn't* like Dale's show'. It's always the artistes who carry the responsibility on their shoulders. Paul recognizes this and is always one of the first to boost your confidence and make sure you are comfortable about what you are doing.

Peter Salmon, the Controller of BBC 1 at the time, agreed with Paul that I was the right man to do the new mid-week lottery shows and I also owe him for having such faith in me when Paul first hatched his plan for *Dale's All Stars with the National Lottery*. The idea was that, in addition to interviewing home-grown talent in the UK, I would also interview some stars in America and the guests arranged for the shows were second to none. In the UK these included Michael Crawford, Jim Davidson, Ronan Keating, Vic Reeves, Bob Mortimer, Michelle Collins, Martine McCutcheon, Jimmy Tarbuck and Lenny Henry.

With the production team in tow, I also went off to Los Angeles to meet celebrities and film stars in their own homes. I might not have been so keen on this idea, though, if I'd known that the journey to LA was going to end in a flight from hell. Three hours after we left Heathrow we were greeted with the kind of announcement you only ever expect to hear in disaster movies: 'This is the captain speaking. Is there a doctor on board?'

A few minutes later, while I was still wondering what all this was about, I looked out of the plane's window and noticed that the sun, which had been on the left-hand side a few minutes ago, was now on the right. 'Good God,' I thought, 'we've changed direction.'

Pushing the button for the stewardess, I asked, 'What's going on?'

'It's nothing to worry about,' she said, smiling. 'One of the passengers is unwell and we're turning back to Prestwick.'

*Prestwick*! I looked at her aghast. Our schedule in LA had been set up with military precision and the stars I was interviewing were expecting me to arrive on time. As I was fretting about this, I suddenly realized that the sun had disappeared *again* and that it was now back on my left. 'All's well that ends well,' I thought, relieved.

But no, our problems were only just beginning. The next thing I heard was that we were on our way to make an unscheduled landing in Iceland, and that before we touched down we would need to fly in circles for about half an hour to jettison the plane's excess fuel.

When we eventually came to a bumpy stop on the tarmac, I peered out of the window at the snowy-white wasteland that was stretching as far as my eye could see, thinking, 'Well, this place is aptly named!' Then, through the howling blizzard and huge flakes of snow, I saw two parked vehicles – a police wagon and an ambulance. Still trying to absorb what was happening, I was then distracted by the sound of raised voices and a torrent of abuse coming from the rear end of the plane. The next moment, amid repeated howls of *'Don't take us off the plane . . .'*, 'two men, who we later heard had been busy abusing drugs and were rapidly becoming a danger to themselves and others, were dragged unceremoniously out of the aircraft and bundled into the waiting police wagon.

Although our problems seemed to be over, in reality they were not. In the time it had taken to land – and remove the two guys – the plane's wings had iced up and, although we did not know this immediately, we were destined to remain on the tarmac for another six hours. As we sat there, suffering from claustrophobia, on what could so easily have been a prop on the filmset for *Ice Station Zebra*, it all became very British. Camaraderie was *the* word. One of the ladies sitting close to me, I discovered, was the manager of the Athenaeum Hotel in London. Another was Engelbert Humperdinck's daughter – an amazing coincidence because, only the night before, Englebert had appeared alongside me on Barbara Windsor's *Hall of Fame*. Yet another – the manageress of the Shutters Hotel in Santa Monica – proved to be an invaluable contact when, later on in the trip, she allowed us to use her hotel as the location for my Bo Derek interview.

The only discord on board, while we waited hour after long hour for the plane's wings to shed the ice, was that the smokers among us were not allowed to smoke. As it was too cold to disembark and puff away on the tarmac, the only thing we could do was mutter, mutter, moan and groan, and stand in the howling gale by the open door. After two or three puffs, most of us were only too happy to return to our seats to nurse our frozen fingers and frost-bitten toes.

The only crumb of comfort was when one of the stewards reminded us that, as the plane was stationary, we could if we wished switch on our mobile phones. Grateful for any kind of displacement therapy, I phoned a couple of friends in England, including Cilla. 'You'll *never* guess where I am,' I said to Cilla.

'You're on the runway in Keflavik, Iceland,' she replied, quick as a flash.

'How on earth do you know that?' I asked, totally and absolutely gobsmacked.

'Because, if you look behind you,' she replied, 'you'll see one of my producers who's just told me you're on the plane.'

It was such a Cilla moment.

When, at last, we landed in Los Angeles, we all breathed a huge sigh of relief. But even that proved to be premature. Another announcement from the captain asked us all to remain seated when the door was opened so that paramedics could board the plane.

'What now?' I thought, stunned.

Then, as I looked round, I saw a stretcher being carried down the gangway and there, lying on it, was somebody *very* dear to me, who had been sitting in another part of the plane. It was Sarah Burrows, my make-up artist! I knew Sarah was nervous of flying at the best of times, but . . .

'What's happened?' I asked, distraught.

'The long journey's been too much for her,' a stewardess replied. 'She's really not at all well.'

'Oh, no!' I cried.

The next moment Sarah, a diamond of a girl, was whisked off to hospital.

Thankfully, two days later, having made an excellent recovery from what proved to be a very nasty chest infection and tummy upset, she was on her way back to London. I was mortified. She had been so looking forward to the trip and meeting some of the stars I was going to interview, and all she had seen was the inside of two Virgin Atlantic jumbo jets, the icy wastes of Keflavik and the four walls of a hospital.

Once in Los Angeles, having found a replacement make-up artist who could remain with us for the rest of the trip, we shot off to the Shutters Hotel in Santa Monica where I interviewed the screen goddess, Bo Derek, who was most famous for the 1979 film, *10*, in which she co-starred with Dudley Moore.

Having got this interview in the can, we then went to see Kirstie Alley from *Cheers*, who now has her own programme called *Veronica's Closet*; Cybill Shepherd, who talked very poignantly about Elvis Presley; English rose, Jane Seymour, now living in Malibu; and veteran film star James Coburn. I also had a wonderful time with Donny and Marie Osmond on the set of their *Donny Marie Show*; and fun in Miami with the singer Gloria Estefan.

One of the artistes we had booked to interview on the last leg of our journey was *Six Million Dollar Man*, Lee Majors, in Miami, on a golf course. But this proved to be a somewhat sensitive situation. The golf course he had chosen for the interview was for men only, but half our crew were women. When we explained this to him, he simply dug his heels in and said he didn't want to be filmed on any other golf course but the one that he had named. As I feel strongly about any kind of discrimination, including sexism, I dug my heels in, too. 'Fine,' I said, 'OK, we won't do the interview.' Once he realized I *really* meant what I said, he changed his mind. But, sadly, it was too late by then to rearrange things.

For me, *The National Lottery* has never ceased to be what it is, the ultimate game show for a man whose dream was to be a game show host. Offering the biggest prizes ever on TV, it's a brilliant show – and I just love the opportunity it gives me to shed the sweatpants and sweatshirts I wear at home to go out shopping with Lynda for some more trendy clothes. One story I often chuckle about when I'm on my way to the studio is that of the couple who went out to buy a bottle of wine after winning £1.5 million pounds, only to realize on their return home that they didn't have a corkscrew. The other one I take great satisfaction in is the survey that discovered that more people play *The National Lottery* than vote in the general election.

Whenever I host *The Lottery*, I step off the set so adrenalized that it takes me quite a while to come down to earth. But I came to earth with a collossal bump, eight days into the new millennium, January 2000, when the last man I had ever expected to gatecrash one of my live shows suddenly crept on to the stage and nabbed me. It was Michael Aspel, the famous red book tucked under his arm, uttering the time-honoured words, 'This is Your Life.'

I don't know how others react at such moments, but the look on my face said it all. I really was stunned. My knees buckled, my hands shook and my mouth gaped open in disbelief. 'Can this be for real?' was my first thought. Then, professional to what I felt *could* be my last breath, I said to Michael, 'Are we still live and on the air?'

'But *of course*,' he replied.

The remainder of that night, which covered the story of how this one-time biscuit factory DJ became a household name, passed, as it must do for so many of Michael's honoured guests, in a total flurry. The stars who turned out for me included Michelle Collins, Davina McCall and Barbara Windsor. There were also contributions from Boy George, Cilla Black, Martine McCutcheon and Jim Davidson. When Garry Bushell reviewed this show in the *Sun*, he simply couldn't resist one of his cheeky PSs: 'Just to clear up any misunderstanding,' he said, 'when talking about Dale's schooling, Aspel *actually* said that Dale had been a *day* boy.'

That was good clean fun, but the *Sunday People*'s coverage was not so amusing. Its front-page headline screamed: DALE'S TURNED HIS BACK ON HIS FAMILY . . . THERE WAS NO RELATIVE ON HIS *THIS IS YOUR LIFE*. Nobody was more upset than I was to discover that, having winkled out my Aunt Lorraine and Uncle Joe, the journalist seemed to have prompted them into believing that I had snubbed them and had then backed this up with quotes that they were 'deeply hurt and disappointed not to have been invited on to the show' or to be 'a member of the audience'. But what the *Sunday People* journalist appeared to have chosen to ignore – and what my lovely Aunt Lorraine and Uncle Joe had not understood – is that the *last* person to know anything about his or her appearance on *This Is Your Life* is the subject of the show. Given that all the preparations are made in secret, because it's meant to be a huge surprise for the person whose life is being featured, that person has no control whatsoever over who is – or who is not – invited. Fortunately, one telephone call from me to my aunt and uncle laid that misunderstanding to rest.

At the beginning of 2001, two executives from Channel 5, Chris Shaw and the Controller, Dawn Airie, spoke to Jan Kennedy about me hosting a new show called *Touch the Truck*. I liked the sound of it instantly. It seemed to me to be a good example of the new breed of television programmes that were being dubbed 'Reality TV'. *Big Brother*, which had first been transmitted the year before, had done very well in the ratings and I have always been a fan of quirky shows.

The idea for *Touch the Truck* had originated in America where it had been done not as a television programme, but as a weekend promotional event for lorries and trucks. It was basically an en-durance test in which twenty contestants, male and female, had to stay awake for five days and nights while keeping their hands planted on a Toyota Land Cruiser. If they fell asleep or overran their ten-minute break every two hours or fifteen-minute food break every six hours, or removed their hands from the truck, they were disqualified. The last person to remain standing and touching the truck won the vehicle. They were allowed to distract each other, and friends could provide encouragement, while in the meantime experts discussed subjects such as sleep deprivation, exercise and endurance, and we also featured some of the people who'd won trucks in America.

Our hour-long show was screened live on five consecutive days from the Lakeside Shopping Centre, Essex. I loved presenting it, but

I have to admit that it was a heart-rending experience watching the contestants going slightly out of their minds with sleep deprivation, and I was worried that they would never be the same again. However, once they'd had a few hours sleep and a good meal they were back to normal, and they all joined in the finale. I did laugh, though, when the guy who won the truck was asked how he felt. 'I don't approve of gas-guzzling trucks,' he retorted. 'And I'm *so* concerned about what this does to the environment I'm going to sell it and launch an eco party with the money.' I thought that was *so* Channel 5 and wished him well.

The unfortunate thing about *Touch the Truck* was that it was screened the same week as *Celebrity Big Brother*, Channel 4's contribution to *Comic Relief.* But for this clash, I am sure that it could have continued and become an even bigger success. Either way, it was very quirky – and I loved hosting it.

By April 2000 Alan Freeman's signature show, *Pick of the Pops* (which had started life on BBC Radio One before moving to Capital Radio) had found its natural home on BBC Radio Two. By this time, having done various shows for Radio Two, including hosting Steve Wright's programme when he was having a break, I'd discovered I really enjoyed being a radio DJ again. When I heard that Philip Swern and Tim Blackmore of Unique Productions – and Mark Lamar, a marvellous entertainer and broadcaster – had all mentioned my name to Jim Moir, Head of Radio Two, to take over Alan's spot when he retired, I was overjoyed. But I was also very nervous. Alan, a hero of mine for as long as I could remember, had stamped his own unique style all over the show and I knew that he would be a very hard act to follow.

'If I do this,' I said to Philip, 'I'll be lynched. Alan's an institution. He's been doing *Pick of the Pops* for forty-odd years. The format is set in stone. Whoever takes over from him can't win.'

'We think you'll be just right for it,' Philip replied.

The only other problem I had with signing the contract for *Pick of the Pops* was that the BBC had instigated a no smoking policy in all its studios. While I appreciate that smoking is a disgusting habit, it's part of Dale, part of what I do, and I just have to have a cigarette every now and again when I'm working. Have I ever broken Auntie's rules? I'm not saying.

I'm very proud to be carrying on Alan's good work every Saturday afternoon between two and three-thirty and, despite my trepidation, I have managed to put my own signature on it. The show's actually doing very well and is still going up in the ratings. I absolutely adore it – and I love working with Philip. Long before I actually met him, I was a fan of his, and I had written his name down hundreds of times in my early radio days. He's a very special man, who wrote and produced hit records in the Seventies, and I'm delighted that he is now a very close friend of mine.

People can only imagine how proud I was, too, when I was asked to present Barbara Windsor's *Hall of Fame* in 2000. This lady, a true show business legend, had been part of my mother's life in the Sixties and had entered mine in the Seventies when I was a fledgling DJ and she was in a play called *Calamity Jane*. When she came into Radio Trent do an interview with me, we hit it off straight away. Since then, the more I've got to know her, the more I've grown to love her and understand *why* she is the star she is. She's never late, always knows her lines, always delivers and deserves all the recognition that she's now given for being one of showbiz's best. Not only was she the bubbly blonde in the *Carry On* films, she's been on Broadway with *Oh What a Lovely War!*, performed in musicals on the London stage and has done, with tremendous aplomb, most of the things that actresses would die to do. The Beeb's *EastEnders* would certainly not be the same without her – and neither would I. We talk constantly on the phone, see each other most weeks and are the closest of friends. A delightfully feisty lady, she knows the business inside out, and has coped wonderfully well with all her life's highs and lows. I can honestly say there's never a dull moment when she's around, and one of my greatest joys these days is seeing how happy she is with her husband, Scott.

The *Hall of Fame* was instigated by the BBC to celebrate the lives of their most revered artistes and Barbara was the very first to be featured. There were anecdotes from people with whom she had acted and she also performed songs from shows she had appeared in. Barbara answered questions from the audience, too, and at the end of the show Ross Kemp, who played Grant Mitchell in *EastEnders*, and I presented her with a *Hall of Fame* statuette. A truly wonderful show, produced by Richard Woolf, it had some really great reviews.

The next show I was offered – and *very* much wanted to do – presented me with a dilemma. Judith Holder, who had given me an early break into TV with the BSkyB show called *Anything for Money*, told Jan Kennedy that Claudia Rosencrantz, a senior executive at ITV, thought I'd be the perfect host for a ninety-minute special called *TV's Best Ever Soap Moments* to be transmitted at the end of August. I was thrilled, but I then had one of the funniest conversations I've ever had with Jan Kennedy about my image.

Claudia, Jan told me, had one niggling point that she'd asked Jan to pass on to me, concerning the colour of my skin. 'Jan,' Claudia had said, 'you simply *must* tell Dale that for this particular project he must *not* look *orange*!'

I understood exactly why Claudia had said this. Throughout my career, because I always like to look tanned, fit and healthy, there had been many times when comics made the tanned mahogany texture of my skin the butt of their jokes. I just happen to be one of those lucky people who tan very quickly and, like most people, I feel at my best with a tan. However, as this had been noted by every comic the length and breadth of Britain, and used so often in their jokes, Claudia had obviously decided that a tanned Dale was *not* on this time. To emphasize her point, she then said to Jan, 'I was having lunch with an artiste the other day who, just like Dale, has a very tanned complexion. We were sitting in a restaurant with oak-panelled walls and I found it almost impossible to distinguish him from the walls! So *please*, Jan, tell Dale I don't want him to look as if he's been burned orange on the new show.'

It did make me laugh! When I rang Claudia to thank her for

the job, she laughed heartily when I said, 'The future doesn't *have* to be orange!' It then proved to be one of the very rare occasions when I actually went before the cameras without any semblance of a tan, and since then I have toned down the colour considerably.

All this, though, proved to be the least of my worries when I first heard about the show. There was another problem. The timing could not have been worse. I'd already arranged to go to Switzerland in July for my facelift and I knew I would need time to recuperate. I was *so* disappointed because I was particularly keen to host this show for several reasons: I hadn't done anything for ITV since *Supermarket Sweep*; it was going to be shown on a Wednesday night, which always has excellent viewing figures, and finally, because it was being filmed on location and involved doing pieces to camera from *Emmerdale*, *Coronation Street* and *Brookside*. In the circumstances, I decided to telephone Michel Pfulg, my cosmetic surgeon, and ask his advice, and was over the moon when he reassured me that I *would* be fit for work within five or six weeks of the operation. 'That,' I thought, 'might be cutting it a bit fine [excuse the pun!], but perhaps he's right.' Then, by great good fortune, we were able to move the date of the operation back a week, which meant I could return from Switzerland with a full three weeks to spare before the start of filming. Every day during this time I used to look in the mirror and pray that the swelling and bruising on my face would have settled down before I went on camera. In all honesty, it could have done with at least another two weeks of healing time but, fortunately, most of the shots were long or wide. Judith, bless her, never said a word, but I'm sure she guessed that I'd had some sort of cosmetic surgery and, this aside, she must have wondered why I'd been unavailable for the pre-production talks.

Like most artistes, I always want to give out the right vibes and not appear difficult or stand-offish to work with, or picky in any way, but there was a problem on this show. We started to shoot *TV's Best Ever Soap Moments* as planned in August and, during this time, in addition to being on the sets of *Emmerdale*, *Coronation Street* and

*Brookside*, I also had to return to London to do a Harry Hill special for ITV. So it was a case of constant travel during what proved to be the hottest week of the year and the one thing you have to avoid when you've just had cosmetic surgery is sunshine. Fortunately, I had managed to secure an air-conditioned limousine, but Judith must have thought I was behaving very strangely indeed. The moment I wasn't needed in the studio – and could have been sitting outside taking in the sun – all I did (a renowned sun worshipper, remember) was run back to the limo and sit in it. The heat in the studio was making my face swell and I needed the car's cool interior, plus constant ice packs, to keep the swelling down. The other problem was the mornings. It takes time for a face to settle down after a night's sleep, but the call time for *TV's Best Ever Soap Moments* was eight o'clock in the morning. The only way I could manage this was to go to bed as early as possible, get up at four, put on the ice packs and wait for everything to settle and look relatively normal.

One way and another, that week was a bit of a nightmare and I'm sure Judith must have guessed why I was behaving *so* out of character. It was a secret that I always intended to take to my grave – with only my make-up artist, who had to redo my make-up for every take, in the know. But now that I'm writing this book, I can see the funny side of it all.

The show itself was a great joy to work on. Apart from the sheer delight of standing in the Rover's Return, in Brookside Close and on the set of *Emmerdale*, I had the chance to relive all the best ever moments. In fact, to this day, *TV's Best Ever Soap Moments* remains one of the shows I'm most proud of but, for the reasons outlined above, it was very touch and go, and certainly the *only* time I've ever been known to prefer life in the shade.


Jan, my agent, is absolutely brilliant. Nobody understands artistes better than she does, but I began to have some serious doubts about her when she rang me and said, 'Dale, would you like to sing a duet with Jane Horrocks on the revival series of *Absolutely Fabulous*?'

'Absolutely not,' I said. 'Dale singing is *not* something that you or I should inflict on the unsuspecting nation.'

'She's obviously forgotten,' I was thinking, 'that we'd already risked my career once in this way when I was asked to sing a duet with Jimmy Nail for *Children in Need*.' I love Jimmy so much – trust him completely – but even so, at the time of the *Children in Need* programme I had said, 'Jimmy, I know what my singing voice is like. *This*, I promise you, is *not* one for me.'

'Well, it *is* for a good cause,' Jimmy replied. 'Let's give it a try.'

Still feeling very insecure, but entering into the spirit of the thing, I agreed.

'There is one song I think you could sing,' Jimmy responded. 'It's the old Lou Reed number, "A Walk on the Wild Side". Lou actually spoke a lot of the words. I'm sure you could manage that. Come up to my house in Hampstead and we'll rehearse it, and I'll take you to see my musical director in Totteridge.'

This particular guy, Danny Schogger, had worked with everybody who's anybody in the music biz. He had a room decorated with gold and silver discs, but I knew he'd be meeting his Waterloo with me. When he sat down at the piano in his house, he said, 'What key would you like the song in, Dale?'

'Pick any key you like,' I said, flustered. 'It makes no difference to me, they all sound the same.'

'There,' Jimmy said, after we'd sung through it once, 'you *can* do it, Dale. I knew you could. Trust me. You'll be fine.'

Back in my car, I rang Jan. 'Darling,' I said, 'I've just had this little rehearsal with Jimmy, who sounds absolutely fantastic, but I honestly don't think I should do this. It'll damage people's hearing.'

'Pull over, park in a lay-by and sing it to me over the phone,' the ever-patient Jan replied.

When I finished my rendition, which had all the melodic qualities of a waste-disposal unit in full gurgle, there was absolute silence at the end of the phone, then I heard a series of stifled sniggers. Jan was literally crying with laughter. 'Well, it *does* need a bit of work,' she said, obviously trying to pull herself together, 'but it'll be all right on the night, Dale!' I knew then that if my agent, who was always the first to support me, could hardly speak for laughing, I was not exaggerating the problem. Thinking I'd rather toddle blindfolded across the M1 than sing in front of millions, I chickened out and decided not to do it.

Recalling this, a year later, when Jan rang me about singing with Jane Horrocks, I said, 'Jan – are you mad? Have you forgotten my rendering of "A Walk on the Wild Side"?'

'No, no, darling,' she replied, 'I couldn't forget *that*. But Jennifer Saunders doesn't want somebody who can sing well.'

'Sing well!' I exclaimed. 'I can't sing at all.'

'That's the point, darling! They want you to do the Elton John and Kiki Dee number, "Don't Go Breaking My Heart".'

'So,' I said, 'not only do they not want me to sing well, they also want me to massacre an absolute classic before millions on a hit TV show.'

'It'll be fine,' Jan said. 'Trust me, I'm your agent.'

There seem to be an awful lot of people in this world whom we are expected to trust.

A couple of days later I spoke to Jonathan Llewellyn, the producer of *Absolutely Fabulous*. 'Jonathan,' I said, 'do you know what you're letting yourself in for? A dying bullfrog makes a better sound than me.'

'It's a sketch set on the set of *The Lottery*,' he said cheerfully. 'It's just a bit of fun, Dale. You don't have to sing, you can speak-sing.'

That sounded familiar.

When I was rehearsing the number to a backing track that had arrived, Jan, whom I'd once again asked to listen in, tried to be reassuring. 'You're coming in just a little too high,' she said, obviously stifling another giggle. 'You just need to change the register.'

The only 'registers' I knew anything about were those that went ping or beep when I was shopping.

When I arrived at the *Ab Fab* studio Alan Yentob, the Beeb's Head of Drama and Entertainment, and Jon Plowman, the show's

Executive Producer, were there. So was Jennifer Saunders who instantly thanked me for entering into the spirit of the thing.

'*Please* don't thank me,' I said, beside myself, 'you haven't heard me sing yet!'

I did a couple of takes with Jane Horrocks, who was an absolute joy, and then the team went ahead and recorded the number. Everyone kept saying 'it's marvellous', but I was thinking, 'Yeah, yeah – pull the other one!' To this day I've not watched that episode. The tape's still sitting there on a worktop in my kitchen, waiting for me to pluck up the courage to insert it into the machine. I'm in no hurry, though, to watch the least fab moment of *Absolutely Fabulous*. And, unlike the adorable bubbly Jane Horrocks, I haven't sung a note since.

Another thing I've never been is a person who enjoys big parties, or networking at celebrity bashes and I never give dinner parties at home. Rarely do I go to dinner at other people's houses. I'm the kind of guy who prefers to meet up for good one-to-one natters in restaurants. When I think about it, this year the only occasions when I have gone to people's homes rather than said, 'Let's go out to a restaurant,' is when I have been invited to a Friday night Shabbos dinner. This is a Jewish tradition where candles are lit, prayers are said, and the food is just out of this world. It takes me back to my childhood when Dad used to light the candles and say the blessing. Jane Lush, the Controller of Entertainment at the BBC, and her husband, Peter, have hosted a couple recently and they have been wonderful. You don't have to be Jewish to enjoy them; in fact, some of the guests Jane has invited include Anne Robinson and Jimmy Melville of Hatrick Productions. My other Shabbos dinner was at the home of Richard Desmond and his wife, Janet, and the other guests were Barbara Windsor and her husband, Scott. The key to a good Shabbos dinner is the food and the nicest thing you can do is compliment the hostess on her chopped liver. In both cases it was home-made and tasted absolutely superb. A rare treat for me. I guess the reason I enjoyed them so much was because with Jewish hospitality, when you go to someone's home you're supposed to feel at home – and in both cases I did.

The exception to my big parties rules was the wedding of Cilla's son, Robert, which proved to be the best-ever bash on my life's social calendar. The service at the gorgeous church in Denham, Buckinghamshire was *very* moving – and could not have been more perfect. As Bobby's funeral had been held there only two years before and most of the wedding party guests had also been present at that, this sad event could have cast a very long shadow over the wedding service and Cilla could have been forgiven for being very over-wrought and emotional. But she was absolutely wonderful and treated the whole day as a celebration of life. Afterwards the reception was held in a magnificent rouche-lined marquee that had been erected in her garden. Normally I only stay a couple of hours, have one glass of champagne and spend most of the time looking for somewhere quiet to have a cigarette. But on this occasion I didn't want to leave, and didn't want the night to end. I enjoyed every single moment, joined in all the merriment, danced the night away and was still there in the early hours of the morning.

'If ever I get married,' I thought (knowing I *never* would!), 'this is *exactly* how I would want everything to be.'

It really was a perfect day and one I will never forget.


There is nothing – as I discovered on Monday 26 November 2001 at the Dominion Theatre, Tottenham Court Road – *anything* quite like a Royal Variety Performance attended by the Queen, the Duke of Edinburgh and other members of the royal household. Famous for its horrendous backstage jitters and on-stage glamour, that year's extravaganza, as Sue Thomas said in *Hello!* magazine, 'rewrote the rule book'. The host of stars who appeared in the flesh gave new meaning to that expression. We are always expected to ensure that there's nothing about our appearance or our acts that could possibly embarrass the Queen, but that evening's presentation turned out to be an occasion when there was literally more flesh on show than ever before and some of it proved to be a good deal more revealing than was intended. During the finale, a troupe of male dancers from the Broadway stage version of *The Full Monty* performed the now-infamous striptease. When the dancers whipped off their thongs, the lighting was meant to ensure that the strippers were only seen in silhouette, but things didn't quite go according to plan. Revealed in all their manly glory, the audience ended up getting an eyeful of full-frontal nudity. Amid all the hoots, cheers and wolf whistles that followed, however, our Queen, wonderful person that she is, managed to remain her usual dignified unflappable self.

As it happened, that was not the only eye opener on that star-studded night. Jennifer Lopez danced flamenco in a beaded Versace evening dress that was seductively split to her thigh, but even she was upstaged by my mates, Lily (Savage), Cilla and Barbara, who stole the show, wearing figure-hugging basques and revealing the kind of shapely legs that twenty-somethings would die for, while singing 'You Gotta Have a Gimmick' from the 1960s musical, *Gypsy*. Cilla then brought the house down when she turned round to reveal a heart, lit with fairy lights, attached to her shapely derrière. If that was not treat enough, the evening then progressed with Denise Van Outen and Claire Sweeney, stars of the raunchy musical, *Chicago*, opting for skimpy sexy outfits, followed by the Hear'Say singers, Myleene Klass, Kym Marsh and Suzanne Shaw, wearing cutaway black dresses that exposed more beauty than they covered. By way of contrast Cher, for her solo performance, was unusually demure in tight-fitting leather trousers and tuxedo jacket. The other entertainers on that memorable night included Elton John, Charlotte Church, Russell Watson, Alessandro Safina, Julian Clary, Craig David, The Corrs, Vinnie Jones, Samantha Mumba, The Americans, Donny Osmond and Jackie Mason – and me.

I can hardly begin to express how awesome and nerve-racking I found it all. I was only too happy to go on stage to surprise the brilliant mimic, Jon Culshaw, when he was impersonating me. But when I realized that I had to learn lines for this I nearly died. As a person whose entire showbiz career has depended on quick-witted one liners, ad libs, or autocues, I was terrified I'd get stage fright and freeze. Before the show I was meant to be sharing a dressing room with Vinnie Jones and Frankie Dettori, but Cilla and Barbara, realizing that it was a first for me to be on stage in that kind of way, and also a first for me to be backstage with total mayhem going on, invited me to come into theirs. While I was sitting on the sofa with Cilla's son, Robert, who was very kindly helping me to learn my lines by listening to me repeating them over and over again, Barbara, completely uninhibited by him or me, was getting ready and pulling on her tights, and Cilla was behind the curtain doing her elaborate eye make-up and changing into her basque. It was an unreal experience.

'Did you get the bottle of champagne and good-luck card I sent to your dressing room?' Cilla asked me.

'No,' I said, puzzled. 'There was nothing like that when I called in.'

That particular mystery was not resolved until much later when Vinnie and Frankie owned up that they'd enjoyed drinking it to soothe their nerves! I could certainly have done with it to calm mine when I was standing in the post-show line-up of stars, waiting to do my bow as the Queen did her walk past. A moment after, Her Majesty had honoured me by stopping to say, 'Hello, Dale. Did Jon Culshaw know that you were going to spring out of the wings and surprise him or was that part of the act?' I had done my best to reply with all due dignity, but having done so, I just saw the funny side of the scene. I went completely to pieces and was overcome by a fit of uncontrollable giggles just as the Duke of Edinburgh arrived alongside me.

One way and another, my first Royal Variety Performance was a night to remember. Sorry, Ma'am – sorry Duke. No offence intended. I always have the giggles when I'm tickled pink – and I was *very* nervous.


By Christmas 2001 I had been fortunate enough to host *Winton's Wonderland* for three years. But that year's Christmas Eve show, which included *The National Lottery*, was renamed *Dale's National*

*Lottery Christmas Cracker*. For this, we changed the format by abandoning all the archive material and game show elements, and made the whole thing much more intimate and Christmassy. For our guest stars we had Anne Robinson whom, despite her intimidating *Weakest Link* persona, we were brave enough to take out Christmas shopping, and I interviewed Vinnie Jones and Cher, and Will Smith, The Corrs and S Club Seven. It all worked brilliantly well, especially as there was all the excitement of the mega lottery draw being done on Christmas Eve, rather than on New Year's Eve as in the past. What a visit from Santa Claus that must have been for the lucky ticket-holders.

Someone – I've forgotten who – once said to me, 'Dale, your philosophy of life should be "yesterday's gone, today is sweet, tomorrow will come".' I wish I could remember that every day when I wake up. My job, as I see it, is to present the best possible programmes I can. But I'm forever worrying that I could do more to leave the audience satisfied. I'm only just beginning to trust that I don't need to try quite so hard. I'm now deliberately reining myself back a bit, becoming a bit less frenetic. I know that what I do for a living is not brain surgery, but I've never been one who rests on my laurels and I'm continually polishing my performance. I look at the icons of the industry, Cilla, Barbara, Bob Monkhouse, Des O'Connor, Chris Tarrant and think to myself, 'These people are *really* famous,' and it always brings a big smile to my face when people in the business say, 'Dale, you're just as well known now.' That's fantastic. And, likewise, it always astounds me when I'm sitting in a restaurant and someone like Elton John, whom I have worked with on many occasions, stops by the table and says, 'Hello, Dale. How are you?' It's also very weird when I'm at home watching something like *Have I Got News for You*, and I suddenly hear Angus Deayton making jokes at my expense. 'My God,' I think, 'I *must* be quite well known for *him* to mention me!'

The truth is my career's been such a roller-coaster, I still can't believe I've arrived where I never thought I would be. Every now and then, when I wake up on the day of a live show, I lie in bed thinking about what is ahead of me and reflecting on all the celebrities I am going to meet on that evening's show. Can this be me, about to go out in front of millions to host another show with all these stars? Sometimes I can't believe my luck, and that I've actually proved to myself that I have the ability to get up and make it happen. It all seems such a far cry from the days when the bailiffs were at the door. I get out of bed, stroll down to the kitchen and make a cup of coffee, and I sit there thinking, '*This* is what I do now, *this* is how I earn my living.' I'm living a charmed life and working with almost every major talent in the business. Although some of these artistes are capable of turning producers' hair white overnight, I find the majority a joy to be with.

Every time a job comes in and Jan asks me if I'd like to do it, whether I want to or not, I think, 'That's nice.' I never ever feel blasé. I've been a *very* lucky guy, and even though I could have done without the bad times when I was so financially strapped that I was frightened to look at my bank statements, those days have simply made me appreciate being in the money even more. I *love* my job, *adore* my life, but I *never* take it for granted. Only a foolish man does that. The moment you begin feeling too secure or start taking yourself too seriously, you're in trouble. That's not what show business is about. You never know for sure when good fortune is going to shine on you or for how long it will last. When I'm on television, the reason I look so pleased to be there is because I am. I love hosting game shows, I love people – and when somebody wins a life-changing prize on one of my programmes, no one is happier than I am. I think it's brilliant.


By the beginning of 2002, having decided to write this book, I had carefully cleared my diary of all television commitments and I didn't plan to be back on the screen until the autumn. But every now and again a show comes along that is totally irresistible. And *this*, despite all my plans, is *exactly* what happened just as I was about to put pen to paper. The Executive Producer, David Young, who, together with his wonderful team, is responsible for so many great television hits, such as *Jet Set, The Weakest Link* and *Dog Eat Dog*, came to me with an idea for a new prime-time Saturday show called *In It to Win It with the National Lottery*, which was going to be known as *Lotto*. By this time he had already taken the idea to Lorraine Heggesey, Controller of BBC One, Jane Lush, Controller of Entertainment Commissioning and Jon Beazley, Senior Commissioning Executive, and they very kindly offered me the job of hosting this show, together with the mid-week lottery.

When they said of *In It to Win It*, 'This is *such* a strong show, Dale, we think you would be perfect for it. And, guess what, you don't have to be *quite* so camp. We want you to be more suave and sophisticated,' I thought, 'This is marvellous.' I was delighted to hear that I could present a new image and that there would no longer be any need for the 'Ooh, er, missus' stuff. As far as I was concerned the days of me bouncing on to the screen like a twelve-year-old were long gone and I welcomed Lorraine's, Jane's, Jon's and David's suggestion with open arms. I couldn't wait to blend the right amount of camp with suave sophistication and genuine care for the contestants. The reason for the success of the show really was the perfect match of executives, plus the lovely producer, Kate Middleditch, and the host. The ratings were phenomenal and it proved to be my biggest hit to date. I will always be grateful to Lorraine Heggesey of the BBC for her confidence in my professionalism and her loyalty. I feel so safe in her hands.

*In It to Win It* was a fantastic quiz that pitched five contestants against each other to win huge cash prizes – sixty or seventy grand was achievable, if they were good. Each question was worth £5000, so if the contestants answered ten questions correctly that was £50,000 in the kitty, but if they got just one wrong then they were back where they started. They could win the opportunity to come back into the game, but if they didn't all their money was shared between the other contestants. So it was all very tense, redolent of Russian roulette!

We've all seen game shows that don't work because the host doesn't bond with the contestants, but I loved the ones I met on the show. My heart beats as fast as theirs during the questions and I wanted them all to be winners. A good quizmaster has his/her own individual style and that's what I've always tried to bring to my shows. The fact that I've succeeded is a wonderful bonus, because I love nothing more in life than doing what I love doing best – my kind of television.

Meanwhile, whoever would have thought that the day would come when *I* muttered those immortal showbiz words, 'I'm worried about overexposure'? But recently I have been. For the last ten years I've gone from one television series to the next, almost without stopping. In the past, if I thought I was going to be off the telly for three months, I'd have thought this was the end of my career, but these days, I think I could take a well-earned two-year break and it wouldn't matter. I could still bounce back when ready. It's weird. I never ever thought I'd hear myself talking like this, but I couldn't bear the viewers to get fed up with me and say, 'Oh, God, it's Dale again. He's *always* on the telly.'

The reality now is that I love my life and I feel very privileged to be living it. I really appreciate being able to sit in the Ivy with my glamorous girls, Barbara, Cilla and Martine. Every time I go into that restaurant I order the dressed crab starter, then the fish cakes, which are the best in the world, or the corn-fed chicken, which is lovely. Being able to live like this is one of the joys that my job brings me.

I could write reams more about my famous friends, especially the adorable Barbara and Cilla, but I'm going to focus now on Martine McCutcheon, Merrill Thomas and Davina McCall who are also very special people in my life.

I first met Martine in the mid-Nineties, when we were both part of a celebrity panel flying up to Manchester to do *That's Show Business*, a Mike Smith entertainment programme. A very intelligent, level-headed girl, with a big heart and romantic nature, I took to Martine in three seconds, and my first impressions were spot on. With Martine, what you see is what you get and ours is a friendship that couldn't fail to blossom. Last year, 2001, she extended her holiday in Spain so that she could spend some time with me when I was there with Cilla. Like me, Martine's a trouper and she's always been very generous about appearing on my shows. She is, of course, still renowned for her part as Tiffany in *EastEnders*, but she's been in showbiz since she was knee-high to a grasshopper, and was trained as an actor/singer/dancer. She was very excited about her singing career when she left *EastEnders* and thrilled about getting the lead part of Eliza in *My Fair Lady*. Unfortunately, I wasn't able to attend the opening at the National, but I promised her that I would be there for the opening night at the Theatre Royal, Drury Lane. When I returned from Spain her mother, Jenny, rang to tell me that Martine had been taken to hospital and I went straight there. It broke my heart to see Martine lying there with drips in her arm, looking so pale and weak. She knew for everybody's sake – not least the members of the public who were so looking forward to seeing her – that she had to get back on stage as soon as possible, but she really had seriously overtaxed her energy during the rehearsals and she was totally exhausted. I know she thought it was the end of the world for her then, but she need not have worried, as she won the Olivier Award for her role in the show. Martine will always be a star because she has oodles of that magical X factor and the public loves her. I've always known that, although she's twenty-three years younger than I am, she's much wiser than me. She's always had an old head on her young shoulders and she deserves the very best. I'm longing for her to meet the man who will prove worthy of her and be the love of her life. I just hope we'll both be lucky at the same time.

Writing about Martine has reminded me that whenever I'm hosting a show I always like to have the studio very cool because it helps to keep me and the audience alert, and because I suffer from perspiration on my forehead. (The *only* place I perspire *would* have to be where it's most obvious, wouldn't it!) I'm not alone in this business of keeping the studio cool. The American host, David Letterman, has the words 'the studio temperature must never rise above fifty-five degrees centigrade' written into his contract, and when you watch his shows you can sometimes see how cold it is because his breath is warmer than the studio. One day, Martine mentioned my let's-keep-it-really-cool rule. 'When artistes, backing singers or dancers are coming on to one of your shows, Dale,' she said, 'the record companies always warn the girls that if they're planning to wear skimpy outfits, they'd better wear plasters on their nipples!'

Oh, dear! I'm quite sure some of the audience leave with hypothermia, too, and for inflicting that suffering on them I'd now like to make a full apology.

I feel as if I've known my lovely TV-presenter friend, Merrill Thomas, for ever. Many's the time she's made my day, cheered me up and given me a new perspective on life. Although I've never really acquired the taste for alcohol, there was one occasion in the late Eighties when I was going through a very low love-life period and got absolutely smashed when I was with Merrill at a book launch at the Langham Hilton. It was a very glamorous occasion, when all the great and the good were there to celebrate the launch of Michael Caine's autobiography. As I was standing with a glass of champagne in my hand, Merrill introduced me to Joan Collins and, while I was talking to this amazing showbiz legend, ultra diligent waiters were keeping my glass constantly topped up. Unaware of this, I just kept on sipping, without noticing that the contents of the glass never seemed to go down. My inexperience with the demon drink quickly caught up with me like a silent express train. By the end of the conversation with Joan, I was absolutely pickled. Merrill, who had never seen me like this, started to propel me out of the room, but we found ourselves exiting at the same time as Brian Forbes and his lovely wife, Nanette Newman. As I had worked with their daughter, Emma Forbes, I stopped them in their tracks. (The familiarity that drink gives you, I discovered, is second to none.) As I was introduced to Nanette, a really first-class actress, with sufficient brilliant reviews to decorate an entire sitting room, I said in a very slurred voice, 'Nanette, it's *such* a joy to meet you. I've always *loved* your Fairy Liquid washing-up commercial.' At this point I felt the pressure of Merrill's hand on my back and heard her saying, 'Time to go, Dale.' I've never met Nanette since, but I still feel mortified when I think of that.

There's a PS to this story for anybody who is ever tempted to ply me with alcohol. If you succeed, the night will end up full of surprises, a bit like the Eastern promise suggested in the Fry's Turkish Delight commercial. In the right circumstances, with the right amount of drink – just three glasses of wine or two single shorts in my case – my inhibitions simply evaporate. A broad smile crosses my face, a twinkle lights up my eyes and I look around the room relying on the kindness of strangers.

I first met Davina McCall, another of my really special friends, when I was invited to present an award at the first MOBO (Music of Black Origin) Awards. When I arrived at the ceremony I was delighted to hear that my partner for the 'Best DJ' award was Davina, the lady who had done *God's Gift*, a late-night cult TV show, which I was totally addicted to. Again, it was one of those rare occasions in life where you meet someone you just love straight away. Due to go on stage immediately after the American star, Mary J. Blige, Davina and I were asked to wait in a narrow corridor. Mary J. Blige duly arrived with more security guards than you could shake a stick at. There were three in front, followed by her backing singers, then Mary J. Blige and five more security guards, all wearing ear pieces and carrying walkie-talkies. Davina and I were flattened against the wall as these people went through towards the stage, without saying a word.

While Mary J. Blige was on stage, Davina and I, still waiting in the corridor, prepared our routine. Then one of the burly six-foot-tall security guards strode over to us and barked, 'Hold the door open. Mary J. Blige is coming through any minute now.' Like fools, we did exactly what he said and stood there holding the two doors open. After about five minutes I suddenly twigged and said to Davina, 'What *are* we doing holding these doors open?'

'I really don't know,' she said, equally bemused.

So we just let the doors close.

About two minutes later the same six-foot security man reappeared and barked at us, 'I *told* you to leave these doors *open*. Mary J. Blige is coming through. Mary J. Blige is . . .'

'Oh, gawd,' we thought and, once again, we opened the doors and stood there for what seemed like an eternity until a flotilla of bouncers appeared, and Mary J. Blige and her entourage stormed through in single file without once looking to their left or right or acknowledging our presence.

Three years later Mary J. Blige asked if she could appear on *Dale's All Stars*. At this time she was promoting a wonderful new single, 'Give Me Love', and was absolutely sensational – a joy and a delight. Sometimes, I think, stars are more a victims of the people who surround them than their own over-inflated sense of self-importance.

After the MOBO event Davina and I kept in touch and often met up for coffee or lunch. A year or so later when she rented a villa in France, I went to stay with her and met her proud parents. I was so thrilled when she met Matthew – now her husband – when she was walking her dog in the park. It really was a romantic story for a girl who lights up a room when she enters and who deserves to be sorted and happy. She's the kind of friend who greets you, saying, 'How are you? Are you all right?' A naturally caring person, she's made my life all the richer for being in it. We've been through each other's ups and downs, and she and Matthew now have a wonderful child and have just moved into a beautiful new house.

So it *is* true that there are a number of famous friends I hang out with regularly, but that's because I'm in showbiz and these are the people I meet. I also have many others who are not high-profile who've been around my life for even longer. Barbara, for instance, is always teasing me about my 'other life', that is, my non-show business friends. One of my dearest mates is Blackburn Rovers' manager, Graeme Souness, who's never seemed to mind that I'm an Arsenal fan. I met Graeme and his lovely wife, Karen, when we were in the same restaurant one night. When they invited me to join them at their table, we chatted and chatted and just bonded. We've been very good friends ever since and speak regularly on the phone. Karen's son, Daniel, and her daughter, Lauren, from her previous marriage are absolute sweethearts, and she and Graeme now have a lovely young son, James. Because Graeme and Karen divide their time between Winchester and Manchester, I don't see them as often as I would like, but when they're in London we always try to meet up and have a meal together. It's great. People always do a double take when I – camp-as-Christmas Dale – walk into a restaurant with macho Graeme, the 'hard man' of football, and Karen. Having had so many hard knocks himself in life, Graeme is a brilliant people manager. And because he isn't in the same business as me and is able to bring a completely fresh perspective to my problems, I love asking him for advice. His answers are always invaluable.

While working on this book and doing *In It to Win It*, I couldn't resist the opportunity to join Graeme, Karen and the children in Spain. They were staying in the beautiful Las Dunas resort in Marbella, where I have spent many happy breaks. So after doing *In It to Win It* on the Saturday, I flew to Spain on the Sunday and was able to spend three fabulous days with them. However, there's a sting in the tail of this story. After a lovely dinner with everybody in a beautiful restaurant, I offered to drop Lauren and Daniel off at the port of Puerto Banus where they wanted to see some of the action. It was a real treat for Lauren to be allowed out so late and I wanted to be sure she and her brother got there safely.

I am *not*, I must confess, good at driving cars I am unfamiliar with and, if the truth be told, I accidentally hit the kerb on a slip road as we were approaching the motorway and the tyre went flat immediately. I'm useless in such emergencies, but Daniel was very macho and started to change the tyre.

'I'd better get a bit of help,' I thought and rang Graeme on my mobile. It was now one o'clock in the morning and poor Graeme, who was just relaxing after a wonderful night out, had to walk half a mile to the car to change the wheel, still dressed in his pristine new white Versace shirt. I didn't have the heart to tell him *why* we had got a flat tyre, but I've come clean now. (Graeme, I'm really sorry. You were a true gentleman, a Sir Galahad. I'm sure the very last thing you wanted after such a lovely evening in Spain was to be sitting on a roadside changing the tyre on a rented hatchback. But, sir, you did, and thank you for that!)

I guess however fortunate we are in our friends, there is always one person who eludes us whom we would die to have met and spent time with. For me that person is Dusty Springfield, who's been a passion in my life since I was a child. Unbelievably, my relationship with her now goes back forty years and, to this moment, a day rarely goes by without me listening to one of her tracks. While I was working on this book in Sarasota, Florida, I used to drive along the ocean roads with the top down in the car, listening to *Dusty in Memphis* and *A Brand New Me*. Her music has been with me through all my good and bad times, and there's always a track that hits exactly the right spot and sorts me out. I'm often asked what my favourite song of hers is, but this changes all the time. To me her songs are like close friends – I love them, know them really well, and they are always there for me. There is not a single one of the 280 she recorded during a career that lasted almost thirty-six years, which I do not know. I have Japanese and American imports of her albums, and I still enjoy her music above all others.

The extraordinary thing – given how many stars I have met throughout my career – is that I never actually met Dusty. The only thing I have now to remember her by is a radio interview I did with her by phone when she was in Los Angeles and I was at Radio Trent. This took place during one of the low points in Dusty's career and, because of the time difference, I had to go into the studio very late at night. I didn't mind one jot. While we were speaking, although I was on cloud nine, I was very aware that she was feeling very vulnerable and was obviously a bit lost just then. Later, when the Pet Shop Boys asked her to record 'What Have I Done to Deserve This?' with them, her name regained the prominence it so richly deserved, and her greatest hits were rereleased and constantly played on the radio. I went to see her many times in concert and adored her more each time. I also saw her once by pure chance in the Seventies when I was in the nightclub, Legends, near Bond Street, in London's West End. I knew she was promoting her record, *Baby Blue*, at this time and I should have gone over and said hello, but I was just too shy and lost my nerve. Fool that I was, I didn't think she'd welcome being pestered by a DJ in local radio, and I missed a unique opportunity to meet her.

Dusty, as we all now know, became a mega star all over the world and, given her incredible commitment to her craft and her insistence on perfection, she deserved all the adoration and respect that was hers, not only from her fans but also from her fellow artistes. A couple of years ago there was an exhibition, just off Trafalgar Square, of her memorabilia. Unable to resist visiting this, I went along to it with my friend, Rob Clark. There were loads of her fans present and, as I was signing autographs for them, a woman introduced herself to me as 'Barbara – Dusty's secretary.' I was *so* pleased to talk to somebody who had worked closely with Dusty throughout almost all the years of her professional life and to ask her all the questions I had so long wanted to ask.

Barbara then introduced me to Dusty's driver who told me of a 1997 occasion in Dusty's life that had involved me. When he had taken Dusty to Sony Records, Soho Square, a place which is very much in my neck of the woods, she had spotted me walking by. Apparently, as she got out of the car she turned to him and said, 'Oh, *look*, there's Dale.' Listening to him telling me this, I was absolutely astonished that Dusty knew who I was. But when I thought about it afterwards I realized that I had mentioned her on just about every radio show and every newspaper interview I'd ever done, and that I'd even talked about her on television. Dusty, it emerged, was just as shy of approaching me as I was of approaching her. When her driver said, 'Why don't you go and say hello to Dale,' she said, 'No – I'm too shy.'

One of my problems is that I walk around with my eyes closed half the time, but I so wish I hadn't that day. Had I seen her I would definitely have gone over and said 'hello'. I still feel sad that we were within a few metres of each other, but didn't meet.

As I was standing in the exhibition, with all the Dusty memorabilia around me and with two people alongside me who had been close to Dusty, I was suddenly overcome with emotion. Rob, taking one look at me, guided me away from the autograph hunters, took me upstairs and sat me down on a chair. I was *really* distraught, and knocked off my feet by an incredible wave of grief. Anybody who'd seen me at this moment would have thought I was barking mad. There I'd been, happily signing autographs one moment for Dusty's fans, then the next I was sobbing my heart out. To have missed the chance to meet Dusty once was silly, but to have missed a second opportunity because I walk about half blind was just too much to bear.

That evening, when I was reflecting on the exhibition, I remembered Dusty mentioning in my Radio Trent interview that she had seen Peggy Lee in concert in New York, and so wished she had had the courage to go backstage and speak to her.

'Why didn't you?' I asked, puzzled.

'Because Peggy Lee wouldn't have known who I was,' Dusty replied.

I could hardly believe my ears. *Of course*, Peggy Lee would have known who Dusty was. But Dusty was just too modest to appreciate that.

She often sang, 'You Don't Have to Say You Love Me' but, Dusty, I *always, always* will.


What about my future? Success, like happiness, is an elusive butterfly. I'm so grateful for the opportunities I've been able to grasp and I'm wise enough and experienced enough to know my strengths as well as my weaknesses. New and exciting opportunities in presenting are constantly arising, but, surprisingly, I *do* fancy a cameo role in *EastEnders*, doing, despite my experience in Spain, butch things in Phil Mitchell's garage: single-handedly jacking up Ford Sierras or lying flat on my back fixing exhaust pipes. Meanwhile, I'm having a great life – and my holidays now follow a much-loved routine. I go to Spain in the summer and spend a great time there with Cilla in her villa; after Christmas, I like to go to Barbados, where all the showbiz camaraderie guarantees all present a fabulous time. On these occasions I stay with Merrill in her beautiful beach-front property and, last time we were there, Cilla was staying next door, Davina and

Carol Vorderman came by for lunch and, one evening, Bob Monkhouse took us all out for dinner. I also adore going to Florida, Marbella and Mauritius, and I treasure the times I spend with my godchildren, Benjamin, Louis, Joshua and Jenna. They are everything to me.

The thing about being on television is that your love life is constantly under the scrutiny of tabloid press journalists who are fascinated by who you are – and who you are not – sleeping with. Martine's love life, for example, has been much chronicled and, true or false, it's still the subject of many column inches. Like Martine, I, too, have had more downs than ups in my love life, but my press coverage has always been along the lines of 'Well, what *is* Dale all about?'

I guess romantic thoughts are particularly poignant on Valentine's Night. This year, 2002, on that night of nights, I found myself without a date and, therefore, with no intimacy to look forward to at the end of the evening. These occasions always involve a difficult decision. Do you spend the evening at home in front of the television, with the answerphone on to pretend you are out? Or do you sit in a restaurant with a friend? I'm not brilliant at being alone on high days and holidays, such as Christmas, New Year's Eve, Boxing Day and Easter. These occasions simply don't work for me unless I'm with someone special. In particular, Valentine's Day always looms large when the person I want to be with on that night (which *has* happened in recent years) is with someone else. So this year I arranged to take Cilla and Martine to the Ivy. When they arrived at my house for a pre-dinner glass of champagne, I gave them each a red rose. It was a magical evening and, in all honesty, I would not have traded my place with them for anyone. The restaurant was full of couples out on a special Valentine's date, and there I was with Cilla *and* Martine.

As we sat down for dinner, the bonhomie across our table was wonderful. Then, to my great surprise, they suddenly started singing to me. Now the Ivy is about as far removed from a karaoke bar as you could find and it takes some guts, even for two of England's foremost songstresses who have both had number one hit records, to sit there, with no accompaniment and sing. But this they did. They sang the Shania Twain song 'You're Still the One' twice to me. The first time the other people in the restaurant could *not* believe it was *Cilla* and *Martine*, two of show business's finest, singing to me, but by the second rendition there wasn't a soul in the place who didn't know I was being serenaded. It has to be the first time the Ivy has ever been used as a stage for two great songstresses and I was unbelievably touched.

I know I've always been a bit of a tease about my sexuality, but I'm ready to tell all now. I've saved the last chapter of this book for the question I'm most often asked:

'Dale – *Are* you, or *aren't* you, gay?'

# 10

## 'Who could be lovin' you
## other than me . . .'

I HAVE ALWAYS viewed the 'is he – isn't he?' question with wry amusement because journalists approach it – and me – in so many roundabout ways. Some are blunt: 'Well, you *are* gay, *aren't* you, Dale?' Others are more ingenuous and say, 'Well . . . *is* there a Mrs Winton?' or 'Are you going to get married and have kids?' I see a certain look in their eyes and I know their editors have said, 'When you talk to Dale, have a good delve. He's never come out; he's always been very ambiguous about his sexuality; and he's never given us a kiss'n'tell.'

I'm wise enough to realize that if you appear on telly and court publicity, there are certain things that people think they have the right to know, but the level of interest in my sexuality always amazes me. I have people coming up to me and saying, 'I *know* who you've slept with . . .' and then, after a bit of coaxing, they name names I've never even heard of. So let's just say that I haven't got to this age without trying most things there are to try sexually, but this has only ever been with people of my own age who are mature enough to know their own minds.

I *have* been coy and a bit of a tease about my private life in the past and, although most people have assumed I *am* gay, I have resolutely refused until now to confirm or deny this. I used to worry about how the public would react to the truth and what effect, if any, too much honesty might have on my career. But these days I just think, 'If people can't accept me for the person I am, there's not much I can do about that.' So I've finally decided to tell how it is in this book.

For years I believed that there's no dignity in being labelled one thing or the other – the sum total of a person is always bigger than any one part. But now I am just happy to be me and I'm ready to address the questions surrounding my private life.

The key word for me is love. I'm a romantic. I want to give and receive true heartfelt passion.

My first kiss was with a girl called Susan Jones when I was all of eleven years old and on holiday in the South of France. I remember her saying, 'Let's have a kiss, Dale' and, when we did, I was surprised by a very strange feeling in the pit of my stomach. I now know that's called sexual awakening! Later, when Michael Aspel collared me for *This Is Your Life*, I discovered they'd tracked Susan down and, as she came on the set, I remember thinking, 'Oh, that was my first kiss.' I also remember having a huge crush on Stefanie Powers when I was fourteen and she was in *The Girl from U.N.C.L.E.* Around the same time I also became totally besotted with Andy Fairweather Low, the lead singer of Amen Corner, when I saw him on *Top of the Pops*, singing '(If Paradise Is) Half as Nice.' So I guess I fancied girls *and* boys from quite an early age. (I'd be mortified to mention my crush to Andy Fairweather Low if I ever bumped into him these days and I never breathed a word to Stefanie Powers when I interviewed her.)

After I left school at sixteen, which coincided with Mum going through a very low phase in her life, I was more than ready to discover the joys that love had to offer. On the one hand I was battling with a difficult home life, always afraid that Mum would commit suicide; on the other I was working as a pub DJ where people were into drinking heavily and having fun, and when one thing led to another it was often sex at the end of the evening.

During that time my dilemma was that I knew I *liked* girls, but I also knew I liked guys. And when I first fell in love at about eighteen, being me, I fell in love with one of each at the same time – a girl called Caroline, and a guy called John. This could be considered bizarre, but that's how it was. I wasn't going through some mind-blowing crisis about my sexuality, I was simply doing what came naturally to me and wavering between the two, unsure with whom I enjoyed being the most.

Although this was the very beginning of the Seventies, when attitudes to relationships were far less liberal than they are now, I never felt under any pressure to compromise how I felt and I didn't feel at all guilty about how I was expressing my feelings. My only concern was that Mum would be upset if she knew, and I considered it an act of kindness to her not to say, 'Actually, Mum, I may end up with a girl, I may end up with a guy, I'm just not sure yet. But I'm not worried about myself in that respect.' There was also – as there usually is at eighteen – a rebel inside me, saying, 'I'm my own person now. I'll do as I please.' So I continued to see the girl *and* the guy. When you're that age there are no boundaries, everything is aspirational and you don't have much baggage. I was just relaxed and open-minded about it all, and thought it was OK. Looking back now, I think I was a well-rounded teenager, in touch with my own feelings.

The problem was that Mum had always said to me, 'There's nothing you can't tell me, Dale, nothing you can't share with me,' but now there was. She was always very happy to discuss her intimate life with me which, although pretty normal nowadays, was comparatively rare in the Seventies. But then the age difference between Mum and me wasn't that great. When I was eighteen Mum was only thirty-seven.

At the time I met Caroline and John, I was a DJ doing two regular gigs. In fact, I met John while I was doing a gig at the Gunnersbury Fair, Ealing. He was very camp and, when Mum met him, she knew at once that he was gay. By this time, because I was so uneasy about keeping things from her, I was thinking, 'I'll tell her everything.' I *so* wanted to sit down and open my heart to her.

But as she was going through her 'Do Not Disturb' era and sleeping a lot of the time, and as I was already walking on eggshells at home trying to balance her ill health with my working life, I couldn't bring myself to do this.

Two things then happened, which I remember very clearly to this day. Having seen a car I wanted to buy in a garage at Spurlings Corner on the Edgware Road, I asked Mum to come and look at it, and as I was doing a lunchtime disco I arranged to meet her there. This was 1972, the time of flared trousers and corduroy caps and coats, and guys didn't have to be gay to carry the then-fashionable clutch or shoulder bags. Trendily dressed, and feeling very much 'the dedicated follower of fashion', I flounced happily into the garage with a shoulder bag swinging from my hip. I must have looked like a pastiche of early Seventies camp and Mum, who had got to the garage before me, burst out laughing.

'What are you laughing at? What's so funny?' I asked, very put out.

'Dale, if you could just see yourself,' Mum replied. 'You're *such* a character. But you don't see it, do you?'

'*See what?*'

I thought I looked great! But I also realized she had caught a glimpse of the camp flamboyant side of me that I usually suppressed at home. By then, I'd become a sort of split personality – Dale as he was expected to be at home and Dale as he really was outside.

'I'm *really* pleased you're so happy being you,' Mum said, still laughing. 'And, to be honest, I wouldn't have you any other way.'

'That's good,' I thought, 'because I'm really happy being me.'

John used to come to my gigs and hang around waiting for me to finish. He was clearly smitten but, as I was very overweight at the time, this couldn't have had anything to do with how I looked! Music was our common bond. I was also happy with Caroline. Dark-haired and comely, she was very caring and sensitive, and Mum really liked her; but, above all, I think Mum was just very pleased that there was a girl around. In the end, though, I got closer and closer to John.

My best friend at this time was a blond and very attractive fellow DJ, Steve Allen, who has remained one of my closest friends to this day. I adore Steve – always have. When I first met him he was living with a 'go-go' girl, called Diane, who later became a Bluebell girl, but he also liked guys. I looked up to him because he was worldly wise, had already left home and was doing his own thing. He knew where *the* clubs and bars were, and he took me under his wing. Because we were always out 'clubbing' together people naturally thought we were a couple, but we never had a physical relationship. We were then – and are now – just like brothers, the best of mates. To this day it makes me laugh when people ask if we are together. I've now known Steve for thirty years and the one thing we never ever argue about is men or women because we never go for the same type and have never found each other remotely attractive.

I first met John shortly after the shoulder bag incident at the garage. By then Mum was definitely becoming a bit suspicious about me. She knew that I liked girls, but she was obviously worried – especially as John was gay and she knew we spoke on the phone every day when I came home from my lunchtime discos. One afternoon, while he and I were having a lovely natter, Mum suddenly came out of her bedroom and flew into a rage. 'Are you talking to John *again*?' she asked angrily.

'Yes,' I replied, startled.

'You know he's gay, don't you.'

'Yes, Mum, I do know he's gay.'

'Well . . . if you know he's gay and you're hanging around with him, that probably means you're going to be gay yourself. I've worked with gay people in the theatre and the movies. They're great fun – and fabulous people to be around – but being gay makes for a very lonely old age. You don't *have* to be gay, Dale. There is an alternative. We *can* get help. This doesn't have to be the way for you. I'm worried about you being lonely in your old age.'

I've never blamed Mum for this out-of-the-blue tirade. It was the way most parents thought then and, young though I was, I understood how she felt. Like most mothers, she wanted what she thought was the best for me – marriage and family life – and, of course, grandchildren for herself. Also, given as she was to making attempts on her life, she wanted to see me settled before she died. She was a very bright, sensitive woman, but I don't think she realized that there are certain things in life, such as sexual preference, that you have no choice about; that whether you are gay, straight, bisexual or asexual, you're born that way. That's how you are. This was a time, though, when gays were taken for all kinds of treatments, including electric-shock aversion therapy, and it was fairly mooted in Mum's tirade that if I was *that* way inclined, I could be straightened out.

When I use the word 'tirade' it doesn't even come close to expressing the monumental argument that ensued that afternoon. On reflection I can see that this was caused by Mum's pent-up frustration that she had not brought up the subject in the past, and it all poured out as the most alarming emotional outburst I had ever experienced. Mum had so many good qualities. She had brought me up so well in terms of how I should behave and treat other people, but at this particular moment she clearly lost it, big time, herself. I was absolutely stunned, and I was also filled with guilt about having caused such a terrible upset when she already had health problems and was severely depressed. So the whole event was a monumental moment in my life. On a quiet, sunny afternoon, when I had simply been enjoying a chat on the phone, I had to confront really big issues, and the tirade, having come seemingly from nowhere, hit me very hard.

After Mum's outburst I was so upset and so confused by the downturn in our relationship that I marched up to my room, packed a few things in a bag, left home and went straight to Steve Allen's to sort myself out. This was my dilemma: I wanted to please Mum because I loved her and I didn't want to disappoint, upset or offend her in any way, but I knew I *couldn't* be the person she wanted me to be. So there I was, bags packed, leaving the luxurious home I loved and taking a step into the unknown. This turned out to be Steve's flat, which he shared with a black stripper called Billy, in (would you believe it!) Queen's Park. Billy was as camp as Christmas and his act, which was incredibly popular on the hen-party circuit, was called 'Billy Ribbon' because he tied a ribbon round It! I guess it was a very *big* part of his act, which was why he always went down so well!

Having bent Steve's ear with my problems at home, I said, 'What should I do, Steve?'

'I've been through all this myself,' he said. 'That's why I left home and got a flat.'

That was the moment when I should have said, 'Right! I'll do what Steve has done.' But I didn't want to do that; didn't feel ready to do anything as drastic as leaving home. Still distraught, I stayed with Steve for ten days.

During this time the man who used to run errands for Mum tracked me down and kept arriving with bits and pieces, like my duvet, changes of clothes and tins of soup, that Mum thought I couldn't survive without. 'Your mother's beside herself,' he kept on saying. 'You *can* go home if you want to. Why don't you give her a ring?'

I was terrified to make any kind of move. I knew Mum's state of mind was already fragile and I didn't want to risk sending her over the edge. After a week, though, I began to feel that I was behaving like a schoolboy. There I was in Steve's and Billy's flat, kipping on their sofa, knowing I couldn't live with them for the rest of my life, but still very fearful of upsetting Mum. After a few more days, though, I decided I had to face the music and return home. The chief question was still: should I tell Mum I wanted to continue seeing Caroline *and* John; or should I put her mind at rest by saying, 'OK, Mum, I'll just see Caroline and *not* John'? Having wrestled endlessly with this problem, I decided I would just go home and say nothing.

When I arrived at the house both Mum and I broke down in tears and were very emotional.

'There's nothing you can't tell me,' Mum kept repeating. 'I am the one person you can trust and I will *always* listen and help in any way I can.'

That was the moment when I should have said, 'Well, actually, Mum, I think I'm gay – and I honestly think that's OK.' But I chickened out and didn't say anything. I bruise very easily and I was still feeling very emotional about leaving home, then returning, and needed more time to rationalize the issues involved. To this day I am someone who fears emotional confrontations and I never lose it unless I am very severely pushed. Then it's a case of batten down the hatches! The '*are* you, *aren't* you?' topic was never referred to again by Mum or me. But it should have been discussed and I really regret not telling Mum more about who I was. I know she was very proud of me for being such a hard worker and a person who always tried to live up to her values, but I also suspect that she knew – and was disappointed – that I was not somebody who was going to settle down and have kids.

After she died, I broke up with John and gravitated towards Caroline for a while. But the relationship didn't last. I still feel bad about that because she really could not have been a sweeter person and I think I broke her heart.


Mum aside, I don't seem to have had any serious hang-ups about my sexuality, and I don't remember having any qualms about what went on between consenting adults in the bedroom. I just thought sex was great, one of the best things in life that was free. The only thing that changes as you get older is the relevance and the emotion that goes with it. When you're eighteen or so, you have a carefree, no-baggage attitude and sex is just sex.

After Mum died I focused even more on my career. It was the only time in my life when I lost my interest in finding a partner. This lasted for at least a year until I left London and went to work for Radio Trent in Nottingham. While I was there, I used to go to nightclubs and became friendly with a couple of girls, but it was always they who made the first moves. About 1979ish, I had a more serious fling with a woman who was having problems with her marriage, but when she turned up at my flat in a very bad state and wanted to move in, I knew I was in trouble. By then I was already wondering why I was persevering with these relationships because I knew that I preferred the company of men.

Perhaps the main reason why it took me so long to get into a serious relationship was because most of my close male friends, including my best friend, Mark Linsey, were *not* gay. My friendship with Mark was then – and is now – one of those rare brotherly relationships that just grows and grows. Throughout our good and bad times, we have always been there for each other, and I was delighted when Mark met Sarah, his wife, and they had my three lovely godchildren. When I think about it, as Mark is someone who always gets it right, I don't know why I don't just let him pick a partner for me and let that be the end of it.

I've always been terribly slow at picking up other people's signals. I virtually have to be pinned against a wall and told in words of one syllable before I realize anybody's interested in me. Over the years, so many friends have said, 'Didn't you realize that X, Y or Z fancied you?'

'Really?' I say, amazed.

Where matters of the heart are concerned, I used to be so like Mum. I always picked the path of most resistance. If a relationship was easy, I could make it run five days; if it was heartbreakingly complex I could make it run five years. On two occasions when I fell in love big time, it was with the kind of person who was just not good for me. This doesn't mean that they were bad people, just that they – and their lives – were far too complex and too complicated even before I came on the scene. On both occasions I knew this before I became involved, but I still said, 'I love that one, and nothing and no one can change that.' Most intelligent people would have backed off, saying, 'Why should I accept this impossible situation? I'm worth so much more,' but *not* me. I used to think, 'Half a loaf is better than none.' But not any more. A loaf *is* better than half a loaf. The time for compromise is over.

I've never been a bit of a lad, never been able to deal with more than one relationship at a time. In truth, I'm incapable of getting out of bed with one person and into bed with another. I have to love and be loved. I know to most people I seem a very confident person, but actually I'm quite vulnerable and insecure where relationships are concerned. I'm also very jealous by nature. But perhaps that has more to do with the fact that in the past I seemed to have had a knack for falling in love with people who already had someone in their life. I hated allowing myself to get into this situation, but I did. I seemed incapable of being more decisive in the beginning and thinking, 'That person's sorted – walk away, Dale, before you get entangled.'

In the Eighties I was involved with someone who had never been in a gay relationship before, and who has since married, had children and lives abroad. It lasted for three years and was one of those occasions when I thought I was happy. I managed to keep the relationship going for a very long time, even though my friends used to say, 'What are you doing with him, Dale? He's not right for you.' In reality he was a very nice man, a true Scorpio who had boundless energy and enthusiasm, and all the physical qualities one could wish for in a lover. I used to walk around with a permanent grin on my face. As it was, I ended the relationship. My dilemma throughout was, 'How can I wave goodbye to this person who thinks so much of me, who constantly tells me how much he loves me and who will do anything for me? If I do, I might never meet anybody else who feels that way about me ever again.' But then I reached a crunch point when I said to myself, 'I *have* to risk that. It's just *too* painful, *too* difficult, and it's sapping me.'

Over the years I have met several people. I cannot mention all of them here, mainly because they quite rightly assumed that I would never kiss and tell. Needless to say, they all touched my life, no matter how briefly. They have also, without doubt, brought something to me. Discovering one's own sexuality is always a journey. You cannot do it alone. The outcome is that I now know what works for me and what doesn't. One thing I've learned about myself is that outrageous flirting is such fun, but I only ever flirt with those I fancy!

In 1993 I met a man who I *really* believed could be my lifetime partner. It happened just as my TV career was getting off the ground. At this time I had become very friendly with Dean who worked for Talbot Fremantle, the television production company that owned the rights of *Supermarket Sweep,* and we often went out for a coffee or dinner. One July night when we were in The Yard, a Soho bar, Dean went to get the drinks. As I stood waiting for him to return, I glanced up and saw, on the upstairs balcony, the most fabulous-looking man I had ever seen, dressed in a blue denim jacket and trousers. When I looked up again he had gone. A few moments later he reappeared just a few yards away from me. He smiled, I smiled, but neither of us spoke. I really am hopeless at making first moves and every bit as bad at chatting anybody up. A few years ago when I invited a guy home for a coffee at the end of an evening, I'd completely forgotten that, in certain circles, this does not mean coffee. As I poured this fellow his drink, I remember him saying to me, 'You are not very good at this seduction business, are you, Dale?'

'No,' I said, becoming all fingers and thumbs – and that was the truth. I really had meant come in for a coffee!

The chap in The Yard, though, was just *so* gorgeous that my interest was instantaneous. I wanted to get to know him. But when he intimated I should go over and say hello, I didn't. Here was the kind of guy who, having been blessed with drop-dead-gorgeous looks, was the original tall, dark and handsome stranger.

'If he wants to come over, he will,' I thought. But he didn't. He just finished his drink and left.

About fifteen minutes later Dean and I decided to leave The Yard and go for a coffee somewhere else. As we walked past The Village, another Soho bar, I saw my Adonis in there. It was very busy but, as there was a gap between him and the next guy at the bar, I made a quick decision, marched in with great deliberation and plonked my briefcase alongside him. 'Hi, can I get you a drink?' I asked, astonishing myself.

'That would be nice,' he replied in a lilt I didn't immediately recognize.

'Are you from Yorkshire?'

'No.'

'Are you Irish?'

'Yes – I *do* have some Irish in me.'

He was very 'cool' in the laid-back sense of the word. I introduced him to Dean and then, astonishing myself again, suggested that we meet for a drink or dinner one evening. By this time, I was like '*Yes!*' and beside myself. 'Shall we exchange telephone numbers?' I asked, opening my briefcase. In contrast to my immaculate grooming that night, this was an absolute tip, full of papers and all manner of what have you.

'Your briefcase is absolutely brilliant!' he said, suddenly bursting out laughing. 'Now I've seen the inside of that, I know you're all right.'

Walking out of the bar, clutching his number, I was terrified I'd lose it. I couldn't wait to ring him and fix a date.

It so happened that the remainder of that evening turned out to be very special for Dean, too. As we walked past the Old Compton Street Café, one of our regular haunts, we saw a guy called Graham in there who turned out to be *the* man for Dean. They are still together – and we are all great friends.

When I got home, although I wanted to telephone my stranger at once, I resisted. I didn't want to appear too eager and, given my low self-esteem where potential lovers are concerned, I was thinking, 'I'm being silly. What will he see in me?'

Three long days later I rang him. 'Hi, it's Dale.'

'Hi, Dale. So you thought you'd wait three days in order not to appear too keen.'

I roared with laughter – he'd got the measure of me.

When we met up for a drink before going out to dinner, I was in for a shock.

'Let's go to Brighton,' he said.

I was not used to taking off just like that with somebody I hardly knew. 'That's a long way . . .' I said, dubiously.

'Yes – but so what?'

'Can't we go somewhere nearer?' I pressed.

He was obviously much more adventurous than me and, to this day, I regret that I didn't just say, 'Yes.'

We ended up in Greenwich. Walking companionably around the park, we chatted about this and that, and I told him I was about to start what I was sure was a life-changing career move on *Supermarket Sweep*. I was so excited about the job which, in addition to being a brilliant, long-awaited, big breakthrough, meant financial solvency. I'd been broke for too long and it meant that I could now exist without worrying about my next day's keep or the phone bill.

Meeting him at that time was phenomenal: my career was about to come good, life was great and just at the right moment I'd met a really fabulous guy. A postmodern artist who sculpted in many different mediums, he was very innovative, but obviously an eternal student. I'm no expert in the arts. People are always surprised that I don't go to galleries and the theatre, that I know nothing about opera or classical music and am not well read in the sense of reading the 'right' books. I consider myself culturally deficient but, having owned up to that, I never pretend to be otherwise. These days I do listen to classical stations more and read better books, but it's because I want to, not because I feel I should.

After our first couple of dates, I knew I wanted to impress this man and make it happen. But I had to go up to Nottingham for three-and-a-half weeks to do *Supermarket Sweep*. At the end of the first week, when I had got into the routine of recording five shows a day, I rang him and invited him to come and join me for the weekend. I was *very* excited. I had my own show and I was booked into a very nice suite in the Royal Hotel.

On the Friday of his arrival I was a nervous wreck. I had told him I had a suite, but I was faced with an embarrassing dilemma. Was he coming up to spend the weekend with me as a friend, or to spend the nights with me? It was a delicate situation to clarify. I rang him and said, 'I know you've bought the train ticket, and that I've told you I'm staying in the Royal Hotel, but I don't know whether you would feel more comfortable with me, or if you would like me to book you a room?'

'Your room will be fine,' he replied in his usual laid-back way.

As I hung up my sense of anticipation and excitement was phenomenal. I couldn't wait for his train to get in because something inside me was still saying, 'I can't believe he's really coming to see me in Nottingham . . .'

When he walked into my dressing room there was one of those awkward moments as he gave me a peck on the cheek. 'What am I supposed to do here?' I thought. Then, as he had arrived during a break between the afternoon and evening recordings, he stayed to watch two of the evening shows. After that, at nine o'clock, I was free until Monday afternoon when I had to return to the studio to continue work.

It was a magical weekend. We went out for a superb dinner that night, visited Wollaton Hall and its beautiful parklands on Saturday and went to Chatsworth on Sunday. By Friday evening I thought I was in love, but I wasn't quite sure; by Monday morning, when he was due to take the train home, I was absolutely certain. 'Do you *have* to go?' I said and, although he wavered, he left to catch his train.

I was bereft, couldn't believe he had gone; and then, because he had a horrible bout of flu, I didn't see him again until I got back to London.

The relationship was wonderful for a time, but it didn't work out the way I had *so* hoped it would. The timing of our meeting wasn't as good for him as it was for me and he had a lot of 'unfinished business' in his life. I was ready to commit and settle down, but he was not. 'I know what you want, Dale. It's the white picket fence, the whole thing . . .' he said warily.

I did. But I soon learned that it takes more than one person to make a permanent relationship work.

We kept in touch, we went on holidays together, and we gave it one brave last shot during a holiday abroad. But however much we tried to compromise with each other, our relationship was too intense, our needs too different. I was always fearful that it wouldn't work and when you are trying so hard to make something right, you invariably do or say the wrong things. To his credit he was able to say, 'This is *not* going to work, Dale,' and my closest friends also said, 'Dale, you simply *have* to accept that you two are *not* compatible.' That just about sums it up. I was absolutely devastated, but we parted company. If any good came out of the end, it was the fact that my whole body went into shock and I shed nearly four stone in weight.

I may have lost what I had so hoped would be the love of my life, but at least I had gained a thirty-four-inch waist in the process, which was fantastic. And I am pleased to say that we are still friends to this day.

After the break-up I had eight weeks to pull myself together before I was due on camera for my new TV show, *The Other Half.* I remember being both shocked and pleased when a newspaper ran an article on me saying, 'What's up with Dale?' In the accompanying photograph I looked painfully thin and gaunt. But then, as I've doubtless said already in this book, my rule of thumb is, 'You *can't* be too thin, too rich or too suntanned!' As I had absolutely no appetite, the weight continued to drop off me. For me, being lovelorn is rather like a bereavement. My whole nervous system was shot to bits. I was wretched, inconsolable and felt that I had somehow failed. But now, when I look back on this affair, I can see that it was a classic on-off, can't-live-*with*-you, can't-live-*without*-you situation. Over the five years that our relationship lasted we were actually more often apart than we were together. My friends were brilliant during this time. Whenever there was a bust-up, followed by yet another recon- ciliation, they said, in the kindest possible way, 'Dale, you've tried *so* many times to make a go of this, are you sure it's going to work this time?' Although it was a very volatile relationship, I was always convinced that it would work. In those days I believed that love conquers all and that, given patience, all would be well. My dear friend, Merrill Thomas, who has seen me through so many trials and tribulations, is an absolute diamond, my three-o'clock-in-the- morning friend, and Barbara Windsor was wonderful. But they were always very dubious that the relationship would work. And Mark Linsey always used to say, 'Oh, *no*! He's not back again, is he, Dale?' I got the distinct impression that when it went wrong for the final time they all breathed huge sighs of relief.

There have been times when the object of my affections has been out of bounds on Fridays and Saturdays. These two particular nights have always loomed large in my thoughts. There I was, going out on the town with Steve Allen and my other mates, thinking, 'Friday nights and Saturday nights are when you, Dale, *should* be going out with your someone special. If he's not with you on those weekend nights because he has other commitments and obligations, there has to be something fundamentally wrong. Seeing somebody on Thursday nights is *not* the same. It helps, but it just doesn't do it.' Sometimes, though, I did settle for not having the person I loved on a Friday or Saturday night, because I'd found myself in a complex relationship where someone else had first claim to him. But not any more. These days if someone is committed to somebody else on those nights, I refuse to be Boy Thursday.

One of my problems in relationships is that I have to give a hundred per cent and that can be frightening for the other person. If they're slightly insecure, or even if they're bullish, arrogant and strong-minded, to be confronted with unconditional love and support can be destabilizing. They don't quite know whether it's for real or not. And there lies the rub. These are the kind of Svengali-type characters who are attracted to me and whom I find so attractive in return. Giving a hundred per cent to a person can also be very seductive in itself. These days, though, because I now know that a little of Dale goes a *very* long way, I'm very much into living alone. Yet . . . I am so ambivalent, so much my usual mercurial Gemini self. What I desperately want is *one* man who will harness my soul. I *have* to have passion in my life. I either have to be madly in love with someone who loves me, madly in love and it's unrequited, or madly in love and it's not going anywhere. I've experienced all of these. And when there *is* passion in my life, I have a certain glint in my eye. A photographer, who has photographed me many times, once said, 'Dale – you have *that* glint in your eye again.' He was right. I did. It was during my second near miss at a permanent relationship.

Why you fancy one person and not another is a very strange thing to unravel. I've never really worked out what it is that makes me respond so powerfully to one person and not to another. In fact, I rarely fancy anybody at first sight and the ones I do find attractive are usually the least gay. When people say to my perceptive friend Rob

Clark, 'What sort of guy does Dale fancy?' Rob raises his eyes to heaven and goes, 'Well, if it looks like trouble and the person just happens to run an allotment, or works on a building site, Dale will be in there.' The truth, though, is that I've never had a particular type, never gone for the most obvious choice of partner. In fact, most of the relationships I have had have been with guys who don't look, behave or even sound gay. It's only when they have suddenly turned round and said, 'By the way, Dale, I *think* I might be a bit gay,' that the penny has dropped. 'Oh, really,' I say.

My ideal remains to be in a happy relationship with one person, and my passion is fuelled just by the thought that one day this might happen. I can be bought with a loving text message, a few kind words and a kiss. Those can keep me going for no end of time. I couldn't bear to be indifferent to passion and I would *hate* to be thought asexual. *That*, for me, would be the worst fate imaginable.

For the rest, I agree with the person who once said, 'Never view your glass as half empty, see it as half full.' I do. But I *love* it when my glass is brimming over. That's the way I am. It comes back to being a person who cannot enjoy having aspirations or just doing the job for myself. When you work very hard to achieve a certain status, you want to share whatever success you have; sharing is what life is all about. There's nothing I'd like more than to get up on a Sunday morning with that special person and say, 'Let's go on Eurostar to Paris for the day,' or, 'Why don't we go to Rome next weekend?' I now have the wherewithal to live life like that and I'm just longing to be swept off my feet. In quiet moments I think, 'I'm a presentable enough looking guy, I've got a successful career, nice house, great car, not to mention a passport and a bit of money in the bank, let's get on with it!'

The upshot of not being married with a family is that my friends are everything to me, and I'm as fiercely protective of them as they are of me. If they're needy, I'm there. I'm proud of that. I work hard at making sure that everybody is happy in my world. If there's a problem I can hear it immediately in their voices, or see it in their eyes, and I say, 'Come on, what's up?' One of the richest relationships

I have had in my life is the one I have with Mark and Sarah Linsey, and my godchildren. When people see how much I love their twins, Ben and Louis, and Joshua, they often say, 'Dale, you'd be a wonderful dad. Why don't you get married and have kids?' The reality is that I adore women and actually spend more time with Barbara, Cilla, Martine, Merrill, Davina and Lynda than I ever do with men, but marriage has never really been an option for me. Many years have now passed since I seriously considered a woman as my partner for life, but I never say never. Where romance and relationships are concerned I don't have any set-in-stone attitudes, so goodness knows who will end up sharing my life. I have an open mind about these things and I'm looking forward to the next chapter of my life which, if my experiences so far are anything to go by, will not go according to any predetermined plan.

The truth is that where relationships are concerned it's taken me a long time to resolve certain issues. In the past, one of these was my overactive sense of responsibility. I've only been truly successful in the last ten years and, up until then, I always felt that *I* had to be the provider, that *I* had to bring financial security to a relationship. I knew in theory that couples could live in a wooden shack, with no hot running water, if they were with the right person, but I never felt at ease with myself when I was impoverished. My current problem is that I now need someone who isn't intimidated by my success because, believe me, this *can* put some people off. The ones you want to be with and who really want to be with you are often afraid of known faces and celebrity. They see your lifestyle and feel they can't compete. And I soon tire of the ones who seek my company for the wrong reasons. I've never been a trophy hunter myself and I'd get no joy whatsoever from being somebody else's trophy partner. I've always thought there must be something fundamentally lacking in a person's character if they go for people for this reason. When I find somebody attractive it never has anything to do with their status, job or income. I don't have a check list. When Jan Kennedy, my agent, helpfully says, 'Dale, I've got a very nice professional man I'd love you to meet,' or a friend says, 'There's this dentist that you simply have to meet,' I always think, 'Just because they're successful professionally doesn't mean that they will be successful as a human being.' *That* is not my criterion and it never has been.

So, apart from the two near misses I've mentioned, I've yet to meet anyone I'd really want to live with on a day-to-day basis. Neil Shand, my scriptwriter, once said to me, 'It's the Mozambique syndrome, Dale.' What he meant was this. You meet someone, go out on a date and end up in bed. But within thirty seconds of the deed being done, you'd rather be in Mozambique. I've not actually experienced this syndrome for many years and I wouldn't want to again. What I want is someone strong who's able to take control and say, 'Actually, Dale, *this* is what we're going to do.' I don't mean take control of my professional life – careerwise I'm very adept, astute and in touch. Jan Kennedy tells me I'm one of very few artistes she knows who monitors ratings, is aware of what everyone else in the business is doing and makes things happen. But at an emotional level I dream of coming home, closing my front door and saying to someone, 'This is as much yours as mine. Isn't it *great*. Let's just enjoy it!'

*But* – and it's a big *but* – I've come to the conclusion that what would really suit me right down to the ground is someone whom I adored and trusted, who had their own place. Then we could visit each other three or four times a week. That would be bliss. I'm not sure I could live seven days a week with anybody now but, as I said before, I never say never. The right person might come along and might change my mind about this. But *if* that ever happens, it would have to be a true soulmate, someone I can really talk to. The worst thing you can do in a relationship is not communicate and whenever I've had a row with someone I can't go to sleep until I've made it right. Mum was always spot-on. She used to say, 'When you get married, Dale, or when you're with someone, *never* have single beds. Always sleep together. Then, if you've had an argument you'll wake up friends.' One of my abiding characteristics is that I'm forever fearful of upsetting someone or saying the wrong thing, and when I do, this is usually brought about by pressure of work, of getting mentally exhausted. I do tend to overanalyse things. I brood about something that someone's said to me for hours, then I simply have to ring them and say, 'You know when you said . . . What did you mean by that?' I'm always worried that I haven't asked the right question at the time or qualified the point they're trying to make. I'm inclined to take what is said as given and that isn't always the best thing to do. Anyone who gets really close to me knows that I'm the kind of guy who can be put right by a phone call or text message. It amazes me when they resist doing this. I'm invariably the one who makes the first move, but I'm learning that it shouldn't always be down to me.

As it is, I'm forever falling in love but that doesn't mean to say it is reciprocated. I haven't actually lived with anyone for years. My relationships have been mainly long-distance ones where I've seen the person on an occasional basis, or long-lasting where the other person has only stayed two or three nights a week. I really have had the most bizarre love life. Maybe my overtly camp demeanour is not always a turn-on sexually. I know what kind of image I've got and, with the best will in the world, nobody looks at Dale Winton and thinks, 'He's going to be a wild animal between the sheets.' People think, 'Oh, he seems *nice*.' But I'm afraid 'nice' doesn't equal 'animal'. The same people would look at George Clooney, Nigel Havers or Robbie Williams and think '*phwoarr*', but I'm afraid my 'phwoarr' factor is not as high as theirs. Sometimes I think I could stand in Oxford Street wearing a fig leaf and sporting three days', stubble, and I'd still look like one of the Nolan Sisters! Once, when I was carrying on like this to a journalist from *Heat* magazine, he very kindly, trying to build up my self-esteem, informed me that I had come fourth in a magazine survey which asked women to name the men in the public eye they would most like to see naked.

'*Really*? That's fab!' I responded. 'You've made my day. I'd like to thank the readers of that magazine for their good taste.' Then, after a pause, I added, 'Now, I suppose you're going to tell me that Mr Blobby was third – and I'll lose my will to live!'

Meanwhile, my career has exceeded my wildest dreams and I'm still close to everybody who has ever been close to me – friends *and* lovers. I love my life. As for the future, my philosophy is 'life is *so* extraordinary, it should be lived to the full.' There are a great number of people who would hate not to know what they will be doing in six months' time, but I am not one of them. I would still like to be working because I thoroughly enjoy my career. Yet I'd like all my close friends and my godchildren to be healthy and happy. As long as I've got enough to live on and I can take care of myself and my godchildren, I'm happy. I work to live, not the other way round.

All I want now is just more of the same, please. Life is a lottery, it's said, and I'm in it to *win* it!

# INDEX